ENGLISH
THE TEXTBOOK

Jane Cooper

Consultant Editor: Carolyn Cunningham

HODDER
GIBSON
AN HACHETTE UK COMPANY

With thanks to the staff and pupils of Firrhill High School, especially Cara Pullar and Keri Millar.

The Publishers would like to thank the following for permission to reproduce copyright material:

Photo credits p. 18 Sashkin/Fotolia and Cobalt/Fotolia; p. 19 anyaberkut/Fotolia; p. 33 epa european pressphoto agency b.v./Alamy; p. 36 Everett Collection Historical/Alamy and Allstar Picture Library/Alamy; p. 70 Facebook/Twitter/Pinterest; p. 74 GL Portrait/Alamy; p. 81 Martin Godwin/The Guardian; p. 106 Simon Price/Alamy; p. 111 RomainQuéré/Fotolia; p. 187 The National Trust Photolibrary/Alamy; p. 201 jeremyculpdesign/Fotolia.

Acknowledgements p. 6: Extract from 'F is for First Date Fashion' by Kate Carter © Guardian News & Media Ltd 2014; p. 7: Extract from 'The Do Something manifesto' by Oliver Burkeman © Guardian News & Media Ltd 2014; p. 7: Extract from 'Bring back the blazers' by Lynsey Hanley © Guardian News & Media Ltd 2010; p. 9: Extract from 'What's happened to home cooking?' by Genevieve Fox © Guardian News & Media Ltd 2013; pp. 40, 44, 46: Extracts from Sandi Toksvig: 'Today we can all celebrate whom we choose to love' © Guardian News & Media Ltd 2014; p. 62: Extract adapted from 'Skype and cheap calls give an illusion of closeness, but homesickness is still real' by Ian Jack © Guardian News & Media Ltd 2013; p. 69: Extract adapted from 'Conscious computing: how to take control of your life online' by Oliver Burkeman © Guardian News & Media Ltd 2013; p. 74: Extract from 'Textual healing', *Sunday Herald* 2013, reproduced by permission of Liz Lochhead; p. 80: Extract adapted from 'Dry bars — is England sobering up?' by John Harris © Guardian News & Media Ltd 2014; p. 85: Extract from 'The big steal' by Rhodri Marsden © Guardian News & Media Ltd 2014; p. 90: Extract adapted from 'The new boom in home tuition' by Daniel H. Cohen © Guardian News & Media Ltd 2013; pp. vi, 95: Extracts adapted from 'Why I can no longer face tutoring the progeny of the rich and aspirational' © Guardian News & Media Ltd 2013; p. 99: Extract from 'Swedish cinemas take aim at gender bias with Bechdel test rating' © Associated Press 2013; p. 102: Extract from 'Cinema programmers beware: feminist films can flunk the Bechdel test' © Guardian News & Media Ltd 2013; pp. 109, 116: 'Waking With Russell' and 'The Thread' by Don Paterson from *Landing Lights* (2003), reproduced by permission of Faber and Faber Ltd and The Permissions Company, Inc., on behalf of Graywolf Press, www.graywolfpress.org; p. 159: Extract from *Mortal Causes* © 1994 Ian Rankin, reproduced with the permission of Orion Publishing Group and Simon & Schuster Publishing Group, a division of Simon and Schuster Inc; p. 160: Extract from *The Big Over Easy* by Jasper Fforde © Jasper Fforde 2005, Hodder and Stoughton Limited; pp. 175, 177, 178: Extracts from *Touching the Void* by Joe Simpson, Jonathan Cape, The Random House Group Ltd; p. 179: Extract from *The Reading Promise* by Alice Ozma, © Grand Central Publishing and Hodder & Stoughton Limited; p. 207: 'Vegetarians With Teeth' from *Hugh Fearlessly Eats It All*, by Hugh Fearnley-Whittingstall, reproduced with kind permission of Bloomsbury Publishing plc.

SQA material is © Scottish Qualifications Authority and reproduced with SQA permission.

Orders: please contact Bookpoint Ltd, 130 Park Drive, Abingdon, Oxon OX14 4SE.
Telephone: (44) 01235 827720. Fax: (44) 01235 400454. Lines are open 9.00–5.00, Monday to Saturday, with a 24-hour message answering service. Visit our website at www.hoddereducation.co.uk. Hodder Gibson can be contacted direct on: Tel: 0141 333 4650; Fax: 0141 404 8188; email: hoddergibson@hodder.co.uk

© Jane Cooper 2015

First published in 2015 by
Hodder Gibson, an imprint of Hodder Education
An Hachette UK company
211 St Vincent Street
Glasgow G2 5QY

Impressions number 5 4 3
Year 2019 2018 2017 2016

Cover photo © Photographee.eu – Fotolia

Illustrations by Barking Dog

Typeset in 13/15 pt Bembo Regular by Integra Software Services Pvt. Ltd., Pondicherry, India

Printed in Dubai

A catalogue record for this title is available from the British Library

ISBN 978 1 4718 3745 6

Contents

Introduction

The Higher course gives you many opportunities to display your English skills. You will be assessed through units you work on in class, by sending away a portfolio of your writing, and also by an exam at the end of the course.

All these different assessments give you an opportunity to develop your skills in the four keys areas of English: *reading*, *writing*, *listening* and *talking*. As you progress through the course, you will have chances to work with literature, with language and with media.

You might be in a class where some pupils are working towards Higher while other pupils in the same class are working towards National 5. Some pupils might start off aiming for Higher but realise that it is a better idea to sit National 5 this year. The courses have the same structure, allowing pupils to drop down to National 5 if they need to.

Some parts of the course are **internally** assessed:

* You need to pass a unit called **Analysis and Evaluation**, which tests your knowledge of what you *read* and what you *listen to*.
* You need to pass a unit called **Creation and Production**, which will get you to *write* and to *talk*.

Both these units will be assessed in school by your teacher. You do not have to do any exams for these units, or send anything away from school to be marked. The units will not be graded, but you will know if you have passed or failed.

Some parts of the course are **externally** assessed:

* You will send away a **Portfolio** of two pieces of writing to be marked by someone outside of your own school.
* You will also sit an **Exam** (sometimes called the **Question Paper**) that assesses different aspects of your reading skills. One of the tasks will test your ability to read something you have never seen before, under exam conditions, and answer questions on it. You will also write a critical essay about a text you have studied in class, and you will answer questions on a set Scottish text that you have also studied in class.

To help you to see as clearly as possible that you are covering all the skills and tasks you are meant to tackle, this book is arranged in chapters that go with each of the units or assessments. Don't panic if that's not quite how your teacher tackles your course. Because the units are based on skills, your teacher may teach you something, or get you to do an activity, or complete a task or challenge, in such a way that you are learning or improving one of the skills and then proving that you've done so.

So, here are some questions that you should be able to answer about any piece of work you do in English this year:

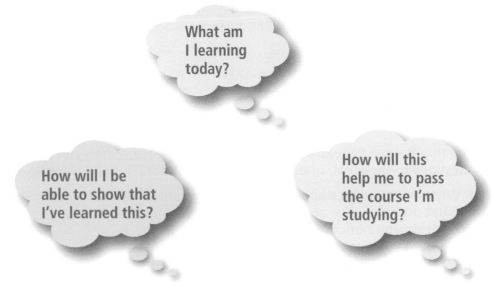

What am I learning today?

How will I be able to show that I've learned this?

How will this help me to pass the course I'm studying?

If you don't understand what you are doing, or why you are doing it, (very politely!) ask your teacher.

How to use this book

Every chapter of the book will begin by telling you what you will be assessed on. On some pages of this book a 'Combined assessment' box will let you know if the task you are doing could be used to help you pass more than one assessment.

One phrase comes up very often. It is mentioned in almost all of the tasks and assessments. We are going to look at this now.

Detailed and complex language

At Higher level, you are expected to be able to understand, and use, *detailed and complex language*. You need to know what this means.

Active learning

Work with a partner. Together, read over the following passage. It is written in detailed and complex language.

Working as a private tutor nowadays is a bit like being a confiseur for Marie Antoinette: no matter how much you spin the sugar into a confection about feeding society, you're really just making life sweeter for the rich. And I should know, having taught a predominantly wealthy elite for over a decade.

Five years into the most thorough economic malaise since the Great Depression, and amid more cuts than you'd find on a straight-to-DVD movie, it should come as scant wonder that one of the few boom industries is private education. In the strata of the recession-proof uber-rich, the private tutor can often appear as simply the next human accessory, summoned before the court to perform.

Yet in a society plagued by the disease of aspiration, it's no longer just about the very rich. Salaried and striving parents are queuing up to fuel the boom in a market valued in excess of £6bn a year, hyperventilating that their kids are being left behind as an already unequal form of education plunges into something that would make the feudal system look like the dictatorship of the proletariat.

You might need to read the extract more than once. When you are ready, answer these questions to show you understand the idea of detailed and complex language:

- What do you notice about the lengths of sentences?
- What do you notice about the number of sentences?
- What do you notice about the vocabulary?
- What do you notice about the writer's ideas?
- What did you notice about the writer's style and techniques?

Try to get used to spotting detailed and complex language. You will find it in newspapers like the *Guardian*, *The Times*, the *Herald* and the *Scotsman*. You will hear it in some television programmes (such as *Newsnight*) and in some programmes on BBC Radio 4.

CHAPTER 1 The Analysis and Evaluation Unit

You must pass this unit to pass the Higher course. (You must also pass the Creation and Production Unit covered in the next chapter.) In this unit you will be assessed on your skills in reading and listening. This chapter will cover these two skills separately, starting with reading.

First, though, we are going to look at two linked ideas that are very important in the Higher course. It makes sense to work on these now, because the easiest way to understand them is by seeing how they come up in what we read or listen to. However, these ideas also apply to what we write or say.

Purpose and audience

You should already be quite familiar with these ideas, as they are an important part of the National 5 course that you have passed already.

- **Purpose** means *what* a text is for — why somebody said it, or wrote it.
- **Audience** means *who* a text is for — who is supposed to read it or listen to it.

To pass the assessments in reading and listening for this unit, you need to be able to identify the purpose and audience of texts produced by someone else. To pass the assessments in writing and talking for the Creation and Production Unit, what you write or what you say must fit your given purpose and be right for your target audience.

Active learning

Here are some possible purposes:

- to examine
- to criticise
- to persuade
- to explain

How many more purposes can you think of? Make a list and share your ideas with the rest of the class. Add other people's ideas to your list.

Now look at the list of purposes you have in front of you.

1   Which of them could be purposes of a **non-fiction** text?
2   Which of them could be purposes of a **fiction** text?

It can be much easier to identify audiences for non-fiction than for fiction. A piece of fiction might be written (just) to entertain, but it might also be created because the writer wants to explore an issue. It might even be written to express the writer's creativity.

For example, think about the two Don Paterson poems in the Critical Reading chapter of this book (pages 105–144). We can very quickly identify a number of possible purposes for these texts:

● to explore the speaker's love for his children
● to consider the effect that being a father has had upon his life
● to capture a particular moment in life
● to allow the writer to use a particular form — the sonnet

Identifying purpose can be trickier if you are given a reading assessment based on just an extract, such as part of a full play or novel. You will get the opportunity to try this later in this chapter.

Active learning

Here are some possible audiences:

● people from a particular age group e.g. pensioners, teenagers
● people from a particular place e.g. Canadians
● people from a particular profession e.g. doctors
● people with a particular interest or hobby e.g. skateboarders

How many more audiences or audience types can you think of? Make a list and share your ideas with the class. Add other people's ideas to your list.

Two different texts can have the same purpose but different audiences. *The Times* and the *Daily Record* are both newspapers. Their purpose is to inform. But they aim at very different audiences. Radio 1 and Classic FM are both music radio stations. Their purpose is to entertain. But they aim at very different audiences. BBC3 and BBC4 are both digital television channels. Each channel produces some programmes that aim to entertain, and some that aim to inform. But they aim at very different audiences.

3   For each of the three examples given above, explain who the two different audiences are.
4   Come up with other examples of two texts that have the same purpose but different audiences.

At Higher level, identifying an audience can mean being a lot more subtle than categorising people by age, gender or interest. It might be that the audience is people with a commitment to social justice, or readers who are interested in issues in society. Also, much journalism is aimed at **the general audience**, readers (or listeners) who are reasonably intelligent, and whose interest can be engaged by something that is well written.

Active learning

This task will get you to identify purpose and audience. You need internet access to do it. Your teacher may set it as a homework task, or you may be able to do it in class by using your smartphone or tablet.

First, pick any two of the following six words:

- bread
- Canada
- elephant
- alcohol
- beetle
- queen

Then, type one of your two chosen words into Google, or another web browser.

Next, go in to each of the first five websites that Google suggests to you — you can ignore any advertising links at the top of the page and just go to the actual sites that other users have brought to the top of the search.

For each website that you look at, decide:

- what the site is about
- what the purpose of that site is
- who the target audience might be

Now, carry out the same exercise with your other chosen word.

For example, the writer of this book googled the word 'castle'. The first website was about Alnwick Castle in the north of England. Its purpose was to persuade people to visit the castle, and the target audience was people who are interested in history. The second website was a Wikipedia page about an American television series called *Castle*. The purpose was to provide information about the programme, and the target audience was people who have watched or would consider watching the programme.

Active learning

This task will get you to show that you can write to fit certain purposes and audiences.

First, get organised. Give everyone in your class the number 1, 2 or 3. You also need lots of small cards, or small bits of paper, in three different colours.

All the **number 1** pupils should use the **first** colour of card. Every pupil should take at least three cards, and write a different **purpose** on each one.

All the **number 2** pupils should use the **second** colour of card. Every pupil should take at least three cards, and write a different **audience** on each one.

All the **number 3** pupils should use the **third** colour of card. Every pupil should take at least six cards, and write a different **subject** on each one.

Now collect all the cards, and shuffle them. Give each person one card of each colour, so that everyone gets, at random, a purpose, an audience and a subject.

Then write a paragraph that fits all of these. For example, here's what happened when someone got the purpose *to inform*, the audience *young children*, and the subject *zebras*.

By Millie

A zebra is an animal. It looks a lot like a horse, but it has black and white stripes. Zebras live in Africa. They have four feet. A zebra's foot is called a hoof.

If you are absolutely sure it is impossible to write a paragraph based on the cards you've been randomly given, tell your teacher. If he or she agrees it can't be done then you can swop one of your cards for a different one.

Finally, read your paragraph to a partner who does not know what was on your cards. Ask this person to guess the purpose, audience and subject.

You can shuffle all the cards and play again if you like.

You will be asked to identify purpose and audience when you are being assessed on reading and listening. The most important thing to remember is that **you must able to justify the purpose and audience you identify.** At Higher level, these ideas can be so subtle, and there can be so many possible answers, that it is really your justification, your support of your answer, that will convince that marker.

You will also be expected to write, and to talk, to suit your chosen purpose and your audience. This will be covered in the next chapter, which is about the Creation and Production Unit. For now, it's time to get on to the main work for this chapter and this unit.

Reading

You have to show all the appropriate reading skills by **understanding, analysing and evaluating** at least one written text. This text should use detailed and complex language. (Remember that you can look back at the Introduction to this book to find out more about what 'detailed and complex' means here.)

You will show your ability to understand, analyse and evaluate what you read by doing these things:

- identifying and explaining the **purpose and audience** of the text
- identifying and explaining the main ideas and supporting details
- applying your **knowledge and understanding of language** to explain the **meaning and effect** of the text. You should be able to explain this in depth and detail, using appropriate critical terminology.

When you do your final unit test, the passage you are given to read may be fiction or non-fiction. It may be recently written or perhaps in more old-fashioned language. If it is a fiction text, it may be in prose or even be a poem or an extract from a play.

What you learn about reading in this unit will build towards the knowledge and skills you will need for the reading for your Understanding, Analysis and Evaluation exam. However, your unit pass for reading can't be used as assessment evidence for any other part of the course.

 Warning

There is one thing you need be careful of. You **cannot** provide evidence of passing your reading outcome by basing this on a text you have studied in class. You cannot, for example, use a critical essay as evidence for a unit pass in reading. This is because, if your teacher has taught you a text, you can't claim that **you** have identified the purpose and audience. You can't show that **you** have identified the ideas and supporting details. It won't truly be **you** explaining the meaning and effect of the writer's language. These would all be things your teacher has taught you as you studied the text. If it's not your own work, you can't use it to pass the unit assessment.

It might be possible to pass your reading outcome by working on an **unseen** extract that comes from a different part of a text that you do have some knowledge of — for example a later chapter in a novel you have read the beginning of — but this is something your teacher will have to consider carefully.

Main ideas and supporting details

As we saw above, you will be assessed on your grasp of the main ideas and supporting details in the text. We are going to use some short texts to get you working on this now.

Active learning

Read the following short piece. As you do so, work out:

1 What is its purpose? Provide evidence from the text to support your answer.

2 Who is the target audience? Provide evidence from the text to support your answer.

F is for First Date Fashion

You've exchanged dozens of emails, perhaps texts and even phone calls, but suddenly reality bites: it's all very well preparing your best conversational openers and show-stopping anecdotes, but what on earth will you wear? The key is, of course, to stay cool. But cool doesn't necessarily mean adopting the latest hipster trends or slavishly following the current magazine diktats. Nor is this the time to debut that spinning comedy bow tie or do-not-adjust-your-set neon dress. It means being yourself, just a slightly glossier, shinier, more well-pressed version.

Everyone, male and female, has something in their wardrobe that makes them feel more confident and gives them a little boost. It's the sartorial equivalent of a stiff drink and a compliment. Wear that. But if you're worried that it'll be too dressy, play it down. Men, put a jumper on top of that shirt. Women, make that dress less formal by adding a cardigan. Do not wear tight new shoes or high heels that you've never worn before or can't walk in. You want to wake up the next day reflecting on a good night, not heading to Boots for blister plasters.

No one has ever regretted a date on the basis of not shopping enough for it. If you need a confidence boost, opt for a new accessory that you wanted anyway and will use again regardless of the romantic outcome of your night out. Keep it stylish, simple and freshly laundered and you can't go wrong.

Kate Carter in the *Guardian*, 1 February 2014

We can see the main idea of this article:

It's important to dress well on a first date.

Active learning

This main idea is backed up by a number of supporting details. List them, using your own words as far as possible to demonstrate your understanding. You should be able to find seven. When you've finished, you can check your answers on page 211.

Active learning

Read the following paragraph. As you do so:

1 Identify the main idea.

2 Using your own words as far as possible, pick out the supporting details.

When you've finished, you can check your answers on page 211.

> Routine is both a blessing and a curse. Without it, the working world would collapse, along with much of the rest of daily life: you'd never keep the house clean, or get the kids to school on time. But regularity exacts a high price — as the grandfather of modern psychology, William James, understood. 'Each passing year converts some of [our] experience into automatic routine which we hardly note at all,' he observed. Life becomes calcified, until 'the days and weeks smooth themselves out … and the years grow hollow and collapse.' Too much routine isn't merely boring; it also contributes to the ubiquitous sense of the years whizzing by as you get older, because so little takes place that's new and therefore memorable. Can you remember what you were doing, say, a month ago? If that was an ordinary week for you, the answer is: probably not. By contrast, when you think back to even the shortest trips to unusual places, they seem to have unfolded at a much more leisurely pace — not necessarily because you were relaxing on holiday, but because you'd disrupted your routine.
>
> Oliver Burkeman in the *Guardian*, 11 January 2014

Active learning

One more task on main ideas and supporting details. First, read the text:

> Good uniforms confer dignity. They give the wearer a chance to take themselves seriously and to convey to others that they ought to be treated with respect. The fact that they're issued as standard, for free, doesn't alter that perception. To give examples, the elegant, quasi-medical tunic worn by Boots shop assistants, and the sharp grey suit worn by guards and ticket officers on the London Overground, dignify the wearer.
>
> Bad uniforms — cheap, second-rate ones — diminish everyone. Poor quality school uniforms, in particular, embody a school ethos that expects little of its students or their parents. Polo shirts and sweatshirts may be cheap and easy to wash, but they're not a uniform designed for unseen

benefits — the benefit of being able to look at yourself in a mirror and say, 'Yeah, I do look smart', of allowing yourself to think, 'Perhaps I'm not thick after all'. Enforcement will be easier but will mean less.

These are most often the uniforms worn by children in largely working-class schools, ostensibly because they're 'more practical' — cheaper for parents and easier to enforce. The less obvious inference is that students may as well prepare for a lifetime of wearing 'practical' clothes. By contrast, I regularly walk past students at the successful Mossbourne Academy in east London, wearing grey blazers and ties, who, in the very act of wearing such a uniform, are transcending their circumstances.

It's precisely because uniforms are presented to you to wear, without choice, that a sense of freedom in other areas is unleashed. Anti-authoritarians, keen on connecting school uniforms with some hidden state agenda to keep the populace compliant, tend to work from the assumption that all order is destructive to the soul. You cannot learn to the best of your ability in a chaotic environment — whether at home, at school, or both.

There is nothing more shameful or frustrating than to turn up at school, desperate for adults to give you the means to become a useful person, to find either that they cannot keep order or that they expect so little of you that they can't be bothered to try. The same goes for uniform: if a code is only half-enforced, it reinforces the notion that you, your aims and by extension, your community, are not worth taking seriously.

Uniforms don't cause the wearer to disappear: conversely, the better it is, the more chance you have to assert yourself within its limits. It doesn't stultify identity, it bolsters it. Students of private and public schools take this for granted. You have to wonder how long it will be before state-school pupils are treated with the same degree of respect, and, in so doing, to treat themselves as people worth respecting.

Lynsey Hanley in the *Guardian*, 20 August 2010

1 What is the purpose of this text? Support your answer with evidence from the text.

2 Who is the target audience? Support your answer with evidence from the text.

3 There are two main ideas here. What are they?

4 Using your own words as far as possible, identify the supporting details for each of the writer's main ideas.

When you've finished, you can check your answers on page 212.

Knowledge and understanding of language

This is the third standard you will be assessed on, along with your grasp of purpose and audience and of main ideas and supporting details. This chapter will not go into detail about this standard. You will find much more about questions that get you to analyse writers' language and style and techniques in Chapter 4, which deals with the reading for Understanding, Analysis and Evaluation exam.

Active learning

In the next few pages you will get the opportunity to try two different reading tasks. These are **not** final assessment tasks. Such tasks have to be kept secure — they can't go in a textbook. But, they will give you a chance to use and practise your reading skills.

Remember you will be asked about purpose and audience. There will be questions on main ideas and supporting detail. You will also be asked about the meaning and effect of language.

The first passage appeared in a national newspaper's glossy weekend magazine.

Homemade used to mean simple, healthy fare. But thanks to food blogs and television, cooking from scratch has become competitive. Welcome to the hell that is haute homemade.

5

I have had enough. I will not plate up. There, I have said it. Plating up has infiltrated the contemporary lexicon. The term once innocently referred to serving food on individual plates, as opposed to letting people serve themselves from serving dishes. Now it means making like you're a Michelin-starred artist and painstakingly arranging individual ingredients on appropriate plates (white and round does not cut it) in such a way as to be visually gratifying. Food must be styled, picture-perfect, plated like a pro.

10

A few weekends ago, I was looking for ideas on what to do with scallops. Friends were coming for supper and I wanted to make an effort. I found a section called Recipes For The Weekend in a glossy magazine. Perfect. But all I could find was Scallops And Ibérico Ham With Parsley Foam. The parsley foam raised alarm bells: it sounded a bit molecular.

15

Then I saw the photograph. A lozenge of green sputum like a slug descending from a concave structure of ham and a single radicchio leaf. Where the foam meets the meat, a forget-me-not has been placed, like a satin rosebud on an old-fashioned undergarment.

20

Who, in their right mind, would make this? Who? The recipe, which comes from a Michelin-starred chef, has a cooking time of four hours, plus freezing time. Four hours. Then you've got to plate up. Weigh that up against how long it would take your guests to eat the thing (four minutes, tops) and you have to ask yourself: what's the point?

25

30

Home cooking, as a term, has got above itself. Home entertaining is the new going out, and it's hell: time-consuming, stressful, expensive. It's no longer good enough to buy ready made puff pastry, you've got to make your own. Make your own bread, too. Mix, knead and roll your own pasta, while you're at it. The home cooking that goes on is, in fact, haute cuisine. Homemade means turning back the clock and spending hours in the kitchen, making everything from scratch and turning ingredients into lifestyle-affirming, narcissistic creations.

35

I came across a food video telling me not 'to unceremoniously plop tonight's dinner on to a plate'. Given that the dinner in question was chicken, veg and mash, it is hard to see why not. I pressed play. Cue some frenetic piano music and the shaming of a 'plopped' dish: a chicken breast, mound of mash, untidy heap of broccoli and messy pile of carrots. The viewer is then talked through 'the art' of plating up. A bit of chicken is laid on a plate, with a bone thrusting skywards and accompanied by nil-by-mouth quantities of veg. Two sprigettes of broccoli, four slices of 'cut-on-the-bias' carrot and one, just one, cauliflower floret are arranged beside the chicken. Where once one might pour some gravy, it's now time to 'pool the sauce and swipe through'. A manicured hand runs the back of a spoon through the rectangle of gravy. No dish is complete without little spots of something unidentifiable and, sure enough, the presenter uses a 'squeezy bottle' to put three Smartie-sized spots between each arrangement of veg.

40

45

50

Cutting up a carrot won't do. You've got to puree the buggers and, once you've done that, according to another video, you've got to 'run your spoon straight through it and you end up with this cool kind of a swoosh'.

55

'I feel like I have to take the day off in order to prepare if friends are coming over,' a friend commented the other day. 'The thing is, I like putting big pots on the table and everyone helping themselves.' While she ploughs her lonely path, the rest of us are doing things that shouldn't be tried at home. I'm talking vinegar balls.

60

These are a must for a 'classic peasant dish' by the Michelin-starred chef Andy McLeish. His poached and roasted pheasant 'is made more impressive with the addition of sherry vinegar pearls', it says in Harper's Bazaar. 'It may take a while to whip this dish up, but it is worth it.' I check the preparation time: three and a half hours. Whip

65

up is not the verb I'd use. The sherry vinegar pearls are part of the plating up. They require agar agar, a chinois, a squeezy bottle, a fine nozzle and not much going on in your life.

70 If you do master the vinegar ball, you'll be in good shape when it comes to preparing the butter to go with your bread rolls. Bread rolls! Yes, some of us still have gluten-tolerant, non-fasting friends who eat the stuff. Obviously you can't slice a bit of Lurpak and squish it into a ramekin. No, you've got to render the butter into
75 individual edible Saturns, smoking it first, moulding it into a ball and lowering a ring of sherry vinegar jelly around it.

Whoever wrote, 'You don't have to be a trained chef to learn the basics of plating', on startcooking.com, is lying.

Startcooking.com says that rule number five of plating up is, 'Play
80 with height.' The photograph shows a pile of rice crouching in one corner of a square brown plate, a medley of chicken and veg beside it. Then the height rule is explained: 'It's good to have a bit of height, but don't overdo it or your guests won't know how to proceed! If you have a mound of mashed potatoes (mid-height),
85 you may want to lean your pork chop against it so that it is standing up (high), with a row of snow peas (low) in front.'

The rules for plating up mention 'your centrepieces', and we're no longer talking candles or, heaven forbid, flowers. The centrepiece should be edible, not disposable. Domestic mistress of the universe
90 Martha Stewart tells us how 'to create an hors d'oeuvre centrepiece that recalls a vegetable patch'. Instead of putting some raw carrots on a plate, a battalion of raw veg is divided up in a planter. Are we children, that everything needs to look like a plaything? Are we scared of food?

Genevieve Fox in the *Guardian*, 14 December 2013

Now answer these questions:

1   Read line 1 ('I have had … have said it.') What tone does the writer establish in this opening line and how is this tone created?

2   Read lines 18–21 ('Then I saw … old-fashioned undergarment.') How does the writer's word choice create a negative impression of the dish? You should examine at least **two** examples of word choice in your answer.

3   Read lines 22–26 ('Who, in their right mind … what's the point?') What are the writer's main arguments against making this dish? Answer **in your own words** as far as possible.

4   Read lines 27–35 ('Home cooking, as a term … narcissistic creations.') Explain at least **two** ways that the idea that 'Home cooking … has got above itself,' in the opening sentence is developed in the rest of the paragraph. You should answer **in your own words** as far as possible.

5   Read lines 42–45 ('A bit of chicken … arranged beside the chicken.') What impression is given of this plate of food and how is this impression created?

6   How do the comments by the writer's friend in lines 56–59 ('I feel like I have to … everyone helping themselves.') illustrate the problems of cooking haute homemade? Answer **in your own words** as far as possible.

7   Read lines 62–69. ('These are a must … not much going on in your life.') How does the writer's language undermine the description of the dish as 'peasant'? You should refer to at least **two** examples of language in your answer.

8   Read lines 70–76. ('If you do master … jelly around it.') How does the writer's language create a contrast between the two different ways of presenting butter?

9   Identify one main purpose of this article. Explain your answer with close reference to the text.

10 Identify at least one possible audience for this article and explain your answer with close reference to the text.

For answers see page 213.

This second task has deliberately been chosen to set you a challenge. Mary Shelley wrote *Frankenstein* in 1818. You will certainly find her language both detailed and complex. Victor Frankenstein, a medical student, has been assembling a creature from human body parts. It is now time to bring his creation to life.

It was on a dreary night of November that I beheld the
accomplishment of my toils. With an anxiety that almost amounted
to agony, I collected the instruments of life around me, that I
might infuse a spark of being into the lifeless thing that lay at my
5   feet. It was already one in the morning; the rain pattered dismally
against the panes, and my candle was nearly burnt out, when, by
the glimmer of the half-extinguished light, I saw the dull yellow
eye of the creature open; it breathed hard, and a convulsive motion
agitated its limbs.

10   How can I describe my emotions at this catastrophe, or how
delineate the wretch whom with such infinite pain and care
I had endeavoured to form? His limbs were in proportion, and
I had selected his features as beautiful. Beautiful! — Great God!
His yellow skin scarcely covered the work of muscles and arteries
15   beneath; his hair was of a lustrous black, and flowing, his teeth of a
pearly whiteness; but those luxuriances only formed a more horrid
contrast with his watery eyes, that seemed almost of the same colour
as the dun white sockets in which they were set, his shrivelled
complexion and straight black lips.

20   The different accidents of life are not so changeable as the feelings
of human nature. I had worked hard for nearly two years, for the
sole purpose of infusing life into an inanimate body. For this I had
deprived myself of rest and health. I had desired it with an ardour
that far exceeded moderation; but now that I had finished, the
25   beauty of the dream vanished, and breathless horror and disgust
filled my heart. Unable to endure the aspect of the being I had
created, I rushed out of the room, and continued a long time
traversing my bedchamber, unable to compose my mind to sleep.
At length lassitude succeeded to the tumult I had before endured;
30   and I threw myself on the bed in my clothes, endeavouring to
seek a few moments of forgetfulness. But it was in vain: I slept,
indeed, but I was disturbed by the wildest dreams. I thought
I saw Elizabeth*, in the bloom of health, walking in the streets
of Ingolstadt. Delighted and surprised, I embraced her; but as
35   I imprinted the first kiss on her lips, they became livid with the hue
of death; her features appeared to change, and I thought that I held
the corpse of my dead mother in my arms; a shroud enveloped
her form, and I saw the grave-worms crawling in the folds of the
flannel. I started from my sleep with horror; a cold dew covered my
40   forehead, my teeth chattered, and every limb became convulsed:
when, by the dim and yellow light of the moon, as it forced its way
through the window shutters I beheld the wretch — the miserable

monster whom I had created. He held up the curtain of the bed;
and his eyes, if eyes they may be called, were fixed on me. His jaws
45 opened, and he muttered some inarticulate sounds, while a grin
wrinkled his cheeks. He might have spoken, but I did not hear;
one hand was stretched out, seemingly to detain me, but I escaped
and rushed downstairs. I took refuge in the courtyard belonging
to the house which I inhabited; where I remained during the
50 rest of the night, walking up and down in the greatest agitation,
listening attentively, catching and fearing each sound as if it were to
announce the approach of the demoniacal corpse to which I had so
miserably given life.

Oh! no mortal could support the horror of that countenance.
55 A mummy again endued with animation could not be so hideous
as that wretch. I had gazed on him while unfinished; he was ugly
then; but when those muscles and joints were rendered capable
of motion, it became such a thing as even Dante could not have
conceived.

60 I passed the night wretchedly. Sometimes my pulse beat so quickly
and hardly that I felt the palpitation of every artery; at others, I
nearly sank to the ground through languor and extreme weakness.
Mingled with this horror, I felt the bitterness of disappointment;
dreams that had been my food and pleasant rest for so long a space
65 were now become a hell to me; and the change was so rapid, the
overthrow so complete!

Morning, dismal and wet, at length dawned, and discovered to my
sleepless and aching eyes the church of Ingolstadt, its white steeple
and clock, which indicated the sixth hour. The porter opened the
70 gates of the court, which had that night been my asylum, and I
issued into the streets, pacing them with quick steps, as if I sought
to avoid the wretch whom I feared every turning of the street
would present to my view. I did not dare return to the apartment
which I inhabited, but felt impelled to hurry on, though drenched
75 by the rain which poured from a black and comfortless sky.

I continued walking in this manner for some time, endeavouring,
by bodily exercise, to ease the load that weighed upon my mind.
I traversed the streets, without any clear conception of where I was,
or what I was doing. My heart palpitated in the sickness of fear; and
80 I hurried on with irregular steps, not daring to look about me.

* Elizabeth is Victor Frankenstein's fiancée.

Mary Shelley, *Frankenstein*

Before you try the questions, did you notice what **isn't** in that passage? Film versions of Frankenstein usually show the creature being violently brought to life on a wildly stormy night. Many of these films show Victor using electricity, perhaps from a bolt of lightning, to do this. Mary Shelley, however, only writes about pattering rain, not a storm, and the phrase 'spark of life' in the first paragraph seems to be a metaphor, rather than any kind of suggestion that Victor used electricity. Nor does Shelley's text describe the bolts in the neck that we are used to seeing in some media images of the creature.

Now answer these questions:

1   Read lines 1–9. ('It was on a dreary night … motion agitated its limbs.') By referring to at least **two** examples, show how Mary Shelley's word choice suggests an unsuccessful outcome of Victor's efforts.

2   Read lines 10–19. ('How can I describe … straight black lips.') Explain, **using your own words** as far as possible, what makes the creature a 'catastrophe'? (line 10)

3   Read lines 21–24. ('I had worked … far exceeded moderation …') How is the reader made aware of Victor's determination to make the creature? You should answer **in your own words** as far as possible.

4   Read lines 26–31. ('Unable to endure … moments of forgetfulness.') How does the context assist you in understanding the meaning of the word 'lassitude' as used in line 29?

5   Read lines 26–53. ('Unable to endure … so miserably given life.') **Using your own words** as far as possible, briefly summarise how Victor spends the night. You should make at least **four** points.

6   Read lines 48–53. ('I took refuge … so miserably given life.') How does the description of the creature as a 'demoniacal corpse' convey Victor's attitude towards the creature?

7   Read lines 67–75. ('Morning, dismal and wet … black and comfortless sky.')

    a   By referring to at least **two** details from the text, show how Victor's fear is conveyed.

    b   How does the image of an 'asylum' as used in line 70 help you to understand Victor's experience that night?

8   Identify one main purpose of this extract. Explain your answer with close reference to the text.

9   Identify at least one possible audience for this extract and explain your answer with close reference to the text.

For answers see page 217.

You have now seen two sample reading tasks. You have had the chance to work on both fiction and non-fiction texts, and with different kinds of language.

In the end, it is up to you and your teacher to know when you are ready to be finally assessed for reading. Remember you will be asked about purpose and audience. There will be questions on main ideas and supporting detail. You will also be asked about the meaning and effect of language.

When the time for assessment comes, your teacher has certain responsibilities:

- He or she must be sure you are reading the right, detailed and complex, level of language.
- Your teacher must give you an assessment that tests you on all the right aspects of reading. This could be by using one of the Unit Assessment Support Packs produced by the SQA. Or, your teacher could make up their own assessment questions based on a text he or she thinks you will appreciate and understand.
- Your teacher must keep a record of evidence that you have passed the assessment.
- Though you do not have to get every individual question right, your teacher must make sure that you have answered enough questions correctly to cover each standard — purpose and audience; main ideas and details; meaning and effect.
- If you do not pass first time, your teacher should give you another assessment. This must be based on a new text at the same level of difficulty, and should ask new questions. You only have to answer the questions that cover the outcome(s) you got wrong in your first assessment.

Listening

So far this chapter has dealt with one of the Analysis and Evaluation skills, reading. Now we are going to move onto the second of these skills, listening.

Of all the four language skills, reading, writing, talking and listening, this is the one you use most in real life. It's the one you get a lot of your entertainment from. It's the one you use most at school in your learning.

Active learning

Think back over all the different speech, sounds and noises you have heard since the start of today. List all the information you have learned today that has come to you mostly through listening, e.g.

I knew I had to get out of the house if I wanted a lift to school when I heard my mum honk the car horn at me.

Until recently though, listening has not been taught or assessed nearly as much as the other three skills of reading, writing and talking.

What you will be assessed on

You have to show all the appropriate listening skills by **understanding, analysing and evaluating** at least **one spoken text**. This text should use detailed and complex language. (Remember that you can look back at the Introduction to this book to find out more about what 'detailed and complex' means here.)

You will show your ability to understand, analyse and evaluate what you read by doing these things:

- Identifying and explaining the **purpose and audience** of the text.
- Identifying and explaining the **main ideas** and **supporting details**.
- Applying your knowledge and understanding of language to explain the **meaning and effect** of the text. You should be able to explain this in depth and detail.

Combined assessment

The work you do for the listening outcome of the Analysis and Evaluation Unit may help you with another part of the course.

You may be able to pass your listening assessment by evaluating the group discussion you take part in for your talking assessment.

Your teacher will make sure that you have covered all the skills each unit asks for and that, for the listening outcome, you have done so by listening to detailed and complex language.

 Warning

There is one thing you need be careful of. You **cannot** provide evidence of passing your listening outcome by basing this on a media text, such as a film or television drama, that you have studied in class. This is because, if your teacher has taught you a text, you won't really be able to show that **you** have identified the purpose and audience. You won't really be able to show that **you** have identified the ideas and supporting details. It won't truly be **you** explaining the meaning and effect of the text. These would all be things your teacher has taught you as you studied the text. If it's not your own work, you can't use it to pass the unit assessment.

It might be possible to pass your listening outcome by working on an **unseen** extract that comes from a different part of a text that you do have some knowledge of — for example a clip from the end of a film version of a play if you have so far only looked at the earlier parts of that same play — but this is something your teacher will have to consider carefully.

It's quite tricky to teach listening in a textbook. Although this book is written to feel as if it is speaking to you, it can't actually make sounds. So, this part of the chapter will give you suggestions of things to listen to, and of ways you can work on these, so that you can improve your listening skills and get experience of suitable texts.

What you could listen to:

Some of the material you might listen to is audio only — purely listening.

For example you could listen to:

- radio news broadcasts
- famous speeches
- a film review or interview from the Radio 5 Live film programme
- a short section from a longer Radio 4 programme such as *Today, Woman's Hour, P.M., Saturday Review, Last Word, More or Less*
- a short section from a longer Radio 4 programme on a particular subject area: the station has programmes about science, the environment, films, politics, farming, food, books, money, and so on

A lot of the material you can listen to is audio-visual — something you watch and listen to.

For example you could watch and listen to:

- other pupils' individual presentations
- group discussions in your class
- a section of a television news broadcast
- film clips
- a clip from a fictional television programme such as a drama or comedy
- part of a television documentary

Three websites may be particularly helpful:

You could listen to TED talks — in which experts talk about a subject they understand well. Go to www.ted.com/talks and you can search by subject to find talks on areas you are interested in. Many of these speakers are from overseas, usually America.

You could also go to 5x15stories.com where you will find British-based speakers giving 15-minute talks, again about topics they know well and are interested in. You can search this site by subject, or by the name of the speaker.

BBC Radio 4 has a regular, weekly programme called *A Point of View*. A speaker gives a 10-minute talk on a subject that has interested them. If you go to www.bbc.co.uk/podcasts/series/pov you will find short summaries of over a hundred of these talks, and a chance to download them as podcasts.

Remember, to be suitable for listening at Higher level, your text must use **detailed and complex** language. The talks on the sites mentioned above — especially the Radio 4 *A Point of View* — will do so.

The rest of this section will give you a number of structures for listening. These will be **generic**. This means they will not be designed to get you listening to a specific text. Instead, you will be given a series of approaches for listening to certain types — genres — of texts. You could try several of these tasks to help you develop your listening skills. Think of them as allowing you to develop your listening muscles.

As you work through these next few pages, remember these three important things:

1	**2**	**3**
This chapter is about passing a **listening** assessment — the words you hear matter more than any visual material that supports them.	If you are doing a listening task to pass your unit assessment, this **must** be based on a piece of text you have not listened to or watched before.	When you are doing a listening task, you can listen to or watch a clip **as many times** as you like. There is no limit to how often you watch it.
It's all right if you mention visual material and media techniques in your answers, but it is up to your teacher when he or she designs any listening assessments to make sure that you could still get the answers right even with your eyes shut.	The questions can be similar to ones you have used before — because they are designed to test the same skills — but the text should be a new one, an 'unheard' one, if you're being finally assessed on it.	You can also rewind and replay smaller sections of the clip as often as you need to. You may make notes as you watch and listen, if you think this will be helpful.

Listening to Shakespeare

You may have studied Shakespeare earlier in school, or be studying one of his plays with a view to writing a critical essay about it in your exam. Or, you may never have read a Shakespeare play, in which case this task really will give you a chance to engage with some detailed and complex language.

Before you can do this task, your teacher needs to do a little preparation.

Teacher's task

First choose one of these filmed versions of a Shakespeare play:

- the 1996 version of *Hamlet* starring Kenneth Branagh and Kate Winslet
- the 2008 version of *Hamlet* starring David Tennant
- the 2012 BBC version of *Richard II* starring Ben Wishaw (released as part of the box set titled *The Hollow Crown*)
- the 2012 BBC version of *Henry IV Part 1* starring Jeremy Irons (released as part of the box set titled *The Hollow Crown*)
- the 2012 BBC version of *Henry V* starring Tom Hiddleston (released as part of the box set titled *The Hollow Crown*)
- the 1999 version of *Love's Labours Lost* starring Kenneth Branagh
- the 1971 version of *Macbeth* starring Peter Finch and directed by Roman Polanski
- the 2004 version of *The Merchant of Venice* starring Al Pacino
- the 1993 version of *Much Ado About Nothing* starring Kenneth Branagh and Emma Thompson
- the 1996 version of *Richard III* starring Ian McKellan

Whichever you choose, it should be one that your class has not seen before, and should not be the movie version of a play your class is studying as a drama text.

Next choose a five- to ten-minute-long extract from the start of the film. This might be just one scene, or might perhaps involve a change of scene. You need to pick a section with a small number of significant speaking characters. As you make your choice, quickly look at the pupil questions below to make sure that they will be able to answer them on the clip you've chosen.

Active learning

First, watch the clip. Remember that you can watch it, or parts of it, as many times as you want. You can also make notes as you listen, if you wish.

Now answer the following questions. You may wish to work with a partner:

1 Purpose
   a What kind of reaction are the makers of this film hoping to get from the audience?
   b What things are said by characters to get that reaction from the audience?
   c Explain how the words said would create that audience reaction.

2 Audience
   a Who would be likely to watch this film? (You could think about age, gender, interests and social class.)
   b Give evidence: explain what it is that makes the film appeal to this audience.

3 Main Ideas and Supporting Details
   a Having watched this opening section, what do you predict the plot of the wider play will be about?
   b By referring to the clip you watched, give reasons to support your answer.

4 Knowledge and Understanding of Language
   a Think about the main characters you have met so far. Pick two of these characters. What is each person like? Support your answers by referring to the characters' language.
   b Pick one character whose feelings are made clear in the extract. What is this character feeling? Support your answers by referring to the character's language.

After you and your partner have finished answering, you can share your answers with the rest of the class.

Listening to radio journalism

Before you can do this task, your teacher again needs to do a little preparation.

Teacher's task

Go to the BBC Radio 4 website and look up the programme *From Our Own Correspondent*. You will find links to editions of the programme going back for many years. Choose one clip, by one journalist, for your pupils to listen to. It may be helpful to pick one that ties in with a current or very recent news story. As you make your choice, quickly look at the pupil questions below to make sure that they will be able to answer them on the clip you've chosen.

Active learning

You are going to hear a piece of radio journalism from a programme called *From Our Own Correspondent*, which is made by BBC foreign correspondents stationed all over the world. These journalists are usually kept busy reporting developing news stories. In their regular work, they have to supply a particular broadcast, of a particular length, and on a particular subject, to fit into a particular radio or television news programme.

FOOC (as it is known to its contributors and listeners) is different. Journalists only contribute to this show if they feel like it. They decide for themselves what they want to say. They might take the chance to tell a wider, deeper, background story, or to focus on a character they have met, or to paint a word picture of a place or situation. They are talking about something they have a personal interest in.

First, listen to the clip. Remember that you can listen to it, or parts of it, as many times as you want. You can also make notes as you listen, if you wish.

Now answer the following questions. This time you should work on your own.

1 Purpose

    a What was the purpose of this broadcast?

    b Support the purpose you identified by giving evidence from the text.

2 Audience

    a What was the intended audience for this broadcast? You may wish to consider age, interest, gender or other factors.

    b Support the audience you identified by giving evidence from the text.

3 Main Ideas and Supporting Details

    a What was the overall subject of this broadcast?

    b What were the speaker's main ideas about this subject?

    c How well did the speaker use supporting details such as information, evidence or personal experience to back up these main ideas? Give reasons and/or evidence to support your answer.

4 Knowledge and Understanding of Language

    a Identify at least two language techniques used in the clip. Quote examples of the techniques in use, and explain the effect the speaker gains from using each of these techniques.

5 Evaluation

    a Did you find this broadcast interesting or not? Refer to details from the programme to explain why.

    b How reliable did the journalist seem? Give evidence to support your answer. This evidence might be based on the words and language they use, or on the way they speak.

Active learning

This final listening task requires some preparation in your own time. Earlier in this chapter, you saw many suggestions of places where you can find clips to listen to and watch.

Homework: Your task is to find a clip you are interested in. This clip should be at least five minutes long. You must be sure that it uses language that is both detailed and complex, as the Higher course expects. Listen to and/or watch the clip, and prepare yourself for the 'classwork' section of this task, which is outlined below.

Classwork: You are going to introduce and explain that clip to members of your class or group. For this you will need to use the classroom computer and data projector, or your own smartphone, laptop or tablet.

- **Introduce** your clip by explaining how you found it, and why you chose it.
- **Show** the clip.
- **Provide evidence** that the language of this clip is detailed and complex.
- **Explain** the main idea of this clip.
- **Outline** at least two supporting details that back up this main idea.
- **Identify** at least two language techniques used in the clip. **Quote** examples of these techniques in use, and **explain** the effect the speaker gains from using each of these techniques.
- **Give** one reason why you like the clip, supporting this with evidence from the clip.
- **Explain** one way in which this communication could have been made more effective, again supporting your answer with evidence from the clip.

In the end, it is up to you and your teacher to know when you are ready to be finally assessed for listening. When that time comes, your teacher has certain responsibilities:

- He or she must be sure you are listening to the right, detailed and complex, level of language.
- Your teacher must give you an assessment that tests you on all the right aspects of listening. This could be by using one of the Unit Assessment Support Packs produced by the SQA. Or, your teacher could make up their own assessment questions based on a text he or she thinks you will appreciate and understand.

- Your teacher must keep a record of evidence that you have passed the assessment.
- Though you do not have to get every individual question right, your teacher must make sure that you have answered enough questions correctly to cover each outcome — purpose; audience; main ideas and details; meaning and effect.
- If you do not pass first time, your teacher should give you another assessment. This must be based on a new text at the same level of difficulty, and should ask new questions. You only have to answer the questions that cover the outcome(s) you got wrong in your first assessment.

CHAPTER 2 The Creation and Production Unit

You must pass this unit to pass the Higher course — just as you have to pass the Analysis and Evaluation Unit covered in the previous chapter. In this unit you will be assessed on your skills in writing and talking. This chapter will cover these two skills separately, starting with writing, and then going on to look at talking in more detail.

Writing

What you will be assessed on

You have to show all the appropriate writing skills by producing at least **one written text**. This text should be clearly **understandable at first reading** — in other words your teacher should not have to re-read anything to try to work out what you mean. Your meaning will be this clear if you choose the right sort of language and vocabulary, and if it is **technically accurate**, which means there should not be mistakes in your spelling, punctuation and grammar.

There are some other choices you need to make too. You must select significant **ideas and content** to include in your writing. And, you must choose a **format and a structure** that suit the **audience** you are writing for and the **purpose** of your piece of writing. Your text should be in detailed and complex language. (Remember that you can look back at the Introduction to this book to find out more about what 'detailed and complex' means here.)

Combined assessment

The writing work you do for the Creation and Production Unit may help you with another part of the course.

- A piece of written work might be evidence of writing for this unit and eventually also go into your Portfolio.
- The subject that you prepare and plan for a piece of writing might also work well as material for an individual presentation, or perhaps for some other kind of talk.

Your teacher will make sure that you have covered all the skills each unit asks for.

It is actually very likely that your teacher will want to combine assessments in this way. There just isn't very much time to cover all the material in the Higher course, so your teacher will almost certainly decide to assess your Creation and Production of writing through the pieces that you need to do anyway for the Portfolio you send away as part of your final assessment.

So, if you want teaching and advice about how to write, and some examples of good writing, turn to Chapter 5 of this book, which deals with the writing Portfolio. The rest of the writing section in this current chapter will mostly look at some of the issues that might affect your performance in writing.

Technical accuracy

As we saw above, your writing has to be understandable at first reading; it must be clearly expressed and make full sense. It also has to be technically accurate, without significant mistakes in spelling, grammar and punctuation.

Even if you go on to make changes to your writing, or to redraft it for your portfolio, if you are using that same piece of writing as evidence that you have passed your unit assessment, you have to be technically accurate at the first draft stage.

But, this book cannot teach you technical accuracy. There just isn't space. If you have difficulties with using language in this way, your teacher will certainly notice this and can recommend other books or exercises you can use.

What we can do here is prove to ourselves that technical accuracy matters. It changes meaning. Look at this sentence:

He baked an extra, large cake

It tells us that a male person, who had been baking cake, made one more cake, and that this additional cake was large.

However, if you change the punctuation, you get this:

He baked an extra-large cake.

Which suggests what you see in the picture.

The writer of this book once received some publicity from a company in which she had invested a lot of money. At the top of the page it said:

Were here to help you!

Can you explain why the writer didn't feel reassured? What went wrong with the company's use of punctuation?

Work your way through the following tasks. Each one demonstrates how important technical accuracy is in affecting meaning.

1 Look at the following sentences. Draw a cartoon to illustrate each one, so that you show the difference in meaning.

> Careful! Children crossing
>
> Careful children crossing

2 At the start of Shakespeare's *Macbeth*, a wounded soldier tells King Duncan about a battle. These are the words the king says about this soldier after he has listened to the report:

> Go, get him surgeons.

What does the king want his staff to do?

Now, imagine the sentence had been punctuated like this:

> Go get him, surgeons!

What does it mean now?

Read the two different versions out aloud so that your tone and pace show the different meanings.

3 Look at the following sentences. Draw a cartoon to illustrate each one, so that you show the difference in meaning.

> This is Andrew. Who could be more attractive?
>
> This is Andrew, who could be more attractive.

4 You go to stay in a small hotel. Which is the right version of the sign on one of the doors?

> RESIDENTS LOUNGE

OR

> RESIDENTS' LOUNGE

What does the wrong version mean?

5 Look at the following sentences. Explain what each means.

> The factory made boys' and girls' toys.
>
> The factory made boys, and girls' toys.

6 Read these two sentences. Both use all the same letters and words in the same order, it's just the punctuation that has changed. Can you explain the two very different meanings?

> Let's eat, Grandma.
>
> Let's eat Grandma!

You might be thinking some of those examples were pretty silly, and they were, but that's the point. Technical errors can make a clever pupil seem rather stupid, so you have to learn not to make them.

Ideally, you will be a skilled enough user of language that you don't make a lot of mistakes as you write. You should also be able to check over your own writing before you hand it in to your teacher, and to notice and correct any errors. If your teacher still finds mistakes when he or she marks your work, you should be able to correct these.

Many schools use a correction code. Teachers put these marks in the margin, to show that there is a mistake on that line of work. Here's one example of a correction code.

sp	spelling	**^**	something missing
caps	mistake in use of capitals	**rep**	repetition
S	sentence error	**✓**	something good
NP	new paragraph	**exp**	not clearly expressed
p	punctuation mistake	**?**	what does this say?

Active learning

You are going to see an example of work which a teacher has marked using the correction code.

1 Identify each specific mistake the pupil has made.

2 Correct the mistakes.

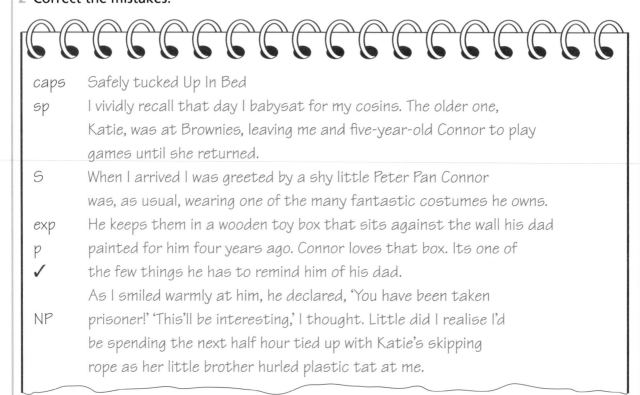

caps	Safely tucked Up In Bed
sp	I vividly recall that day I babysat for my cosins. The older one,
	Katie, was at Brownies, leaving me and five-year-old Connor to play
	games until she returned.
S	When I arrived I was greeted by a shy little Peter Pan Connor
	was, as usual, wearing one of the many fantastic costumes he owns.
exp	He keeps them in a wooden toy box that sits against the wall his dad
p	painted for him four years ago. Connor loves that box. Its one of
✓	the few things he has to remind him of his dad.
	As I smiled warmly at him, he declared, 'You have been taken
NP	prisoner!' 'This'll be interesting,' I thought. Little did I realise I'd
	be spending the next half hour tied up with Katie's skipping
	rope as her little brother hurled plastic tat at me.

By the way, if any of your writing contained as many mistakes as that extract, you would certainly not pass the standard for technical accuracy.

Read the next part of the piece. Decide where the teacher would mark errors. What would the teacher write in the margin each time?

'Stop chucking toys' I yelled, as a Barbie narrowly missed poking my eye out. Connor stopped lobbing and insisted quietly, ' They are cannonballs!'

Nevertheless I managed to untie myself and get him to help me tidy up. I wrestled him into a firemans lift and he squeeled and wriggled as I carried him up the stairs, threatening to tickle him if he didn't get straight into his pyjamas.

This was actually a fairly easy task as over the month or too since I had started babysitting the children had learned to get changed when I told them to. In fact they are always very well behaved when i look after them. They are always good when I'm in charge.

Occasionally Connor and Katie will mention their dad in passing conversations, such as, 'I have sums to do tonight.' PAUSE 'Daddy was good at sums.' This never fails to make my throat tighten. I still get angry that two young, innocent children could lose their dad so suddenly.

They were both still under five years old when my uncle had a major heart attack and didn't recover, my auntie was in her late thirties and my uncle David was only thirty-seven. He was perfectly fit and healthy, led an active life, and loved his family more than anyone else I know. I think that's why, when we got the phone call, I couldn't believe the bad news. It still seems so unfair. Remembering times I spent with him makes me think abut how I saw him — a tall, strong, clever man who never failed to make people laugh I always looked up to him.

As the kids grow up they remind me more and more of dad. Connor looks like him in every way and Katie has his bright eyes and sharp mind.

Now that you have a better idea about what technical accuracy means, let's go on and look at one other important idea.

How your work will be assessed

In order to prove that your writing has met the standard required by the Creation and Production unit, your teacher will formally assess it.

- The work has to be done under controlled conditions. This means it will be done in school or college so your teacher knows it is your own work and sees how you have done it.
- Your teacher can give you advice and guidance.
- Your teacher can support you as you prepare and plan. He or she can discuss your ideas with you and give you advice and support in making notes.
- Your teacher is not allowed to give you key ideas, specific wording, or a detailed plan or structure.
- Your teacher cannot correct your work in detail. This means he or she cannot show you exactly what your mistakes are or how you should fix them.
- If you do not pass the assessment first time round, you can have another go. But, this might mean starting again with a whole new task. Your teacher will make clear what you should do to be reassessed.

Types and genres of writing

 Warning

Remember that the genres of writing you are most likely to tackle in school are *not* dealt with in this chapter. Short story writing, personal writing, two-sided argumentative writing and one-sided persuasive writing are all covered in depth in Chapter 5. You can look there to find teaching and advice about them.

There are other types and genres, of course. The unit support notes for teachers mention dramatic monologues, film screenplays and journalistic reports, as well as the kind of pieces you will learn about in Chapter 5.

Other forms of writing include website or wiki pages, blogs, letters (both formal and informal), diaries, and playscripts.

If we covered each of these here in all the depth you might expect from a Higher textbook, the book would become enormous. And, as we've seen before, it's very likely that your teacher will assess your writing work for the Creation and Production Unit by considering the pieces you write for your Portfolio — pieces which are dealt with in the next chapter.

But, if do you want to produce something else for the Creation and Production Unit, here's a piece of advice:

YOU CAN'T BE A WRITER IF YOU AREN'T A READER.

Pupils, even Higher English pupils, sometimes say, 'I don't like reading.' English teachers really can't understand that sentence. To an English teacher, saying, 'I don't like reading,' is as bizarre as saying, 'I don't like people,' or 'I don't like food.' The world is so full of things to read, there must be something out there that you'd like. And:

YOU CAN'T BE A WRITER IF YOU AREN'T A READER.

If you look at Chapter 5 about the Portfolio, you'll find it's full of examples, short extracts and complete pieces, of the sorts of texts you'll be trying to write. Similarly, if you decide you want to write a wiki page, or a news report, or a diary entry, to prove you've met the standards for writing in the Creation and Production Unit, you need to read wiki pages, or news reports, or diaries.

After all, you wouldn't join an orchestra if you'd never listened to any music in your life. You wouldn't decide to become a chef if you'd only ever eaten toast.

There's lots of advice in the next chapter, but remember:

YOU'LL NEVER BE A WRITER IF YOU AREN'T A READER.

Talking

So far this chapter has dealt, briefly, with one of the Creation and Production skills, writing. Now we are going to move onto the second of these skills, talking, in more detail.

You have to show all the appropriate talking skills by actively participating in at least **one spoken activity**. What you say should be clearly **understandable at first hearing** — in other words your listeners should not have any difficulty understanding what you mean. Your meaning will be this clear if you choose the right sort of language and vocabulary.

There are some other choices you need to make too. You must select significant **ideas and content** to use as you talk, and you must choose a **format and a structure** that suit the **audience** you are talking to and the **purpose** of your talk. You should speak in detailed and complex language. (Remember that you can look back at the Introduction to this book to find out more about what 'detailed and complex' means here.) Your teacher will also be looking at your **non-verbal communication**, things like eye contact and body language.

The spoken activities you take part in should be of some length — after all you need to speak for long enough to let your teacher see you demonstrate all the skills.

Your teacher may use a number of different methods of assessing your work, and of recording these judgements. He or she could:

- make a video or audio recording
- assess your work against a checklist
- make notes of what he or she observes

The talking work you do for the Creation and Production Unit may overlap with some other part of the course.

- You might be able to pass your assessment in listening by listening to someone else talking, or by evaluating and answering questions about a group discussion that you have watched or taken part in. There is more information about this in the listening part of Chapter 1, which is the chapter about the Analysis and Evaluation Unit.
- If your teacher plans to assess you for talking through a group discussion, this opportunity might arise from other work you are doing in class. For example, if you are discussing a text you are studying for the Critical Reading exam, your teacher might assess your talking skills as you do this.
- You might choose to give an individual presentation to your class about the topic you research and prepare for your discursive essay. There is more information about this in Chapter 5, which is the chapter about the writing Portfolio.

Your teacher will make sure that you have covered all the skills each unit asks for.

Spoken activities

We saw above that you need to demonstrate your skills in talking by taking part in at least one spoken activity. This might mean:

- a presentation to an audience
- a pair or group discussion
- a debate
- a video or audio podcast

Even if you are mainly just standing up at the front of the room giving an individual presentation, you should be *interacting with* the audience, not *talking at* them. You need to engage and involve the audience, and show that you are involved with them. We will cover how you can do this as we work through this part of the chapter.

Some people do feel very nervous about talking, especially about individual presentations to an audience. That's completely understandable. For every raging, egomaniac extrovert in your class who just loves being listened to, there's going to be someone who wishes the carpet would open up and swallow them.

But the reason talking is assessed in the Higher English course is because it is a valuable life skill, one you will use in your further study, at work, and in your daily relationships.

As the most common tasks used for the assessment of talking are individual presentation and group discussion, we will deal mainly with them.

Individual presentations

You might deliver your individual presentation to your whole class. However, it is also possible to talk to a smaller audience, perhaps by speaking to a group while the rest of your class is working on something else. If you are particularly anxious about individual presentation, discuss with your teacher whether you can be assessed in this way.

But, the best way to overcome nerves is by being ready. So, in this part of the chapter we will focus on the three Ps of **preparing**, **practising** and **presenting** your talk.

First though, an inspirational example:

Malala Yousafzai speaking to the United Nations in 2013

Malala Yousafzai was a schoolgirl in Pakistan when she became known for campaigning for the right of girls to have an education. She wrote a blog for the BBC, was filmed by a US documentary crew, gave media interviews, and was nominated for the International Children's Peace Prize.

One morning, Taliban gunmen boarded Malala's school bus. They asked for her by name, and shot her in the head. Critically ill, she was brought to Britain for surgery and intensive medical support.

Far from giving up her campaign, she became the focus for a world-wide movement to give all children everywhere, and especially girls, an education. In October 2014 Malala became the youngest person ever to win the Nobel Peace Prize and has been named as one of the 100 most influential people in the world. She met the Queen, and US President Barack Obama, and marked her sixteenth birthday by making a speech to the United Nations.

So, if Malala Yousafzai can speak to hundreds of people at the UN, under the gaze of the world's media, just seven months after an assassination attempt, and can do so in English — which isn't even her first language — what's stopping you from talking to your classmates?

We're going to use that event as an example. First, your teacher needs to do a little preparation.

Teacher's task

- Google 'Malala UN speech' to find the film of this event.
- Your pupils will also need a written version of the speech, which you can find by googling 'Malala UN speech transcript'.
- Each pupil in your class also needs a copy of the next page of this book to write on.

Active learning

Start by working on your own. The whole broadcast speech is quite long. Get your teacher to play it up to the 6 minute, 50 second point, just before Malala talks about her feelings for the Talib who shot her.

As you watch, make notes on your sheet to record your observations. The wording on the page comes from the assessment standards for talking at Higher, which means your teacher might also eventually use a copy of this page to assess you.

For example, under the heading for language choice, you might notice her repeated use of the 'Honourable … Respected …' form of address. Under the heading for ideas and content you might notice her gratitude to those who have helped and supported her.

Now join up with someone else and compare your notes. What did your partner spot that you did not?

Next, still working with your partner, read the transcript of the speech. This will really let you focus on two features: the speaker's ideas and content; and her language choice. Add to your notes on the sheet.

Speaker:

      ⬭

Topic:

      ⬭

Significant ideas and content, using a format and structure suitable for purpose and audience:

Knowledge and understanding of language, shown by language choice

Non-verbal communication

Speaker communicates meaning at 1st hearing? Tick/cross ☐

Going deeper

You can do this task again on your own by watching or reading other inspiring examples.

- If you'd like to read the text of a historical talk, look for the Gettysburg Address, delivered by Abraham Lincoln in 1863 during the American Civil War. This famous oration is just ten sentences long.
- For another US presidential source, search out John F. Kennedy's inauguration speech from almost a century later in 1961.

John F. Kennedy speaking at his presidential inauguration

- To read the words of a man unafraid to lay down his life, find Nelson Mandela's statement from the dock at his trial in 1964. This is a very long speech, but the last few paragraphs have become especially famous. Or, look for the shorter speech he gave when inaugurated as South Africa's president in 1994.
- If you want to watch a British politician and gifted speaker, check out Tony Benn.
- For a speech by a younger, female speaker, look for actress Ellen Page talking to the Time To THRIVE conference.

Ellen Page

Now that you are thoroughly inspired, it's time to work on the first of the three P stages mentioned earlier.

Preparation

The best way to use this section on individual presentations is to prepare one as you work through the next few pages. Before you start to do this, it's helpful to know two things:

1 **Who** will your audience be? Your whole class? A small group? Some other audience altogether?
2 **What** will your talk will be about?

Your teacher can help you clarify the *who*. Let's take some time to think about the *what*.

You know that you have to use detailed and complex language. Also, your audience will most likely consist of Higher English students, who should be listening to detailed and complex language. One way to make sure you use this sort of language is by picking a subject that is, in itself, detailed and complex.

Your teacher may give you a topic, or at least an area to think about. Here are some other suggestions. For some of them, you'll see how they might be an evolution of, or a move on from, topics you might have covered in National 5.

At National 5 you might have spoken about a favourite film, speaking about what happens, who is in it, and why you like it. You could still focus on just one film, but deal with it far more deeply, with thorough analysis and by making use of appropriate film studies terminology.

You might choose a film director and present an introduction to his or her work. This would include looking at aspects of this director's style, recurring themes and ideas in the work, and so on.

Or, at National 5 you might have spoken about a book. Again, you could still deal with just one book at Higher, but taking a far deeper and more critical approach.

You could choose to discuss the work of a particular writer. This would include looking at aspects of this author's style, recurring themes and ideas in their work, and so on.

You might talk about a writer you are studying for your Critical Reading exam. For instance, once you have become familiar with some of this author's work you could investigate a new area: a new poem or short story, a later extract from a novel or play. In your talk you would share your discoveries with the class, thereby introducing them to that text or extract.

You could deliver a revision lecture to your class about a text they have studied for the exam.

Your talk might be based on the research you have done for the discursive essay that goes in your Portfolio.

You might pick an issue that is currently in the news and present a deeper viewpoint: for example if a conflict has broken out somewhere, you could research and explain the underlying historical causes; if the government has launched some new policy or programme you could investigate the ideas behind this.

These are just some suggestions. Any topic that gets you to be thoughtful, critical or analytical is likely to be a rich source for your talk.

The first step is to create a rough outline for your Presentation. The easiest way to do this is to make a list of headings. For example if you were talking about a writer, your headings might be:

- Introduction — who this is, why I chose him/her
- Brief overview
  - biographical detail
  - significant works
- Key themes and ideas — how these are handled
  1
  2
  3
- Key aspects of style
  1
  2
  3
- Critical responses/reception
- My own response to this author
- Conclusion

You can then write out what you want to say under each of these headings. Even at this stage, try to do this by writing notes rather than full sentences. Use short phrases, key words and bullet points. This will lower the risk of you just getting up and reading your notes out to the audience. This isn't a reading aloud assessment, it's a talking one!

Here's an idea for you to think about:

The holy grail of public speaking is rehearsed spontaneity.

Have a chat with your partner. What do you think this means? If you understand this, you will understand what the preparation and practice stages are for.

Now that you have your raw material, let's look at how to shape it into a successful Presentation, one you know you have rehearsed, but will come across as spontaneous.

Good openings

You want to engage your audience right away — to draw them in, or intrigue them, to get them thinking or to startle them.

Look at the two openings below. Which one do you think belongs to the National 5 Presentation, and which one begins a Presentation by a Higher student?

> **'First, do no harm,'** said Hippocrates, which is all very well for him sitting quietly in ancient Greece, but rather more daunting for a sixteen-year-old in an ill-fitting set of scrubs.

> **Doctors, nurses, patients...** As you've probably guessed I spent my work experience week in a hospital.

You should have spotted that the first one is the Higher one. While both speakers draw the audience in, the National 5 speaker starts by saying something rather predictable. The Higher speaker, though, shows off knowledge of the foundation of all medical ethics, then undercuts that seriousness with the self-deprecating image of herself in the borrowed hospital clothes.

There are many ways you can give your opening impact. Here's writer and broadcaster Sandi Toksvig:

> A man once offered two camels for my hand in marriage. I was making a documentary in the Nubian desert in Sudan when I caught an older gentleman's eye. He made the offer to my male producer, who very kindly suggested he would split the proceeds with me if I agreed. Never one to rush a decision, I went off to look at the proffered creatures. I'm no camel expert, but they seemed rather dapper for fellows with many miles left in them. In the end, however, I graciously declined and we all had mint tea instead.

Toksvig starts with a very striking opening sentence, a statement the audience can't ignore. She goes on to tell a story, as an introduction to her text.

So, by looking at the opening from the pupil who did her work experience in a hospital, and from that by Sandi Toksvig, we already have five techniques you can use:

1 use a quotation
2 use humour
3 paint a picture with words
4 make a striking statement
5 tell a story

You could also do one or more of these things:

6 ask a question, either a rhetorical one or one you do want the audience to answer
7 share a thought or observation
8 jump right in to the middle of the action

Look back at the notes you have made so far for the Presentation you are preparing. Rewrite your opening to have more impact on the audience.

Language and vocabulary

One of the things the assessor will be looking at is the language and vocabulary you choose to use. These, remember, should be **detailed and complex**.

First of all, you should **vary your vocabulary**, choosing interesting, less common, words rather than more ordinary and predictable ones. So Sandi Toksvig in her opening used words like 'proffered', 'dapper' and 'declined' rather than the more straightforward 'offered', 'smart' and 'refused'.

Active learning

This pupil is talking about his favourite film director. His language at the moment is a little unsophisticated. Can you re-write this section of his talk to make the language more detailed and complex? You should be helping him to do these three things:

1 use more interesting vocabulary

2 avoid repetition of the same words or phrases

3 use longer and more complex sentences

Wes Anderson's next film was his most successful so far. This film was *The Grand Budapest Hotel*. In my opinion it is also his best. Every frame is full of detail that makes you wish you could rewind it and watch it again. Wes Anderson has used lots of bright, light colours such as pinks, creams and blues. These colours almost make the film feel like a bright and tasty box of chocolates for the viewer to pick from. This is very suitable as one character works in a bakery making incredible cakes and pastries. Part of the plot involves two characters using the bakery van to sneak their way in to the hotel.

As well as working on varying your vocabulary, and using more complex structures, think about how you will use language to shape your Presentation and give it direction. Words like *therefore*, *furthermore* and *however* can act as links and connections within your talk. (You will find a lot more of these useful words and phrases on page 205, in the section of this book that deals with discursive writing.)

Look back at the notes you have so far for the Presentation you are preparing. Check over your vocabulary. Are there places where you could vary words? Remember variety can mean both avoiding boring repetition and also showing the breadth of your word choice. Are there places where you could use longer, more complex, sentences?

As well as generally varying your vocabulary, there are other language techniques you can use to engage your audience and give impact to your talk.

Register

Register is the choice of language you make to suit your purpose, your audience, and the situation in which you are speaking. At its simplest level, register is often about choosing how formally to speak. As being assessed is one of the most formal parts of school life, you should be choosing a fairly formal register for your individual presentations, and for group discussion.

That doesn't mean informality is always wrong, just that your choice of register is a choice about technique. What you say has to work as an interesting speech, and you should always be trying to engage your audience while fulfilling your purpose. But, it can be hard to handle detailed, complex ideas if you use overly simplistic and informal language.

This pupil is giving a revision lecture about the poetry of Don Paterson. Read the two possible versions of what he might say:

We have to concede that he's a great writer. He moves us to feel his emotions at the same time as dazzling us with his mastery of technique. Paterson's grasp of the sonnet totally updates it. We can see how the form can be used for life and death issues — it's far more than a sweet little box of love and romance.

You have to say he's a great. He makes you feel his emotions at the same time as basically just dazzling you with his technique. His take on sonnets is totally now. You can see how they can be used for important stuff.

Did you notice the second bubble uses *you*, a lot? Using *you* in speech, and in writing, can be a problem. It's rather vague, and too impersonal. The pupil is talking about a poet he has studied. Why is he using *you* as if only the audience know about Paterson? If you are talking about yourself, say *I*. If you are talking about people in general, say *we* or *us* to involve the listeners.

Register goes a little further than just choosing how formal to be. You should also be able to use a little bit of slang, or dialect, or informality, to gain certain effects and to make your speech vivid: this would give evidence of your ability to choose the best words at the best time. If your Presentation is about the rich variety of language used in modern Scotland, then the use of Scots would be highly appropriate. If, however, your Presentation is about Hilary Mantel's evocation of the court of Henry VIII in her *Wolf Hall* series of novels, then the use of Scots would be inappropriate.

Furthermore, your choice of register may also involve using specialist vocabulary: words, phrases and terminology that pertain to a certain subject matter or area.

Active learning

Look at the groups of words and phrases. Which subject or area of interest does each belong to?

A mise en scène, representation, institutional factors

B jurisprudence, precedent, duty of care

C enjambment, assonance, rhyme scheme

D bond, hedge fund, annuity

E grind, carving, wipe out, 360

F fold, sauté, ballotine

For answers see page 220.

While it's important that you use a register that suits your subject matter and your purpose, remember that, for the sake of your audience, you might need to define or explain some of the terms you use. If you use specialist language they can't understand that's not communication, it's just showing off.

Humour and anecdote

One of the easiest ways to win over your audience is to give them something to laugh at — especially if that something is you. Being funny to order may sound like a hard thing to do, but we all make our friends laugh all the time in real life by using **anecdotes**. An anecdote is a brief story, often an amusing one.

Look back again at the introduction by Sandi Toksvig that appeared on page 40. She's telling a personal, gently humorous anecdote. But, she goes on in the rest of her text to discuss the more serious subject of how marriage, and society's definition of marriage, has changed in recent years.

You don't have to personally star in each anecdote that you use. An anecdote can just as easily be something you observed, or an experience that you know happened to someone else. Nor do anecdotes all have to be funny. If you listen to correspondents on longer radio news programmes like Radio 4's *Today* or *PM* you will often hear them telling anecdotes about one person's experience as a way of illustrating a wider story. For instance, an anecdote about the millionth Syrian refugee to be registered by the United Nations was used as part of an explanation of the ongoing civil war in that country.

Hyperbole

This is the more formal and literary term for exaggeration, and it's another technique that can bring life to the language of your talk. Here's the next paragraph of Sandi Toksvig's piece. Can you spot the hyperbole?

> I wonder what the world would have made of me if I had suddenly become the wife of a Nubian nomad about whom I knew nothing? He was a man, I was a woman. Did that make it a pleasing union for all concerned? I suspect even the most rabid proponent of 'traditional' marriage might think not, but the offer was entirely in keeping with the origins of matrimony. Historically, marriage had nothing to do with love. It was a legal contract and was all about alliances, getting the right in-laws and adding to your property. Things have changed. Now marriage is about love, or at least it should be.

Active learning

Go back to your notes again. Decide if there are places where you could use anecdote or hyperbole.

Rhetorical questions

We have already seen how you can use questions — rhetorical or otherwise — to engage your audience at the start of your talk. These can also be used throughout to challenge your listeners or to get them thinking. You can see one in the Sandi Toksvig paragraph above:

> He was a man, I was a woman. Did that make it a pleasing union for all concerned?

'Of course not,' think the audience members, realising how much more there is to marriage than biology.

Emotive language

One technique that can be particularly helpful in serious or persuasive talks, or in ones dealing with controversial subjects, is to use **emotive language**.

Emotive words are strong ones, ones that rouse the listeners' emotions. If you read tabloid newspapers, listen to politicians, or read the advertising sent out by charities, you will often find a lot of emotive language in use.

Active learning

Some emotive language aims to cause negative emotions such as anger or disgust. Look at the words in the box on the left. How many similar ones could you add to the box on the right?

disturbing
terrifying
horrendous
scandalous
contemptible
alarming

Some emotive language aims to cause more positive emotions. Look at the words in the box on the left. How many similar ones could you add to the box on the right?

excellent
superb
remarkable
astounding
magnificent
extraordinary

Active learning

Go back to your notes. Try to find a couple of places in your Presentation where you could change statements into rhetorical questions, or where you could use emotive language.

Good endings

Endings matter too. When you did National 5, you probably concentrated on making sure that you wrapped up clearly so that the audience knew that you had finished. You will have made sure that you summed up your Presentation, and perhaps thanked the audience or invited questions.

You need to do more at Higher. Think of it as **finishing with a flourish**.

Do you remember the techniques we said you could use for your opening? Many of them will also work equally well for endings, particularly:

- quotation
- making a striking statement
- asking a question
- sharing a thought or observation

There are other ways you can make your ending effective too. You could refer back to something you mentioned earlier in your Presentation. You could bring the whole thing back round by returning to a detail from your start.

Here's the ending of Sandi Toksvig's text. Having discussed how marriage, and society's view of it, has changed, she looks ahead to her own upcoming celebration:

> Marrying is one of the greatest things that has ever happened in my life. I know it's traditional to have doubts on the big day, but I confess to just one tiny niggle. I am worried that I am never going to get that camel.

You could also refer to a person, story, or example that cleverly embodies or epitomises an idea that was in your talk.

Active learning

Look back at the notes you have so far for the Presentation you are preparing. Rework your ending so that you can finish with a flourish.

Using notes

There's nothing wrong with using notes. However you do have to use non-verbal communication, such as gesture and body language, and the way you handle your notes can affect these.

Your notes are there to support you if you need them. You should never just read your Presentation out — this is not what you are being marked on. The best way to avoid this is to keep your notes as short as possible, so that you **can't** just read them.

On page 39 you saw the outline for a talk about a writer. Let's focus on the section giving a brief overview of the writer's life and work. The outline for that point looks like this:

- Brief overview
  - biographical detail
  - significant works

Imagine you were going to talk about George Orwell. You want the audience to hear something like this:

Orwell was born Eric Arthur Blair in Bengal, then part of British India but now the independent nation of Bangladesh, in 1903. He later described his background as, 'lower-upper-middle-class'.

The family returned to England when Orwell was three. He was sent to boarding school aged eight on a scholarship, and later went to Eton, also on a scholarship: facts which demonstrate both how clever he was, and how little money his family had. One might assume that attending Eton – an exclusive and prestigious private school which has produced 19 British Prime Ministers – would have turned Orwell into an establishment figure. On the contrary, he always felt like an outsider, unworthy and very aware of how little money his family had.

After school, rather than going to university, he joined the Indian Imperial Police and served in Burma from 1922 to 1927. He spent much of his time there feeling disillusioned and frustrated, and returned to Britain, 'conscious of an immense weight of guilt that I had got to expiate'.

After leaving Burma he lived for a while among poor and marginalised people in Britain and France, taking low-paid and dirty jobs. He wrote about this later in a book called *Down And Out In Paris And London*. He spent most of the rest of his life writing, not only essays but also journalism, longer non-fiction books and novels. Two of his most famous books are *Animal Farm* and *1984*, and in the latter he created two ideas that have become part of our culture, the notion that Big Brother is watching us, and the idea of a Room 101 where the things that upset each of us most can be found.

If you get up to deliver your Presentation with all these words written out, you may just read them. The next step is to reduce the notes to key words, first by underlining or highlighting the most important words and phrases.

Orwell was born <u>Eric Arthur Blair</u> in <u>Bengal</u>, then part of British India but now the independent nation of Bangladesh, in <u>1903</u>. He later described his background as, '<u>lower-upper-middle-class</u>'.

The family returned to England when Orwell was three. He was sent to boarding school aged eight on a scholarship, and later went to <u>Eton</u>, also on a <u>scholarship</u> — facts which demonstrate both how clever he was, and how little money his family had. One might assume that attending Eton – an exclusive and prestigious private school which has produced <u>19 British Prime Ministers</u> – would have turned Orwell into an establishment figure. On the contrary, he always felt like an <u>outsider</u>, unworthy and very aware of how little money his family had.

After school, rather than going to university he joined the Indian Imperial Police and served in <u>Burma</u> from <u>1922 to 1927</u>. He spent much of his time there feeling disillusioned and frustrated, and returned to Britain, '<u>conscious of an immense weight of guilt that I had got to expiate</u>'.

After leaving Burma he lived for a while among poor and marginalised people in Britain and France, taking low-paid and dirty jobs. He wrote about this later in a book called <u>Down And Out In Paris And London</u>. He spent most of the rest of his life writing, not only essays but also journalism, longer non-fiction books and novels. Two of his most famous books are <u>Animal Farm</u> and <u>1984</u>, and in the latter he created two ideas that have become part of our culture, the notion that Big Brother is watching us, and the idea of a Room 101 where the things that upset each of us most can be found.

However if you speak from notes like these, you may still have to do a fair bit of scanning to find your key words. The next step is to write them out on small cards or slips of paper. Using strong colours and large print, write out your key words. You can also use layout to show the connections between ideas.

Your last card might now look like this:

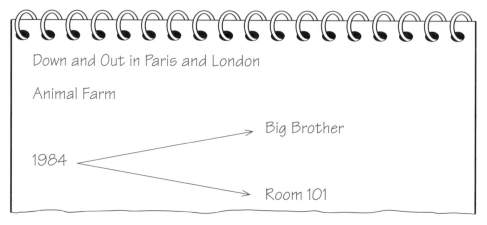

By the time you get to this stage, you'll know your material so well that a quick glance down at the few words in your notes will bring up all you want to say.

Using props

As we saw earlier, you are being assessed on your interaction with others: you are not just talking *at* them. The more ways you can find to interest your audience, and to engage with them, the more interactive you are being.

It can be a very good idea to use props in your Presentation. For instance if you are talking about an author, you could bring copies of books by that person. If you are exploring the background of a current news story, you could bring papers whose headlines show them covering that issue.

Holding a prop gives you something to do with your hands, which may help you control signs of nerves. Passing a prop around is interesting for the audience and connects you more strongly to them. If your Presentation is well prepared, then using props may even remind you of everything you want to say, and help you to speak without notes.

Using PowerPoint and other technology

If you are speaking to your whole class, or some other roomful of people, rather than a small group, you may decide to use a PowerPoint to accompany your Presentation. This can be a fantastic way of bringing more interest and interactivity to your talk.

A word of warning here. Many PowerPoint users make a classic mistake. Instead of talking to the audience, they just read out what can be seen on the screen.

This is just repetition, and it will bore your audience. Instead, use PowerPoint to support your words, and don't feel the need to have a slide for every single thing you're going to say. The pupil talking about Orwell could put up a picture of the writer, or a map showing the locations of Bengal and Burma.

The same goes for DVD clips, YouTube videos, and any other visual material. They should be doing something you cannot do in words, not repeating something you have already verbalised.

You shouldn't use PowerPoint, or any other technological prop, unless you are absolutely sure how it works, and how it operates in your school or college. Even if you know how it would run on your computer at home, even if you know how to bring up a clip on your own DVD player, make sure you get a chance to set up and practise on the equipment you'll be using at school.

Now that you have your notes set out on cue cards, have chosen any props, and have made your PowerPoint or other visual aids, your talk is prepared. It's time to think about the next two stages.

Practising and presentation

We're going to look at these two steps together, because any practice of your talk is, in itself, a little presentation.

Eye contact

Eye contact is one of the key aspects of non-verbal communication.

If you've produced good notes as discussed already, then you are on your way to good eye contact, because you should not *need* to keep looking down. If you feel that you might *want* to keep looking down, there's a section coming up on dealing with nerves that you'll find helpful. If you want to look up, but you're not sure how to, keep reading.

If you are talking to your whole class, your teacher will be part of the audience. If you're speaking to a group, your teacher will be sitting among you, or nearby. As you talk, the teacher will assess you: maybe by making notes or following a checklist, or by filming your talk.

Lots of pupils make the mistake of staring at the teacher, or at the camera. Some others look at a friend, because they know that person will support them. Others just look straight ahead.

Try this instead. Imagine you are a lighthouse. Although you are standing still, your eyes – the lamp of the lighthouse – can move, sweeping across the class like the light sweeps across the sea. Whenever you are able to look up for a few seconds, sweep your eyes across the class, taking in most of the room. You might notice that this is what your teachers do when they talk to their classes. The reason this works so well is that it makes everyone in the audience feel they should pay attention to you all the time, because they know you could look at them at any second.

Active learning

This game will give everyone in the class a very quick chance to practise eye contact. Everybody needs a small slip of card or paper. Get each person to write down a nice, simple, straightforward common noun and then fold their paper in half. Get someone to collect the cards in a bag.

One by one, each person should take a card, and talk for 30 seconds about the word on it. (You may need to give people a minute or two to think about what they are going to say.)

When each person comes up to speak, they should try to keep their eyes on the audience at all times, moving their eye contact around the room like a lighthouse as they do so.

Body language

This is another aspect of non-verbal communication, one that is rather more significant if you will be standing up talking to your whole class than if you will be sitting presenting to a smaller group.

Think of a television presenter who is good at their job. (It should be someone who stands up to speak, and doesn't just read from a prepared script, so not a newsreader.) Now try watching them with the television sound muted so you can focus on only what they do and not what they say. Make a list of the gestures they use. Can you work out, from their gestures alone, what they are talking about, or how they feel about that subject? Can you tell how they feel about any other people in the studio, or in the shot, with them?

You should find that the television presenter's body language helps him or her to put across the message. Unfortunately, bad body language can also lower your mark, and there are a few things to avoid.

Some people fidget terribly. All sorts of 'head' fidgets, like earring twisting, ear rubbing, nose scratching and hair twiddling are really your subconscious mind trying to send your hands to cover your mouth and stop you talking. These fidgets muffle what you say, and they display your nerves to the whole audience.

Some people, both girls and boys, hide behind their hair. If yours is long, tie it back. If your fringe tickles your eyes, just for as long as you are up there talking, don't keep flicking your head to get it out of the way — you'll look like a pony being annoyed by a fly!

Some people stand awkwardly, twisting their arms behind their backs or crossing their legs while standing up to talk. Try to plant your feet firmly, about shoulder-width apart. Otherwise the audience won't be able to concentrate on your Presentation, they will just be waiting to see you tip over sideways.

If your classroom has a lectern or book stand, try putting your notes on that. You could even borrow a music stand and use it. This way you can lightly place your hands on the stand, and move them when you want to make a gesture. If you have to hold on to your notes, keep them in one hand and use the other for gestures.

Gestures

These are any movements that you make that support the meaning of your Presentation. It can be a little bit hard to plan these — if they work, it is usually because they have come naturally. Let me give you some examples:

- A pupil talking about film director Alfred Hitchcock slapped his own (much slimmer) stomach while talking about Hitchcock's famously recognisable fat silhouette, which Hitchcock used almost as a logo.
- A pupil discussing the history of politics in sport gave the Black Power salute given by two American athletes at the 1968 Olympics.

Any uses of good eye contact, suitable body language, or appropriate gesture will make your Presentation more interactive. They connect you to the audience and make the listeners feel more interested.

Voice

We've thought a lot about visual elements of your Presentation: props, PowerPoints, eye contact and body language. But your voice is a key tool. It needs to be varied and interesting. There are several ways you can do this:

- vary the speed of what you say, speaking more slowly to create moments of emphasis and tension, or to highlight what is most important, speaking a little more quickly to indicate excitement
- increase the volume of your voice at moments of excitement
- speak a little more softly to draw your audience in
- use intonation for emphasis, leaning more heavily on the most important words: this is the spoken equivalent of using bold in your writing
- use a rising tone to suggest questions

If your audience sat there with their eyes shut, they should still find you fascinating.

Active learning

Find a partner. Ask this person to sit with their back to you. Practise your talk, or a section of it, so that your partner can hear you but cannot see you. Ask for feedback on your use of voice. Then swop roles and do this again.

Other ways of interacting with your audience

Remember the best way to engage your audience is by giving an interesting Presentation that they feel they want to listen to. The advice so far about visual aids, body language, eye contact, and voice will all help you with that. However here are a few other hints and tips to help you get the audience on your side:

- As mentioned above, one way to do this is by showing them something. This can be something electronic that you show on screen, or a real prop you pass round.
- Try asking them questions, not only rhetorical ones but perhaps also one where you clearly expect one or two of them to answer.
- Use a quiz, perhaps at the start of your Presentation, to find out how much they know about your subject, or at the end to see what they have picked up and learned from you.
- Get them to raise their hands to vote on something you've said, or to show that they have had a similar experience to the one you are describing, e.g. 'How many of you have ever read a novel with a historical setting?'
- Give them the opportunity to ask you questions at the end.
- Get them to laugh, and show them you appreciate that laughter by not talking over it.
- Use language that includes them, e.g. 'I'm sure **we** have all at some point in **our** studies this year found **ourselves** puzzled by **our** first encounter with a new text.'

Dealing with nerves

Although we've left this to last, it's actually the first thing that comes to mind when many people find out they have to do a Presentation. If you've followed all the advice in this chapter so far and prepared well, that should help you to feel less nervous and more skilled. Remember also that you do not necessarily have to talk to a whole room full of people, and that if this is a worry for you, you should discuss it with your teacher. Another way to defuse nerves is to practise on other people.

Pair up with someone else from your class and practise your Presentations on each other. Ask your partner to time what you say. Then ask them to tell you two things that were good about the talk, and one thing you could improve. Also, ask for one suggestion of a way you could add length and detail to your Presentation.

Now join up with another pair to make a group and all take turns to practise again. This will help you to get to know your material even better, as well as giving you a chance to practise lighthouse eye contact. After each person has spoken, give the same kind of feedback mentioned above.

When you get up to give your actual Presentation, remember this: **The audience wants you to succeed.** They know you, and they want you to do well. They also want to be a good, receptive audience for you, because they'll have their own talks to do too, and they'll want you to be part of a friendly and receptive audience for them when their turn comes.

Think of your talk as being shaped like a little hill:

SPEAK

SMILE   SMILE

STAND   STAND

STAND there, nice and still

SMILE at your audience

SPEAK to them, giving the Presentation you've prepared and practised

SMILE again at the end

STAND and wait for the applause

You're ready to do your Presentation now. Good luck!

Group discussion

If you've worked through the section on individual presentation, then you already know a lot of what you need to do in group discussion too.

However the group situation does introduce a few differences:

● You may have less choice of what you talk about. Your teacher will probably provide you with a discussion topic or set of questions.

- You will probably have less time to prepare for group discussion than for an individual presentation. You may be given some advance notice, and if so you should use that time to gather together ideas and points, but you won't be preparing language in the way you might do for the sort of solo talk opportunity we have just learned about.
- You may or may not get to choose the other people who are in the group with you.
- You may be given a particular role to play in the group during the discussion.
- You need to show that you know how to behave in a group situation, respecting and interacting with the others in your group.
- You must make sure you contribute enough to the discussion that your teacher can find evidence to assess you on. At the same time though, you must not take over the group. That's a tricky balancing act.

We'll deal with particular group roles later. First, let's look at how body language and spoken language can be used to show that you are taking account of others in your group.

Active learning

Imagine you had these two people in your group. Which person's body language shows that they are taking an active part in the group? Which one seems to have opted out?

So we can easily see how your body language shows that you are actively taking part. However, you need to go beyond that.

During the discussion you should be doing more listening than talking. Listening doesn't mean staying quiet for as little time as possible until you can wedge in something that you have already decided to say. What you say when you do speak might support, develop, or challenge what you hear when you are listening. If you disagree with what you have heard, there are ways to express this without giving offence or seeming arrogant, and it's perfectly all right to disagree, even quite firmly, so long as you can do so respectfully too.

Active learning

The comments in the speech bubbles fit into two groups.

1 Some phrases show that you support the previous speaker and agree with what he or she has said.

2 Some of them will let you express disagreement, so that you can challenge the previous speaker.

First, work out which comments belong in which group.

I agree with you because …

On the other hand …

I don't agree because …

I think you're wrong because …

But in my opinion …

You're right to say that …

Next, see how many more ways you can think of to begin:

1 comments or sentences that show support for a previous speaker

2 comments or sentences that allow you to appropriately challenge another speaker

As well as being able to support and challenge other group members, you should also be displaying these skills in your responses to others:

- developing
- summarising
- refuting
- justifying

Copy and complete the following table to show your understanding of these concepts.

Concept	What this concept means	What Pupil A might say	How Pupil B could respond
developing			*That's not the only reason why the government should address this. It also matters because …*
summarising			*You seem to be saying …*
refuting	Using evidence to prove that someone else is wrong.		
justifying	Using evidence to prove that you are right.	*I'm afraid I don't agree. I think X's films are overrated because …*	

Any comments or points you make during group discussion should be developed in some detail and should be backed up and supported.

Roles and contributions

In some group discussions you may be asked to take on a certain role. If so, make sure you understand what is expected of you. Here are some of the more common roles:

- **The chair** should lead the discussion and keep it moving along. The chair should also solve any conflicts or arguments and should try to encourage any shy group members, while trying to stop confident speakers from dominating. By the way, if your teacher expects your group to have a chair, he or she will be watching to see that other group members are acknowledging that chairperson.
- **The leader** has a similar role to the chair, but may also be responsible for reaching a decision or conclusion or having the casting vote if the group cannot reach a consensus.
- **The reader** may be asked to read out instructions, information or questions to the group.
- **The recorder** takes notes of what is said. Near the end of the discussion it is a good idea to read your notes back to the group so that they can agree the reporter has kept a fair record.
- **The reporter** may be asked to give a verbal report back to the whole class on what the group talked about.
- **The timekeeper** may be responsible for keeping the discussion moving, or for ensuring that you reach a conclusion or solution within a given time.

Your own teacher may use different titles for some of the roles, but these are the main responsibilities that people are generally asked to carry out in groups. Just make sure you know what is involved in any role you are given, and you'll be all right.

You may also notice that someone in your group is not contributing much, or is having trouble getting a word in. Since your teacher will also be assessing whether group members are all taking turns, you need to find a way to draw out that quiet person (or perhaps to encourage other group members to become a little quieter!) Try using some of these phrases to help you:

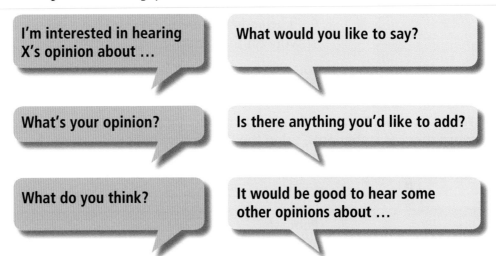

I'm interested in hearing X's opinion about …

What would you like to say?

What's your opinion?

Is there anything you'd like to add?

What do you think?

It would be good to hear some other opinions about …

Other spoken activities

At the start of the talking section of this chapter, we mentioned two other sorts of spoken interactions: **debates**, and video or audio **podcasts**. We'll take a fairly brief look at each of these now.

Debates

Debates are ideal for tackling controversial topics. A debate takes some time and preparation but can allow your teacher eventually to assess a number of people during one event.

There is a set of classic rules that a debate usually follows.

1   You debate a controversial subject. This is called the **motion**, and is usually phrased as a statement. For example:
    - This house believes that Romeo and Juliet are entirely responsible for their own deaths.
    - This house believes that British society is still deeply illiberal.
2   There are two sides.
    - The **proposition** side supports the motion.
    - The **opposition** side speaks against the motion.
3   The two sides take turns to put their points.
    - The first proposer makes a short speech in favour of the motion.
    - The first opposer makes a short speech against the motion.
    - The second proposer makes a short speech adding more points and ideas in favour of the motion. This person may also pick up on points made by the first opposer.

- The second opposer makes a short speech adding more points and ideas against the motion. This person may also pick up on points made by the proposers.

4 This pattern can go on for as long as groups have been able to come up with new points to make. This relies on groups and speakers preparing very thoroughly *before* the debate takes place.

5 At the end of the debate:
- Someone from the proposition side sums up their position.
- Someone from the opposition side sums up their position.

6 The audience members who have been watching the debate now vote on the proposition.

Active learning

Find a partner. Try to come up with at least three suitable topics for a debate. Make sure you word them as statements, using the 'This house believes…' style. Remember that, at Higher level, you need a motion challenging and complex enough to get you using detailed and complex language. Share your ideas with the rest of the class.

Podcasts

We live in a technological world. Our everyday life is full of types of text that didn't even exist when the writer of this book was studying for her Highers: wiki pages, websites, SMS messages, tweets, and so on. Podcasts are another kind of text, another thing made of language, that you can listen to or produce. So, in theory, you could have your talking skills assessed through a video or audio podcast you've produced.

However there are some possible complications.

Anything you use as evidence that you have passed a unit assessment should be done under what is called 'controlled conditions'. This means that your teacher needs to be able to oversee the process, so that they know you have done the work yourself. You can't just produce the podcast at home and bring it in to school or college to play to your teacher.

So, if you think you would like to be assessed on the basis of a podcast, check this with your teacher:

Does your school or college have IT facilities you can use, so that your teacher can oversee you producing the podcast?

That's the end of this chapter. Writing and talking are essential skills for life and for work, which is why we focus on them so much in school. You should now feel more ready to be assessed on these skills, and more able to show, through your use of detailed and complex language, how well you have mastered them.

CHAPTER 3 Reading for Understanding, Analysis and Evaluation

Reading for Understanding, Analysis and Evaluation is the formal name for the skill your teacher might also call 'close reading'.

You will be tested on this by sitting an exam in early May. Although this exam comes at the end of your Higher course, you will probably want to work on these skills throughout the year.

What you will be assessed on

In the exam you will be given two non-fiction passages, perhaps pieces of journalism or extracts from books. They will be written in the detailed and complex language you have come to expect at Higher.

You will have **one hour and thirty minutes** to read the passages and answer **30 marks'** worth of questions. These will be divided up as follows:

- **Passage 1** will be longer — usually around 850 words. It will be followed by a series of short questions. Each question will probably be worth 2, 3 or 4 marks. The total number of marks available for Passage 1 will add up to 25 marks.
- **Passage 2** will be shorter — usually around 600 words. It will be followed by just one question. This question will be worth 5 marks. It will get you to summarise the ideas and/or language of both passages, and to show your understanding of the relationship between these texts.

The exam tests your ability to **understand** the writer's ideas, and to **analyse** and **evaluate** the language he or she uses to put those ideas across. You will also be expected to summarise the writer's ideas. You have, of course, already done all of these things at National 5 level; the difference is that you will be a working at a more challenging level, and with more complex language.

This chapter will introduce you to the skills you need to pass this exam, and to some of the types of questions you may be asked. You will see explanations and worked examples and then have a chance to try questions for yourself.

This chapter will teach you suggested approaches to questions. Although you will learn how to tackle various sorts of question, you cannot assume that all these question types will come up in the exam you sit. The examiners base their questions each year on what suits their chosen passage, not on a list of question types. Also, many of the questions you will meet don't easily fit into any particular type, and so there can't be a straightforward formula for answering them. The most important advice for the exam is always going to be:

ANSWER WHAT THE QUESTION ASKS!

Using your own words

If you can put something in your own words, you have understood it; if you don't understand something, you won't be able to express it in your own words.

This will be emphasised in some of the questions where you may see **in your own words** or **using your own words** written in bold. Questions that ask you to *identify* or *explain* also expect you to use your own words.

This skill is so important that, even when the question does not say that you must use your own words, it is still best to do so as far as possible. A good general approach is to quote from the passage only when you know that you are going to go on and analyse the language of that quotation. We'll look at these more analytical questions later in the chapter.

Read the following article about homesickness:

Skype gives an illusion of closeness — homesickness however is as real as ever

1   Nostalgia used to be considered an illness. A word with a refreshingly certain etymology, it was coined by a Swiss medical student, Johannes Hofer, who in 1688 joined together two Greek words, *nostos* for homecoming and *algos* for pain or ache. The Swiss also knew it as *mal du Suisse* or *Schweizerheimweh*, later translated into English as the nationally unspecific '*homesickness*', a mental and physical malady that was found particularly among Swiss soldiers in foreign armies. It was to these mercenaries, fighting on the lowlands of France and Italy and missing the peaks and valleys of their homeland, that Hofer applied his impressive new word. Stomach pain, fever, anxiety, headache? Rather than blaming bad water, unfamiliar food or the sound of muskets, military doctors now diagnosed nostalgia: a yearning for the past, and not in a general, sentimental way (as it now tends to mean), but for a specific time and place: in this case, one where the sufferer might once have woken to the tinkle of cowbells.

2   The top deck of a number 19 London bus is a good place to listen to nostalgia, though of course you cannot be sure. The

phone conversation that lasts the half-hour from Tottenham Court Road to Finsbury Park might be about grandma's delicious Christmas recipe for roast carp, or how auntie prepared couscous in the High Atlas, but then again it might just be about *The X Factor* or nuclear physics. Somali, Bengali, Russian, Bulgarian, Moldovan, Latvian: the averagely insular native English speaker on the number 19 can easily hear all of them (and more) without understanding a word.

3 **Whatever the people on the bus are talking about, they are talking about it with someone who shares their language and — probably — their customs and traditions and country.** An interesting question then arises: has technology — mobile phones, Facebook, Skype — lessened nostalgia or increased it? Does technology give the illusion of closeness, or does it sadden the caller by reminding them sharply of what they have left behind (which is why parents were discouraged from phoning their children too often at English boarding schools)?

4 More thought than you might imagine has gone into this question and others like it, universities being what they are. Researchers at the University of Southampton, for instance, have developed the Southampton Nostalgia Scale, a universally accepted measurement produced from a standard list of questions such as 'Specifically, how often do you bring to mind nostalgic experiences?' The answers available to be ticked range from 'at least once a day' to 'once or twice a year'; as the university defines nostalgia as 'typically a fond, personally meaningful memory', it seems inconceivable to me that such recollections could be rationed in any human being to once a week, never mind once a year. And yet, as a US history professor, Susan J. Matt, recently pointed out in the *New York Times*, certain kinds of modern personality find it better to suppress or eliminate the backward glance. Explicit discussions of homesickness are now rare, Matt writes, because the emotion was typically seen 'as an embarrassing impediment to individual progress and prosperity. This silence makes mobility appear deceptively easy.'

5 **In the 19th century, by contrast, immigration made America the most openly homesick society in the world.** 'Victim of Nostalgia: A Priest Dies Craving for a Sight of his Motherland', ran a headline over a story about the death in 1887 of an Irishman in Brooklyn, demonstrating that neurology had hardly moved on since 17th-century

Switzerland. But who could deny that mobility carried high emotional costs? By 1900, American commentators wanted to believe, in the words of one of them, that homesickness had grown less common 'in these days of quick communication, of rapid transmission of news and of a widespread knowledge of geography'. Facts denied such a hopeful view — according to Matt, at least 50% of migrants from Greece and southern Italy went home (not necessarily, of course, from nostalgia) — and she is sceptical that new technology has made much difference: **like the phone call from the fretful parent to the boy or girl boarder, frequent contact may actually heighten feelings of displacement**.

6   Matt feels that the persistence of homesickness shows the limitations of the cosmopolitan philosophy that 'celebrates the solitary, mobile individual and envisions men and women as easily separated from family, home and the past'. It may do, but that looks to be a poor brake on the migratory urge. A recent Gallup World Poll suggested that 630 million adults or 14% of the world's adult population would move abroad permanently if they had the chance, while another 1.1 billion would move temporarily for better-paid work.

7   **The multilingualism of the London bus remains the most obvious manifestation of this great multicultural city.** Twenty years ago, the measure of difference was how people looked. With the mobile and cheap calls rates, it has become how people sound.

8   For those of us who were here before, another kind of nostalgia presents itself. **We remember the years**

when the top deck was filled with cigarette smoke and passengers who, if they spoke at all, confined themselves to small remarks about the football or the weather.

9   This kind of nostalgia — the way we were — can be the seedbed of the narrowest nationalism, and therefore we must watch our step. To anyone who has sat for half an hour behind a shouter in Russian, however, the memory of men in hats coughing quietly over their Capstans can seem as seductive and beyond reach as a tinkling cowbell did to a Swiss trooper struggling across a mosquito-infested plain.

Adapted from an article in the *Guardian* by Ian Jack,
20 December 2013

By the way, you may think this is a very London-centric passage to use in a textbook for Scottish schools. Although he does not mention it in this passage, Ian Jack's regular readers would know that he himself is Scottish, and moved to London some years ago. So he too is someone who left 'home' to move to that faraway city.

This sentence from paragraph 7 of the article:

The multilingualism of the London bus remains the most obvious manifestation of this great multicultural city.

could also be expressed as:

The fact that people on the bus speak so many different languages is the clearest example of what a mixture of cultures London is.

Active learning

Several other sentences or parts of sentences in the article have also been printed in bold. Rewrite each one in your own words. You don't have to change every single word, and you may find that some long sentences can be reworded better as two or even three shorter ones.

Showing your understanding

You won't meet a question in the Higher exam that just asks you to put part of the passage in your own words. The reason you need to use your own words, as we've seen before, is to prove your understanding. The exam questions will usually want you to demonstrate your grasp of the writer's ideas and of what the passage is saying.

Active learning

Answer the following questions, using your own words as far as possible, to show your understanding. The number of marks available for each question will suggest how many details or ideas you need in each answer.

1 Re-read paragraph 1. According to the writer, what is the difference between the original meaning of *nostalgia*, and what we now understand this word to mean? **2**

2 Re-read paragraph 3. Explain the two different ways in which the use of modern technology may have affected our feelings of nostalgia. **2**

3 Re-read paragraph 6. How does the remainder of the paragraph elaborate upon the idea that there is '*a poor brake on the migratory urge*'? **2**

For answers see page 220.

Context questions

You may be asked to work out from the **context** what a word or expression means. The examiners think that you probably will not know the given word, but that you can work it out from what surrounds it in the passage.

Context questions might be worded like this:

Explain in your own words what is meant by _____ in this context.

How does the context of lines X–X help you to work out what is meant by _____?

Work out from the context what is meant by _____ in line X.

Look again at paragraph 1 of the article about homesickness:

> Nostalgia used to be considered an illness. A word with a refreshingly certain etymology, it was coined by a Swiss medical student, Johannes Hofer, who in 1688 joined together two Greek words, *nostos* for homecoming and *algos* for pain or ache. The Swiss also knew it as *mal du Suisse* or *Schweizerheimweh*, later translated into English as the nationally unspecific '*homesickness*', a mental and physical malady that was found particularly among Swiss soldiers in foreign armies. It was to these mercenaries, fighting on the lowlands of France and Italy and missing the peaks and valleys of their homeland, that Hofer applied his impressive new word. Stomach pain, fever, anxiety, headache? Rather than blaming bad water, unfamiliar food or the sound of muskets, military doctors now diagnosed nostalgia: a yearning for the past, and not in a general, sentimental way (as it now tends to mean), but for a specific time and place: in this case, one where the sufferer might once have woken to the tinkle of cowbells.

Now here's a possible question:

How does the context of this paragraph help you to work out what is meant by *etymology*?

As you can see, the word *etymology* in the passage is followed by a description of how the word *nostalgia* was *coined* by the joining together of two Greek words. This suggests the writer is using *etymology* to mean the origin of a word, where a word comes from or how it arose. So, here's an answer to the question.

> The word 'etymology' as used here means the origin of a word. This can be understood from the context because the word 'etymology' is followed by a discussion of how the word 'nostalgia' was 'coined' by the joining of two Greek words.

You cannot be sure that you will meet a context question in your exam, but, if you do, it will usually be worth two marks. You earn the first mark for showing what the word means, and the second for showing how you could work this out from the context. Your answer should therefore be in two sentences, with the second including some short quotations from the context.

This pattern will give you one way to structure your answers:

- The word/expression '_____' as used here means _____. This can be understood from the context because …

Active learning

Answer these context questions:

4 Look back at the paragraph on page 66 again. Using the formula given above, show how the context helps you to understand the meaning of the word *malady* as it is used here. **2**

5 How does the context of the paragraph help you to understand the word *mercenaries* as it is used there? **2**

For answers see page 221.

We have now looked at questions that ask you to show your understanding of the passage, and at questions about meanings in context. More examples of these will come up as you try other passages. For the moment, it's time to meet another type of question.

Word choice questions

In the exam, word choice will often be mentioned alongside other techniques. You may get a question that begins:

Analyse how the writer's use of language …

or

Analyse how the writer conveys …

and then later in the question be given the instruction:

You should refer in your answer to such features as sentence structure, word choice, imagery, contrast, tone …

So, although we are going to take the chance here to focus on word choice as a distinct technique, do remember that in the exam it will usually be referred to alongside others, and that it may be up to you to decide which features of the writer's language merit your analysis. (You will get the chance to practise questions like this later in the chapter, after we have looked at more of the individual skills.)

Of course all words that a writer uses are chosen in some way, but when we talk about **word choice** as a technique we mean that certain words are very carefully and deliberately chosen to obtain particular effects, or to suggest particular meanings.

Most words have two levels of meaning, a **denotation** and a more complex **connotation**. The denotation is the basic, simple, straightforward meaning. The connotations of a word are the ideas that the word suggests to us.

For example *wrote, scribbled* and *inscribed* all have the same denotation.

They all tell us that someone used a hand-held implement to mark words upon a surface. However they all have different connotations. *Wrote* is merely factual; *scribbled* suggests speed or carelessness; *inscribed* implies that the words were put there with great care, and were perhaps engraved into the surface. The context in which words are used will help you to know more about which exact connotation to go for.

Active learning

You will see pairs or trios of words. In each group, the words have the same basic denotation, but different connotations. For each group, work out the denotation they share, and the different connotations of the individual words.

doggie	hound	canine
pupil	scholar	student
book	tome	volume
procure	get	obtain
meticulous	controlling	
enthusiast	fanatic	
conservative	fundamentalist	
teased	taunted	
castle	fortress	

Now pick one of the pairs or trios of words that you examined. Draw two or three cartoons to illustrate the different connotations, just as the ones you saw above illustrate *wrote, scribbled* and *inscribed*.

When you answer word choice questions you will usually need to identify and quote the carefully chosen words the writer uses, then explain and examine their connotations.

Read the following news article about how the internet gets our attention:

The compelling web

1   The dirty secret of the internet is that distraction and interruption is immensely profitable. Web companies like to boast about 'creating compelling content', or offering services that let you 'stay up to date with what your friends are doing', 'share the things you love with the world' and so on. But the real way to build a successful online business is to be better than your rivals at undermining people's control of their own attention. Partly, this is a result of how online advertising has traditionally worked: advertisers pay for clicks, and a click is a click, however it's obtained. A website such as Mail Online doesn't care, at least in the short term, if you're 'hate-reading' — clicking in order to share your friends' outrage.

Facebook doesn't really mind if you click a link by mistake because it's tweaked the design of the site overnight without telling you. Advertising aside, commandeering people's attention, so that they click compulsively, is just a surer way to survive in the hyper-competitive marketplace of the web than trying to convince them intellectually that they ought to click a link, or that they'll benefit in the longer term from doing so.

2   And let's be honest: this war for your attention isn't confined only to Facebook or Twitter or Pinterest, or to the purveyors of celebrity gossip or porn. Higher-minded publications feel the same pressures. 'We're living in a moment when even institutions that used to be in the business of promoting reflection and deep thinking are busy tearing up the foundations that made these things possible, in favour of getting more traffic,' says Stanford University technologist Alex Pang, whose book on 'contemplative computing', *The Distraction Addiction*, will be published in August. 'Even universities and churches end up doing this when they go online, never mind newspapers and magazines.' The compulsiveness is given extra force, in social media, by the fear of missing out.

3   To explain what makes the web so compelling — so 'addictive' in the colloquial sense, at least — the advocates of what has become known as 'conscious computing' usually end up returning to the psychologist B. F. Skinner, who conducted famous experiments on pigeons and rats at Harvard University in the 1930s. Trapped inside 'Skinner boxes', equipped with a lever and a tray, the animals soon learned that pushing or pecking at the lever caused a pellet of food to appear on the tray; after that, they'd start compulsively pecking or pushing for more. But Skinner discovered that the most powerful way to reinforce the push-or-peck habit was to use 'variable schedules of reward': to deliver a pellet not every time the lever was pushed, but only sometimes, and unpredictably.

4   There's a slightly depressing view of the web according to which we're essentially just Skinner pigeons, compulsively clicking in hopes of a squirt of dopamine, the so-called 'feelgood' hormone in the brain. Once you've learned about Skinner, it's impossible not to see variable schedules of reward everywhere you look online. When you click *refresh* on your

email, or when you check your phone, you're not guaranteed a new message; when you visit Facebook or open Twitter, you might or might not find an update of the sort you'd been hoping for. This might even help explain the appalling quality of so much online content. Nine times out of ten, when you click on a Huffington Post link — 'PICTURE: Kate and Wills as OAPs', 'Simon Cowell Just Got Weirder' — it's a tedious disappointment. But if it predictably lived up to expectations every time, you might actually feel less compelled to click.

5   By far the funniest, or maybe the most horrifying, illustration of this situation is Cow Clicker, a Facebook game created in 2011 by the game designer Ian Bogost as a satire of undemanding 'social games' such as FarmVille. In Cow Clicker, you clicked on your cow and it mooed, and that was it: you then had to wait another six hours to click again, unless you were willing to part with real money (or virtual money, accumulated through clicking) for the right to click again immediately. Bogost's joke became a surprise hit: at its height, Cow Clicker had more than 50,000 users, some paying $20 or more for pointless 'improvements' to their cow, such as making it face the opposite direction.

6   'After a while,' Bogost told a US radio interviewer, 'I realised they're doing exactly what concerned me about these games' — becoming 'compulsively attached'. 'I began to feel very disturbed about the product.' Eventually, a few months after the launch, Bogost eliminated all the cows in a Rapture-like event he called the Cowpocalypse. After it, users could keep playing only by clicking on a bare patch of grass — and some actually did. Responding to a player who complained that Cow Clicker was no longer 'a very fun game', Bogost replied, 'It wasn't very fun before.'

7   It's this vicious Skinnerian cycle that conscious computing seeks to break. That's why one of the simplest pieces of advice — to check your email at fixed points during the day — works so well: if you're checking only occasionally, you're virtually guaranteed the 'reward' of new messages, so the lure of the variable reward dies away, and with it the constant urge to check. Something similar is going on with services such as iDoneThis, which lets you track the work you've accomplished by responding to a daily email. When it launched, its founder Walter Chen had the capacity to process the emails only once a day, so to put a positive spin on things, and mainly as a joke, he added a note: 'iDoneThis is part of the slow web movement. After you email us, your calendar is not updated instantaneously.

But rest up, and you'll find an updated calendar when you awake.' It's hard to imagine Mark Zuckerberg approving a feature that actively encouraged making fewer visits to Facebook. But maybe we'd all be a bit happier if he did.

Adapted from an article in the *Guardian* by Oliver Burkeman, 10 May 2013

Now look at this worked example of a word choice question:

Q Analyse how the writer's word choice in the final sentence of paragraph 1 *('Advertising aside ... from doing so.')* emphasises the power of the internet. 2

A The writer uses the word 'commandeering'. This suggests that the internet has taken over the users, and that it controls them rather than them being in control of it.

Active learning

Now answer the following word choice questions about this passage.

1 Re-read paragraph 1. Explain how the writer's word choice conveys the strength of competition between web companies for users' attention. 4

2 Re-read paragraph 2. Explain how the writer's word choice in the rest of the paragraph supports his statement that 'this war for your attention isn't confined only to Facebook or Twitter or Pinterest, or to the purveyors of celebrity gossip or porn.' 3

3 Re-read the first sentence of paragraph 4 ('There's a slightly depressing view ... in the brain.') What is implied about the nature of the rewards users get for their use of the web, and how does the writer's word choice suggest this? 4

4 Re-read paragraph 6. What was Bogost's attitude to the game he had created, and how does his word choice convey this attitude? 4

For answers see page 222.

Active learning

Earlier in this chapter you learned about how to answer questions on meanings in context. Each question is worth 2 marks. Using the formula you learned, show how the surrounding context helps you to understand the meaning of the following words:

5 *satire* in paragraph 5 2

6 *rapture* in paragraph 6 2

For answers see page 223.

Active learning

Earlier in this chapter you learned about how to answer questions that show your understanding of the ideas and information in the passage. Now answer these:

7 Re-read paragraphs 3 and 4. How do the examples given by the writer in paragraph 4 elaborate on the idea of 'variable schedules of reward' as introduced in paragraph 3? 2

8 Re-read paragraph 5. How can the Cow Clicker game be understood to be both 'the funniest' and 'the most horrifying' example of the compulsion to click? 2

For answers see page 224.

You will have more opportunities to work on word choice later in this chapter. Now let's move on to a technique that, in reading, rests upon your understanding of word choice.

Tone questions

It's easy to understand what we mean by **tone** if we think of a speaking voice. When you hear someone speaking, you can tell if they are angry, confused, excited or fearful. These tones in the speaking voice are created by factors like the volume and speed of the speech, which words the speaker puts emphasis on, and how fluently or hesitantly the words come out.

It's a little harder at first to see how we can identify tone in written English, when there are no sounds, only words. But, skilled writers can create a tone by word choice alone.

Teacher's task

Twelve tones are mentioned below. Prepare enough separate cards for each member of your class to get a card each: this will probably mean you need two or three cards for each tone. On each card, write a different tone. Hand these cards out around the class, making sure your pupils do not show or tell each other what it says on their cards.

Active learning

Four tones have already been mentioned above:

| angry | confused | excited | fearful |

Here are some more:

| defeated | hopeless | scathing | sceptical |
| critical | matter-of-fact | humorous | emphatic/definite |

Your teacher should give each person a card with a tone on it. Don't let anyone else know what is on your card!

You have five minutes to write a short paragraph in this tone. Then, to make sure that you have created that tone through word choice alone, swap your writing with someone else. Get them to read it and to tell you what they think the tone is.

As we saw earlier with questions on word choice, in the exam, tone will usually be mentioned alongside other techniques. You may get a question that begins:

> **Analyse how the writer's use of language …**

or

> **Analyse how the writer conveys …**

and then later in the question be given the instruction:

> **You should refer in your answer to such features as sentence structure, word choice, imagery, contrast, tone …**

We are going to take the chance here to focus on tone as a distinct technique, but do remember that in the exam it will usually be referred to alongside others, and that it will probably be up to you to decide which features of the writer's language merit your analysis. (You will get the chance to practise questions like this later in the chapter, after we have looked at more of the individual skills.)

When you are answering on tone you will probably have to do a mixture of these different things:

1 **identify** a tone
2 **quote** words which create that tone
3 **explain** how the words you have quoted create the tone

Read this piece by Scotland's Makar (national poet) Liz Lochhead about growing old and poetry:

Liz Lochhead

Textual healing

1 The subject of how to care for the elderly and those suffering dementia has been very much in the air lately. We're all aware that the UK has an ageing population, whose care will have to be funded from a dwindling tax base. Some 10 million people in the UK are over 65 years old. (Hell, I'm joining them on my next birthday, my 66th, later this month. Me, in my mock Converse trainers and leopard-skin Bob Dylan bunnet, trying to convince myself that I'm an artist and I don't look back. Omigod, I'm actually, technically, One of Them.)

2   In 20 years' time, it's estimated there will be 15.5 million of us in the UK who are over 65, the number increasing to 19 million by the middle of this century. Little wonder the subject of how to pay for care proves so daunting to politicians. We hear the elderly described in terms of being a 'burden' on the welfare state. But if caring for the old is a burden society has to bear, then it had better bear it gladly.

3   The issue of funding often aggravates the complicated feelings – resentment, among others, let's face it – that 'the elderly' trigger. The people you meet in care homes when some combination of duty, family ties, honouring old friendship takes you there, come, of course, from an incredibly diverse range of backgrounds. They are retired doctors and nurses and teachers who once taught you, and joiners and butchers and builders and former soldiers; folk that never got a start and were 'on benefits' all their lives; parents, neighbours, widowers and divorcees; folk that 'fought drink', or were made redundant at 50. They were fly-men, head-hunters, bank clerks and church-goers and socialists and atheists and pacifists and harmless biddies and bonny-fechters, folk who followed their team and total chancers and ballroom dancers… They were big readers or avid cinema-goers or opera enthusiasts or rock fans or jazzers or into am-dram. They were artists or writers or musicians themselves.

4   It's hard, but we need to look closer, see the old as individuals. Their experience should be, could be, an asset. To us. And to them. They have a right to continue to enjoy things they've taken part in throughout their lives. They may be having to move into residential care, but their lives are not over. Maybe they will even finally have the chance to deeply engage with something that hasn't meant much to them so far. Creative solutions should be called upon — and I have to believe that poetry, language at its most naked and most playful, must be a useful tool.

5   The Scottish Poetry Library and the Scottish Storytelling Centre have been collaborating on the pilot scheme of what we all hope is to be an ongoing project called Living Voices. Into care homes and sheltered housing complexes in three regions, they have been taking poetry old and new – wonderful texts full of recall, reminiscence, rhythm, rhyme, pieces spilling over with immediate, now, living, sensuous detail and distinct voices.

6   I'm told that a raw wee elegy for my mother, *Sorting Through*, detailing the universal, painful, intimate experience of dealing with a loved-one's things in the immediate aftermath of loss — a poem that I might have flinched away from reading aloud in such a setting myself — has been immediately popular and stimulated a whole lot of talk and communication. So it's not a matter of 'don't mention the war'. It's proven to be quite the reverse. They want words that deal with reality.

7   Certainly, a session can legitimately be about nothing more than pure escapism and entertainment. Pleasure. People who can't remember what happened half-an-hour ago can just come out with whole screeds of what, long, long ago, they learned by heart. And then they remember the English teacher who taught them it, and his skelly eye, and his fancy for the music teacher that everybody knew all about, and they remember who they were sitting next to in the class and what she did to Archie Esslemont with the point of her protractor and what their granny came out with when they did the poem out loud for everybody at teatime …

8   The scheme has proved its effectiveness. Well, we've long known that music and memory go hand in glove — music is memory, according to neurologist Oliver Sacks in *The Man Who Mistook His Wife for A Hat* — and, lo, poetry seems to work in exactly the same way. There is loads of anecdotal evidence from staff in the homes about marked, even miraculous, shifts of mood and engagement in certain individuals. One man who had been very withdrawn (depressed?) now 'joins in everything and has a lot to say to the others. Really connects'.

9   Of course, I'm not old. My survival strategy? Denial. Denial and a pair of rockabilly brothel-creepers in viper-green, tartan or leopard-skin. My hair might be white but, hey, I can think platinum blonde if I like. I'll be playing with words, reading, drawing, 'keeping creative' if I can. Just as long as those proteins and neurons Alois Alzheimer discovered aren't already busily clotting and fusing and forming themselves into those terrible, twisted, tangled trees in my brain.

Adapted from a piece by Liz Lochhead in the
Sunday Herald, 1 December 2013

Here are two possible tone questions on the start of this passage, along with suitable answers. Notice that in one of the questions you have to identify the tone, while in the other you only have to show how it is created:

Q1 How does the writer establish an authoritative tone in the first paragraph?   2

A1 She uses formal vocabulary such as 'dwindling tax base' and statistics, for example saying how many UK residents are over 65 years old. The seriousness of this word choice, and the apparent reliability of the figures quoted, combine to make her sound authoritative.

Q2 What is the tone of the bracketed section in this paragraph, and how is this created?   2

A2 The tone is a self-mocking one. This is created by her use of the phrase 'trying to convince myself' as if she knows she cannot keep pretending she is not growing older.

Active learning

Now you try these tone questions:

1 How does the writer establish a persuasive tone in paragraph 4?   2

2 What is the tone of paragraph 6 and how is this established?   3

For answers see page 224.

Just before we move on from the idea of tone, a word of advice. If you are asked to identify or name a tone, don't ever just say that it is positive or negative. That's far too vague. You need to say something much more exact. What kind of positive tone is it? Praising? Happy? Encouraging? What kind of negative tone is it? Critical? Despairing? Angry?

Active learning

Earlier in this chapter you learned how to tackle word choice questions. Now answer these:

3 How does Lochhead's word choice in paragraph 2 emphasise the challenge of caring for the growing elderly population?   **2**

4 How does the word choice in paragraph 6 convey the experience of loss?   **3**

For answers see page 225.

Active learning

Earlier in this chapter you learned how to tackle questions that show your understanding of the ideas and information in the passage. Now answer these:

5 Re-read paragraphs 7 and 8. Identify any four benefits of the poetry sessions with elderly people.   **4**

Hint: To make it easy for the marker to see and reward your good work, and to help you keep track that you have done everything the question asked you, set out your answer for this question as a list of bullet points.

6 Re-read paragraph 9. Identify two ways in which the writer responds to her own increasing age. You should use your own words as far as possible.   **2**

For answers see page 226.

Imagery questions

Writers use images to strengthen what they say by putting all sorts of pictures in the reader's mind. Imagery is not the same thing as description. A **description** tells us what something is like. An **image** shows that one thing is somehow like another. The comparison tells us more about the thing that is being compared. Similes, metaphors and personification are all different sorts of image, though most of the images you will be asked about will be metaphors.

To get us thinking about images, and how they add to our understanding, let's think about all the studying and preparation you have to do as a Higher pupil. On any particular night, you might have an English essay to write, a Maths test to study for, some French vocabulary to learn, and a chapter of your History textbook to read. If all this were true, you could quite justifiably say:

I have a mountain of homework to do.

How is your homework like a mountain? There's a lot of it. It's a big challenge. It will take a lot of effort on your part. So, if you were to analyse the image of your homework as a mountain, you could do it like this.

Just as a mountain is high and hard to climb, so the amount of homework I have to deal with tonight is enormous and will be really difficult.

Of course there are ways in which your homework is not like a mountain. You don't need to strap on an oxygen tank before you deal with it. Special clothing and footwear are not required. There's no snow on your French jotter. When you answer imagery questions, you are looking for the **similarities**.

There is a method for analysing images. You begin with what the image **literally** is like, or **literally** means. Then you go on to the **metaphorical** meaning, showing how that image applies to and adds meaning to the subject under discussion.

The following structure can help you organise your analysis:

Just as … (explain the literal meaning) … so … (explain the metaphorical meaning)

You can see that method being used above, in the image of the homework mountain.

Active learning

Two particular images are very commonly used. You will hear them all the time in conversation, and see them constantly in the press.

- People dealing with serious illness are often said to be involved in a 'battle'.
- Participants in many competitive television programmes describe their progress through the contest as a 'journey'.

First, using the *Just as … so …* method, analyse each of these common images.

Then, work with a partner. Try to come up with two rather more original images to use for dealing with illness, or competing in a television contest.

Finally, give your new images to another pair to analyse using *Just as … so …* If they can do this, you have probably come up with good, and therefore very welcome, images.

As we saw earlier with questions on word choice and on tone, in the exam, imagery will usually be mentioned alongside other techniques. You may get a question that begins:

> **Analyse how the writer's use of language …**

or

> **Analyse how the writer conveys …**

and then later in the question be given the instruction:

> **You should refer in your answer to such features as sentence structure, word choice, imagery, contrast, tone …**

We are going to take the chance here to focus on imagery as a distinct technique, but do remember that in the exam it will usually be referred to alongside others, and that it will probably be up to you to decide which features of the writer's language merit your analysis. (You will get the chance to practise questions like this later in the chapter, after we have looked at more of the individual skills.)

Read this article about a rather unusual bar:

Dry bars — are we sobering up?

1   'Alcohol is omnipresent,' says Catherine Salway, handing me something called a Beetroot Coco-tini. 'You can't even go to the cinema now without considering having a glass of wine. But I thought: "There's a way to cut through that, and do the opposite."'

2   Salway is 40, and the founder of a new 'gastrobar' called Redemption, located at the foot of the Trellick Tower on Golborne Road, west London. The decor is stripped-down and chic: bare brick walls, neon signs and furniture that a

neighbouring social enterprise has made out of other people's junk. Sight unseen, you'd think you were in a reasonably typical urban hostelry.

3   But that's not quite true. The food here is 'pretty much' vegan, but what really sets the place apart is a completely alcohol-free drinks menu. The basic idea, Salway tells me, is to offer people a chance to 'spoil yourself without spoiling yourself', and provide a sanctuary of sober calm in the midst of a booze-dominated culture. As she sees it, moreover, her business is on the crest of a wave — as evidenced by a handful of similar projects in other British towns and cities, and statistics that suggest our national dependence on the bottle may at last be starting to wane, not least among people under 30.

Catherine Salway in her dry pub, Redemption

4   Until 2011, Salway was the chief brand director for the Virgin Group. She was also drinking a lot, a habit that developed when she first arrived in London in the giddily hedonistic mid-90s. By now, though, an existential hangover had kicked in: 'I was overweight, drinking too much, pretty miserable. And I thought: "I could just sit here grinding away, doing corporate jobs, or do something meaningful."'

5   The idea for Redemption came to her when she was holidaying in a yogic retreat in Goa ('very cliched,' she smirks). No booze was available — which, she was surprised to find, gave everyone she was with a pronounced feeling of liberation. 'It was only by alcohol not being present at all that we were freed from it,' she says.

6   And so, via an initial 'residency' at a venue in Hackney followed by the opening of permanent premises here in September 2013, a new business came into being. With backing from two individual investors and over £50,000 of

her own money already staked, Salway says she wants to open up two more branches of Redemption in London. In time, she would like to expand abroad.

7   'Loads of people have told me I'm going to fail: particularly big property moguls from London, and traditional investors — mainly men over 50,' she says. 'A lot of people said to me: "You're mad — London runs on alcohol. It's fuelled by alcohol." And I said: "Well, not everybody, and not all the time."'

8   For all the collective angst about Britain's drinking habits, our consumption of booze does seem to be changing. According to the Office for National Statistics, the share of people who report having a drink in the previous seven days has been falling for at least eight years: 72% of men and 57% of women did so in 2005, but by 2013, the respective figures had fallen to 64% and 52%, and the amount of alcohol consumed by people on their 'heaviest' day had also come down.

9   As Salway explains, it's generational differences that suggest something really is up. According to NHS data, in 1998, 71% of 16 to 26-year-olds said they'd had a drink in the week they were questioned about their habits — but by 2010, that figure had fallen by around a third, to 48%. 'People in their early 20s and teenage years are growing up with parents who get lashed all the time, and that's uncool,' she says. 'I've also heard that there's a lot of displacement through use of technology. Kids aren't going out to get drunk because they've got so much to stimulate them.'

10   On the night I visit Redemption, among the customers are a trio of twentysomethings, slurping apple mojitos around a long table. Jennifer Moule, 28, and Alicia Brown, 27, are both secondary school teachers; 28-year-old Yassine Senghor manages a club, and is therefore well aware of what a contrast to the prevailing model of socialising this place represents. 'The fact that there's no booze makes everything easier,' says Moule, who is splitting her time between chatting, and marking essays on *To Kill a Mockingbird* and *The Crucible*. 'You're not distracted: the evening won't turn into something else.'

11   I mention the idea that their generation is less boozy than its predecessors, hoping for some proud statements of 21st-century puritanism. But no. 'I had a bottle of malbec last night with my boyfriend,' says Moule. 'Well, he had a glass, anyway.'

12   'But that's what makes this place perfect,' says Brown. 'If we were anywhere else, we'd order a bottle, not just glasses.'

Adapted from an article in the *Guardian* by John Harris, 21 March 2014

Active learning

Paragraph 3 contains three images:

1 'a sanctuary'

2 'the crest of a wave'

3 'a handful of similar projects'

Using the *Just as ... , so ...* method to help you, explain what each image means and analyse its effect.   **2 marks for each**

4 Re-read paragraph 4. How does Catherine Salway's use of imagery convey her feelings about her former career?   2

5 Re-read paragraph 7. How is imagery used to suggest the importance of alcohol as part of London life?   2

For answers see page 226.

Active learning

Earlier in this chapter you learned about how to answer questions about meanings in context. Now answer these:

6 How does the context help you to understand the meaning of '*omnipresent*' as used in paragraph 1?   2

7 How does the context help you to understand the meaning of '*displacement*' as used in paragraph 9?   2

For answers see page 227.

Active learning

You also learned how to answer questions that allow you to show your understanding of a writer's overall ideas and argument. Now answer these:

8 Re-read paragraphs 8 and 9. **Using your own words as far as possible,** list the evidence that suggests that 'our consumption of booze does seem to be changing'.   4

Hint: Bullet point your answer.

9 Re-read paragraphs 10 and 11. In what way is the group of customers described both a good and a bad example of the trend towards lower consumption of alcohol as discussed in the article?   2

For answers see page 228.

Link questions

You may be asked a **link question**. These often ask you to say how a sentence **creates an effective link** between one paragraph and another; or how a sentence, or paragraph, acts as a link in the writer's ideas or argument. These questions are usually worth two marks and you usually need to answer them in two parts:

- Show how one part of the sentence **links back** to the previous paragraph.
- Show how another part of it **refers forward** to the new paragraph.

For example, a **link question** based on the news article you have just read about alcohol-free bars might go like this:

> **How does the sentence 'But that's not quite true.' form a link between paragraphs 2 and 3?**

To answer this, you need to re-read this section of the passage:

> 2   Salway is 40, and the founder of a new 'gastrobar' called Redemption, located at the foot of the Trellick Tower on Golborne Road, west London. The decor is stripped-down and chic: bare brick walls, neon signs and furniture that a neighbouring social enterprise has made out of other people's junk. Sight unseen, you'd think you were in a reasonably typical urban hostelry.
>
> 3   But that's not quite true. The food here is 'pretty much' vegan, but what really sets the place apart is a completely alcohol-free drinks menu. The basic idea, Salway tells me, is to offer people a chance to 'spoil yourself without spoiling yourself', and provide a sanctuary of sober calm in the midst of a booze-dominated culture. As she sees it, moreover, her business is on the crest of a wave — as evidenced by a handful of similar projects in other British towns and cities, and statistics that suggest our national dependence on the bottle may at last be starting to wane, not least among people under 30.

A good answer to this question would be:

> The word 'that's' links back to the idea of a typical city pub as found at the end of paragraph 2. The expression 'not quite true' introduces the writer's explanation of what makes the bar unusual, which is explained in paragraph 3.

This answer would get two marks because it has two parts to it, one linking back, the other referring forward. You could, if you find it helpful, use this formula for link questions.

The word/expression '_____' links back to _____ which was discussed in _____.

The word/expression '_____' introduces the idea of _____ which is going to be discussed in _____.

Read the following news article about plagiarism in the digital age:

The big steal

1   When novelist John Gardner used the phrase 'opening the throttle at the last moment' in his 1983 book *Icebreaker*, it's unlikely that he sat back and congratulated himself on being the first to have written it. Innovation wasn't what he was aiming for, after all; he was just trying to describe someone driving a scooter. But Google Books, that vast indexing project, informs us that Gardner's was the only book to contain this phrase until another, *Vestige Of Evil* by Len Vorster, appeared on Amazon in 2011. A section of the novel, one of two books self-published online under that name, featured other phrases that were no longer unique to *Icebreaker*, such as 'the ice and snow were not as raw and killing as this' and 'the slope angling gently downwards to flatten'. The many coincidences were startling, though if it wasn't for the internet, nobody need ever have known.

2   In fact, if it wasn't for the internet, there might never have been a *Vestige Of Evil*. Vorster appears, like millions of others, to have been inspired by the sheer quantity of online content and the new opportunities for digital self-expression. With a potential audience of billions, the prospect of contributing can be thrilling; meanwhile, the moral responsibility we traditionally attach to creative expression has been downgraded by the sheer ease of copying someone else's work. Today, technology covertly assists us: ctrl+C to copy images, prose, code, video and more, ctrl+V to paste. The consequences of this can range from sly postings of other people's witticisms on Twitter in pursuit of retweet glory, to print-on-demand books that are merely duplicates of other books. Driven by a combination of greed, confusion, ignorance, pressure, laziness and ambition, an increasing number of people are looking at stuff other people have

done and thinking, 'Wow. That's really good. I'll pretend that I did it.'

3 'It's a problem for me, it really is,' says Edward Champion, managing editor of an American blog, *Reluctant Habits*, which has frequently expressed contempt for plagiarists. He expounds at length on the subject, relishing his rhetoric. 'When you see someone desecrate this wonderful, noble medium by not being assed to try to find a new form of expression,' he says, 'it's basically a writer signalling utter contempt for the reader.'

4 It's an opinion shared by British thriller writer Jeremy Duns, whose work in exposing and publicising cases of written theft has earned him something of a reputation as a plagiarist's scourge. 'When I was in my 20s,' he says, 'I was one of the editors at a magazine for English-speaking expats in Belgium, a kind of *Time Out* wannabe. I found out by pure chance that our film reviewer had plagiarised all his reviews from IMDb [the Internet Movie Database] for years. But even though it was verbatim plagiarism, the editor hadn't really wanted to sack him. I was shocked. If you're really annoyed by something and people say, 'Oh no, it's not wrong at all', then you get even more annoyed. So I tend to be like a dog with a bone.'

5 The act of uncovering and investigating acts of plagiarism is becoming easier by the day. Search engines, online plagiarism checkers (of varying quality) and the viral publicity opportunities afforded by social media all play their part. Plagiarism searches can be compelling, like addictive puzzles where positive results elicit mental fist-pumps of delight. (It's unlikely that the unwieldy phrase 'mental fist-pumps of delight' will be plagiarised, but I've set up a Google Alert in case.) Still, it's laborious, unpaid work. 'It takes discipline,' Champion says. 'You have to sit for hours looking through documents, and it can be a tedious task.' The act of proving plagiarism can also be unnerving, according to Duns, not least because getting it wrong exposes you to legal action for defamation. 'You open yourself up to a certain amount of abuse,' he says. 'It's a lot easier to leave it all alone. And sometimes I do try to leave it alone,' he adds. But both men seem independently driven by

their displeasure. 'What keeps us going,' Champion says, 'is what we're going to discover.'

6   These searches aren't restricted to words; content-based image retrieval — i.e., searching for images using the image itself — has been crucial in exposing cases of photographic plagiarism. Nearly every professional photographer has a story about their copyright being violated, but that violation can also blur into plagiaristic acts, where photographers simply pretend that other people's work is theirs. Corey Ann, a wedding photographer based in Ohio, was appalled when she heard of a photographer advertising their services on Groupon in 2010 using someone else's work, and she became involved in exposing it. 'Afterwards,' she says, 'people started coming to me when they found out their work was being used. I needed a place to put it all, to show who was doing it and who was affected by it.' The result was stopstealingphotos.com, which documents as many cases as Ann has time to publish. Other websites, such as logothief.com, which exposes the work of designers who have been, shall we say, a little overinspired by others, fulfil a similar function. 'If these things are in a central location that everyone can see,' Ann says, 'it has more impact. It draws attention to what's happening, and hopefully it deters people from doing it.'

Adapted from an article in the *Guardian*
by Rhodri Marsden, 21 March 2014

Active learning

Answer the following link questions about the article:

1 How does the sentence, 'It's an opinion shared by British thriller writer Jeremy Duns,' form a link between paragraphs 3 and 4?   2

2 How does the sentence, 'The act of uncovering and investigating acts of plagiarism is becoming easier by the day' form a link between paragraphs 4 and 5?   2

3 How does the sentence, 'These searches aren't restricted to words' form a link between paragraphs 5 and 6?   2

For answers see page 229.

Active learning

Earlier in this chapter you learned about how to answer questions about imagery and about word choice. Now answer these:

4 How does Edward Champion's word choice in the third sentence of paragraph 3 ('When you see … a new form of expression.') convey the strength of his feelings about plagiarism? **2**

5 a How does the imagery of the opening sentence of paragraph 4 ('It's an opinion … a plagiarist's scourge.') emphasise the impact Jeremy Duns has upon the plagiarists he exposes? **2**

b What does the imagery of the final sentence in this paragraph add to the reader's understanding of Jeremy Duns? **2**

6 Re-read paragraph 5. What does the word choice of the second sentence ('Search engines … all play their part.') convey about how publicity spreads across the internet? **2**

Now answer these other questions that test your understanding of the ideas and information in this article.

Hint: Use bullet points whenever appropriate to clarify and organise your answers.

7 Re-read paragraph 2. What, according to the writer, are the reasons why plagiarism has now become so common? **4**

8 Re-read paragraph 5. Why might people be put off discovering and exposing plagiarism? **4**

For answers see page 231.

Sentence structure questions

Sentence structure is how a sentence is made and built up. Very often, pupils get structure questions wrong because they don't actually answer the question. Many pupils end up rehashing the content of a sentence when they should be examining its structure.

Structure is not the same as content. The structure of the bag you take to school might be canvas, stitched together and then attached with leather straps and metal buckles; its content might include books, pens, a packet of crisps and your phone.

A number of smaller techniques contribute to sentence structure:

- **Length**: Look at whether a sentence is noticeably long, or noticeably short, especially if its length contrasts with the length of other sentences nearby.
- **Listing**: What is being listed and what does this list suggest?
- **Repetition**: What is being repeated and what does this repetition suggest?

- **Parenthesis:** This can be created with a pair of commas, a pair of brackets, or a pair of dashes. What is the extra information inside the parenthesis about and what is the effect of this?
- **Word order:** Have any words been put in a position in the sentence that particularly creates emphasis?
- **Colons or semicolons:** What do these divide the sentence into? What do colons introduce?
- Type of sentence: is it
    - a statement?
    - an instruction?
    - a minor sentence?
    - a question?

Has the writer used this particular type of sentence to have a particular effect upon the reader? What is this effect, and how is it created?

Look at this extract from the article you've already read about older people and poetry:

> The issue of funding often aggravates the complicated feelings — resentment, among others, let's face it — that 'the elderly' trigger. The people you meet in care homes when some combination of duty, family ties, honouring old friendship takes you there, come, of course, from an incredibly diverse range of backgrounds. They are retired doctors and nurses and teachers who once taught you, and joiners and butchers and builders and former soldiers; folk that never got a start and were 'on benefits' all their lives; parents, neighbours, widowers and divorcees; folk that 'fought drink', or were made redundant at 50. They were fly-men, head-hunters, bank clerks and church-goers and socialists and atheists and pacifists and harmless biddies and bonny-fechters, folk who followed their team and total chancers and ballroom dancers … They were big readers or avid cinema-goers or opera enthusiasts or rock fans or jazzers or into am-dram. They were artists or writers or musicians themselves.

Here are two possible sentence structure questions on this extract, along with suitable answers.

Q1 What is the effect of the use of repetition in this paragraph?   2

A1 The writer repeatedly uses 'They were' at the start of sentences. This creates the impression that the residents of care homes have lived a huge variety of different and interesting lives and have contributed to society in many ways.

Q2 Show how the structure of the first sentence allows the writer to communicate with her readers.   2

A2 The writer uses parenthesis '— resentment, among others, let's face it —' to speak directly to the reader. This address to the reader is emphasised by the use of 'let's' within the parenthesis, which draws the writer and readers together.

As we saw earlier with questions on word choice, tone and imagery, in the exam, sentence structure will usually be mentioned alongside other techniques. You may get a question that begins:

Analyse how the writer's use of language …

or

Analyse how the writer conveys …

and then later in the question be given the instruction:

You should refer in your answer to such features as sentence structure, word choice, imagery, contrast, tone …

We are going to take the chance here to focus on sentence structure as a distinct technique, but do remember that in the exam it will usually be referred to alongside others, and that it will probably be up to you to decide which features of the writer's language merit your analysis. (You will get the chance to practise questions like this later in the chapter, after we have looked at more of the individual skills.)

Now read this article about private tutoring:

The new boom in home tuition

1   'Earn £800 a week tutoring in Kazakhstan,' read one email I received earlier this year. Another began, 'Do you fancy going to the Bahamas for three months?' Summers in St Tropez, Hong Kong and Tuscany were also up for grabs.

2   Some may dismiss these emails as spam. In fact, they are a few of the 'international opportunities' offered by Bright Young Things, a British agency specialising in 'private bespoke tuition'. Such assignments require at least four hours of work a day − teaching English, for example, or preparing children as young as five for entrance exams to a British private school.

3   Private tutoring is that rare thing: a booming British industry, in demand at home and abroad. The online education resource EdPlace estimates, not entirely convincingly, that British parents spend as much as £6bn a year on private lessons for their children. A recent Ipsos Mori poll for the Sutton Trust found that 24% of all young people in the UK

have received private tuition at some point; in London, the figure rises to 40%.

4 Across the country, and especially in the capital, agencies have sprouted in the hope of benefiting from this boom. Some have prospered. But more significantly, tutoring has become a career — and for young people working in the arts, it is increasingly a second career, supplementing their creative endeavours.

5 As a young journalist who has just started working freelance, I recently joined these ranks. Last month I attended a training day alongside postgraduate students, former teachers and recent graduates at a loose end — as well as young writers, actors and journalists.

6 At a time of high unemployment, hiring freezes and unpaid internships, it's not hard to see the appeal of a job paying between £25 and £40 an hour (and even more at some high-end agencies). For me, tutoring promises to be a far more dependable source of income than writing, for which it will leave plenty of time. It is also livelier and less solitary — and, unlike many forms of casual labour, intellectually stimulating.

7 For young adults in the creative industries, tutoring has become a long-term means of supporting their other work. 'Virtually all of my friends who are working creatively in the arts tutor,' says Edward Kiely, a comedian who has been tutoring for almost two years. He tutors between 17 and 19 hours a week, which is enough to support his writing and performing. 'I never thought that there'd be enough out there for it to be a full source of income,' he says.

8 Tutoring has become a kind of inadvertent private subsidy for the arts. Until recently, an aspiring novelist might have signed on or worked as a copywriter, and a drama school graduate might have turned to temping or waitressing. Now, if they have a good degree, they have an option that offers higher wages for fewer hours.

9 If the hourly rates are tutoring's main attraction, the independence and flexibility it allows are also important. Although agencies play a key role in finding clients and processing payments, tutors are essentially self-employed. For Jackson Gordon, a songwriter, his work as a musician is entrepreneurial — 'you are your own boss'. To work in

a conventional office job alongside that 'is such a weird clash of values'. With tutoring, hours can be negotiated: 'Once you've built a relationship with your families, they're usually up for tutoring on a week-to-week basis,' says Henry Eliot, a writer who also edits a magazine about London. For musicians or actors who might have to travel for a concert or attend an audition, such flexibility makes it easy to keep two careers going.

10 Some tutors have concerns over the levels of pressure their students — many of them still at primary school — are under, stoked by a combination of their parents and their schoolmates. And although some tutees attend state schools, many tutors I spoke to expressed misgivings about work that tends to aid already privileged, wealthy people. 'You're further enhancing the educational capital of people who already have the cards stacked in their favour,' says Kiely.

11 The Sutton Trust estimates that 31% of students from better-off families have had some private tuition, compared to 15% from less well-off families. Not-for-profit organisations such as the Manchester-based Tutor Trust offer free tuition to students from poorer backgrounds. The Trust trains its tutors, who work a free hour for every six they are paid, and connects them with disadvantaged schools around Manchester.

12 Despite their reservations, most of my interviewees said they enjoy tutoring and are grateful for the opportunities it has given them. The alternatives, for Davis, would have been ushering and bar work, 'which would have been damaging to my career' because they require more time for less money.

13 Others would give up teaching if they could afford to, but accept they might have to wait a while. For myself, as a freelance journalist just starting out, it's hard to imagine being able to manage without an additional source of income.

Adapted from an article in the *Guardian* by
Daniel H. Cohen, 26 October 2013

Active learning

You are going to try some sentence structure questions on this passage.

1 How does sentence structure in paragraph 1 engage the reader? **2**

2 What is the effect of the author's use of parenthesis in the second sentence of paragraph 3 ('The online education resource … for their children.')? **2**

3 How does the sentence structure of paragraph 5 convey the popularity of tutoring as a career? **2**

4 How does the sentence structure of paragraph 6 emphasise the challenges of the graduate job market? **2**

For answers see page 232.

The comparison question

At the start of this chapter you were told that the Reading for Understanding, Analysis and Evaluation exam would consist of two non-fiction passages. So far though, we have only looked at one passage at a time. The question types you have been learning about, and the questions you have tackled, have all been designed to prepare you for Passage 1 of that exam.

It's time now to learn about Passage 2, and the final question.

Passage 2 will be shorter — usually around 600 words compared to the 850 or so in Passage 1. It will be followed by just one question. This question will be worth 5 marks, and will get you to make a comparison between the ideas and content of two passages.

You have 90 minutes altogether in the exam, which is quite a generous amount of time. Try dividing it up like this:

- Use the first hour to read Passage 1 carefully, and to answer the questions on it.
- Use the remaining half hour for Passage 2 and the comparison task.

The examiners want you to have the ability to follow, and summarise, the key ideas running throughout an article or passage. They also want you to be able to see the connections between ideas, and to be able to take a step back and look at texts more widely, as opposed to the very detailed scrutiny that some of the other questions demand. So, the final question on the exam paper will give you a lot to think about.

Picture yourself in the exam. You've been there for an hour, and you've just finished answering the questions on Passage 1. You now know that passage and its contents really well. You have read the whole passage through at least once at the start, and have probably read most of it over and over again in short sections as you answered the questions.

It's time for Passage 2.

Above the passage you will see a short introduction, something like this:

> **In the second passage below, the writer discusses his own experience of tutoring.**

You'll then find this instruction:

> **Read the passage and answer the question which follows. While reading, you may wish to make notes on the main ideas and/or highlight key points in the passage.**

And then you'll see the passage. This next piece of advice is going to sound rather odd, but it's important, which is why it's set out to grab your attention:

DON'T READ THE PASSAGE YET!

Why not? Because you don't know yet what the final question in the exam is, and if you don't know that, then you don't know how you should read that second passage, or what you should be looking out for as you read it.

So, look down at the bottom of the page to find the question. Let's assume that in this case it says:

- Both writers discuss the private tuition industry. Identify key areas on which they agree. In your answer, you should refer in detail to both passages.   5

You may answer this question in continuous prose or in a series of developed bullet points.

Now you know what you must do, and what you can or might do, to answer this question.

You must:	You can, or might:
<ul><li>know Passage 1 really well already</li><li>read Passage 2 very carefully</li><li>identify the areas on which the two writers agree</li><li>refer in detail to both passages to give evidence supporting these areas of agreement</li></ul>	<ul><li>make notes as you read Passage 2</li><li>underline parts of Passage 2</li><li>highlight sections of Passage 2</li><li>answer in continuous prose, if you want to, OR answer in a series of bullet points if you'd rather do it that way</li></ul>

Active learning

You're about to see a Passage 2 that follows on from the tutoring passage you have just been working on.

First, as you saw explained above, remember to skip to the end and read the question **before** you read the passage, so that you know what you are reading for.

Then, read the passage, as the instruction says.

In the second passage below, the writer discusses his own experience of tutoring.

Read the passage and answer the question which follows. While reading, you may wish to make notes on the main ideas and/or highlight key points in the passage.

1   Working as a private tutor nowadays is a bit like being a confiseur for Marie Antoinette: no matter how much you spin the sugar into a confection about feeding society, you're really just making life sweeter for the rich. And I should know, having taught a predominantly wealthy elite for over a decade.

2   Five years into the most thorough economic malaise since the Great Depression, and amid more cuts than you'd find on a straight-to-DVD movie, it should come as scant wonder that one of the few boom industries is private education. In the strata of the recession-proof uber-rich, the private tutor can often appear as simply the next human accessory, summoned before the court to perform.

3   Yet in a society plagued by the disease of aspiration, it's no longer just about the very rich. Salaried and striving parents are queuing up to fuel the boom in a market valued in excess of £6bn a year, hyperventilating that their kids are being left behind as an already unequal form of education plunges into something that would make the feudal system look like the dictatorship of the proletariat.

4   Amid terror tales of two-year-olds receiving elocution tutorials, and salacious reports of super tutors creaming £1,000 per hour, the method for ensuring your child makes it with the likes of Old Etonians David Cameron, the Archbishop of Canterbury and Bear Grylls appears simple: start 'em young and pawn your granny to do so.

5   I began tutoring with no formal teaching qualification, just a respectable degree from one of the world's top universities and a knack for working with a child without leaving either one

of us in shreds. Soon I was called to the sort of west London streets I thought had been dismantled once Mary Poppins had finished filming. The class of degree was less important than the whispered name of the university. I repeatedly watched parents hypnotised by the dubious dream of some sort of intellectual osmosis, passing accomplishment like a cold, from tutor to pupil.

6   What made the process endurable was being called on every so often by a normal family, for whom tutoring was an expensive and rare gift that succeeded in helping an already able child fulfil their potential. Sometimes I worked for the council, or on a donation-only basis, or for free. Helping those who were living proof that money does not happiness make, the ones struggling to cope with their parents' divorce, excluded and facing depression, made tutoring feel, if not as moral as curing cancer, then at least something marginally less dirty than selling arms to Bahrain.

7   Of course, one-to-one tuition is an amazing process. The problem is that under the current system, already polarised between the wafer-thin few and the frantic, competing many, children already excessively advantaged are being further preferred. In many cases, the next step for such kids is to have the tutor turn up and sit the paper for them.

8   Invariably it's the parents who could do with an education. I'm thinking of the media mogul who, in addition to his five-storey Mayfair house and Oxfordshire mansion, kept a château in the Loire valley, closed up throughout the year, save for the two weeks in the summer when it was needed. Recently I was offered any financial incentive I cared to mention to continue working for the sons of a convicted billionaire murderer.

9   The malaise with private tutoring is not the absence of regulation. The agencies I've worked for have been tightly run with all tutors CRB checked, and for every passing private-school graduate who fancies earning some cash between gap years, there are scores of tutors from local comps; intelligent, kind, and warm-blooded enough to understand how to be interested in someone's emotional wellbeing for longer than the duration of a gin and tonic.

10 No, the real problem is that we continue to panic buy into a system so fatally unequal and personally exhausting and then wonder why there remains an issue with the lessons our kids are learning.

Adapted from a piece in the *Guardian*,
3 May 2013

Question

- Both writers discuss the private tuition industry. Identify the key areas on which they agree. In your answer, you should refer in detail to both passages. 5

You may answer this question in continuous prose or in a series of developed bullet points.

Active learning

In the exam you can, as we've seen, write on, highlight, or underline parts of your exam paper. You can do this on Passage 2 and also on Passage 1 as you track down the shared ideas.

However your teacher won't want you writing on this book, so you may need to read this passage, or both passages again.

When you're ready, note down three areas the writers agree on. Here's one to get you started:

Both writers agree that private tuition can be well paid.

Write this one down in your notebook, and add at least two more you have spotted by yourself.

Next, compare your list with a partner's. How many more can you each add?

Once you've identified the key areas on which the two writers agree, you are ready to support these areas by making detailed reference to both passages. The best way to set this out is by stating the comparison, and then quoting or referring underneath to support this.

Both writers agree that private tuition can be well paid.

Daniel H. Cohen refers to an email he received offering him £800 a week to tutor in Kazakhstan. He goes on to say that tutors can earn 'between £25 and £40 an hour' and says that the pay can be 'even more at some high-end agencies'.

The second writer refers to 'salacious stories of super tutors creaming £1000 per hour'

The (sometimes very) large sums involved show that working as a tutor can be lucrative

Good answer!

Do you remember the exam paper saying you could answer this question in 'a series of developed bullet points'? The pupil above has written one 'developed bullet point' — he has found one area of agreement between the writers and evidenced it thoroughly.

Suppose instead he had written this. It's not wrong, but it's not as good.

Both writers agree that private tuition can be well paid.

Daniel H. Cohen refers to an email he received offering him £800 a week to tutor in Kazakhstan.

The second writer refers to some tutors earning '£1000 per hour'.

A decent start, now develop this.

Active learning

Go back to the list you made of the areas on which the two writers agreed. Working with the passages beside you, so that you can gather in the evidence you need, create a **developed** bullet point for each area of agreement.

When you have finished, your teacher might ask you to hand them in for marking, or you could swap with another pupil and mark each other's.

Although this question is worth 5 marks, that does not mean you have to find five areas of agreement. Think again about the differences between the fully-developed example of a bullet point that you saw above, and the not wrong, but not nearly so good, one. The mark scheme that the examiners follow says that if you can write about three areas of agreement, and do so with full use of evidence, not just quoting but also supporting those quotations with explanations, then you can earn 5 marks for this question.

This example question asked you to look at the points on which the two writers were in agreement. The question in your exam might not be quite like this. It might, for example, ask you to discuss the key areas on which two authors disagree. As always, the most important advice is:

ANSWER WHAT THE QUESTION ASKS YOU!

Active learning

You have now learned about questions on word choice, tone, imagery and sentence structure. You have learned how to answer questions about linking, and how to ascertain the meaning of words from their context. You've learned how important it is to use your own words, and have answered questions that let you show your understanding of writers' ideas and arguments.

You will now see a two-passage Reading for Understanding, Analysis and Evaluation task.

All the way through this chapter you have been reminded that although you were learning about some question styles (such as word choice, sentence structure, tone or imagery) separately, they would probably be mentioned together in the exam. Question 2 and Question 4c on page 102 are examples of this type. Try this approach. Once you have decided which feature or features of language you are going to answer on, use headings to organise and clarify your answer.

If you've found two different techniques or language features to write about, use two headings.

This task should take you 90 minutes. Remember always:

ANSWER WHAT THE QUESTION ASKS!

When you have finished, hand your work in to your teacher for marking.

The following two passages focus on sexism and gender in film.

Passage 1
The first passage, taken from the *Guardian* newspaper, considers one way of rating films.

Read the passage and answer the questions which follow.

1   You expect movie ratings to tell you whether a film contains nudity, sex, profanity or violence. Now cinemas in Sweden are introducing a new rating to highlight gender bias, or rather the absence of it.

2   To get an A rating, a movie must pass the so-called Bechdel test, which means it must have at least two named female characters who talk to each other about something other than a man.

3   'The entire *Lord of the Rings* trilogy, all *Star Wars* movies, *The Social Network*, *Pulp Fiction* and all but one of the *Harry Potter* movies fail this test,' said Ellen Tejle, the director of Bio Rio, an art-house cinema in Stockholm's trendy Södermalm district.

4   Bio Rio is one of four Swedish cinemas that launched the new rating last month to draw attention to how few movies pass the Bechdel test. Most filmgoers have reacted positively to the initiative. 'For some people it has been an eye-opener,' said Tejle.

5   Beliefs about women's roles in society are influenced by the fact that movie watchers rarely see 'a female superhero or a female professor or person who makes it through exciting challenges and masters them', Tejle said, noting that the rating doesn't say anything about the quality of the film. 'The goal is to see more female stories and perspectives on cinema screens,' she added.

6   The state-funded Swedish Film Institute supports the initiative, which is starting to catch on. Scandinavian cable television channel Viasat Film says it will start using the ratings in its film reviews and has scheduled an A-rated 'Super Sunday', when it will show only films that pass the test, such as *The Hunger Games*, *The Iron Lady* and *Savages*.

7   The Bechdel test got its name from American cartoonist Alison Bechdel, who introduced the concept in 1985. It has been discussed among feminists and film critics since then, but Tejle hopes the A rating system will help spread awareness among moviegoers about how women are portrayed in films.

8   In Bio Rio's wood-panelled lobby, students Nikolaj Gula and Vincent Fremont acknowledged that most of their favourite films probably would not get an A rating. 'I guess it does make sense, but to me it would not influence the way I watch films because I'm not so aware about these questions,' said Fremont, 29.

9   The A rating is the latest Swedish move to promote gender equality by addressing how women are portrayed in the public sphere. Sweden's advertising ombudsman watches out for sexism in that industry and reprimands companies seen as reinforcing gender stereotypes, for example by including skimpily clad women in their adverts for no apparent reason. Since 2010, the Equalisters project has been trying to boost the number of women appearing as expert commentators in Swedish media through a Facebook page with 44,000 followers. The project has recently expanded to Finland, Norway and Italy.

10   For some, though, Sweden's focus on gender equality has gone too far. 'If they want different kind of movies they should produce some themselves and not just point fingers at other people,' said Tanja Bergkvist, a physicist who writes a blog about Sweden's 'gender madness'.

11   The A rating has also been criticised as a blunt tool that does not reveal whether a movie is gender-balanced. 'There are far too many films that pass the Bechdel test that don't help at all in making society more equal or better, and lots of films that don't pass the test but are fantastic at those things,' said Swedish film critic Hynek Pallas.

12   Pallas also criticised the state-funded Swedish Film Institute — the biggest financier of Swedish film — for vocally supporting the project, saying a state institution should not 'send out signals about what one should or shouldn't include in a movie'.

13   Research in the US supports the notion that women are under-represented on the screen and that little has changed in the past 60 years. Of the top 100 US films in 2011, women accounted for 33% of all characters and only 11% of the protagonists, according to a study by the San Diego-based Centre for the Study of Women in Television and Film.

14   Another study, by the Annenberg Public Policy Centre at the University of Pennsylvania, showed that the ratio of male to female characters in movies has remained at about two to one for at least six decades. That study, which examined 855 top box-office films from 1950–2006, showed female characters were twice as likely to be seen in explicit sexual scenes as males, while male characters were more likely to be seen as violent.

15   'Apparently Hollywood thinks that films with male characters will do better at the box office. It is also the case that most of the aspects of movie-making — writing, production, direction, and so on — are dominated by men, and so it is not a surprise that the stories we see are those that tend to revolve around men,' Amy Bleakley, the study's lead author, said in an email.

Adapted from an article in the *Guardian* newspaper,
November 2013

Questions

1   Re-read paragraphs 1 and 2. According to the writer, in what way have Swedish cinemas gone beyond filmgoers' usual expectations of movie ratings? You should use your own words as far as possible.

2

2   Analyse how the language of paragraph 3 emphasises the gender bias of most films. You should refer in your answer to such features as sentence structure, word choice …   4

3   By referring to at least two features of language in paragraph 5, analyse how this paragraph conveys the current depiction of women in film.   4

4   Re-read paragraphs 9 to 11.

    a   Identify two further instances of Sweden's desire to promote gender equality. You should use you own words as far as possible.   2

    b   How does the sentence, 'For some, though, Sweden's focus on gender equality has gone too far' at the start of paragraph 10 form a link at this stage in the article?   2

    c   Analyse how the use of language in paragraphs 10 and 11 emphasises the opinions of those opposed to the use of the Bechdel test. You should refer in your answer to such features as sentence structure, word choice, imagery, tone …   4

5   Re-read paragraphs 13 and 14. Identify any four details given in these paragraphs that support the claim in the first sentence of paragraph 13, You should use your own words as far as possible.   4

6   Evaluate the final paragraph's effectiveness as a conclusion to the passage as a whole.   3

For answers see page 233.

Passage 2

In the second passage below, the writer considers how quite unexpected films can be judged unsatisfying by the Bechdel test. Read the passage below and answer the question which follows. While reading, you may wish to make notes on the main ideas and/or highlight key points in the passage.

1   With its excellent health care, superb state-sponsored child-minding provision, and greener-than-Kermit environmental policies, Sweden is practically the canary in the coalmine for putting politically correct policies into practice. It therefore comes as no surprise that cinemas in Stockholm are the first in the world to make gender representation a factor in an unofficial ratings system, pledging to give an A rating to films that pass the Bechdel test. So should feminists and other folk of a liberal minded persuasion round the world be throwing their copies of *The Second Sex* in the air with joy, and blessing the Swedes' hand-knitted socks?

2   The Bechdel test was invented in the mid-1980s when Alison Bechdel's comic strip *Dykes to Watch Out For* featured a character

who refused to watch a movie that didn't have at least two women who talk to each other about something besides a man. It's a notion rather beautiful in its stringent simplicity, which is why it's stuck around, come to be taken so seriously, and even applied to forms of media other than film. Bechdel actually introduced it in wry light-hearted fashion, via two women debating in the street what to go see at the cinema. The punchline was that the only film that the character who proposed the theory saw as qualifying was Ridley Scott's *Alien*, which was already five or six years old at the time the strip was published.

3 Today, if sticking to the letter of the Bechdel test, there wouldn't be much more at regular multiplexes for the characters to choose from, especially given the dominance now of effects-driven, male-demographic-skewed blockbusters. Ellen Tejle, the director of one of the four cinemas in Stockholm to adopt the Bechdel-driven rating system, said that the campaign has been aimed at opening viewers' eyes to how rarely they see 'a female superhero or a female professor or person who makes it through exciting challenges and masters them,' and that 'the goal is to see more female stories and perspectives on cinema screens.'

4 Well, good for her and the other theatre managers, and good for the Swedish Film Institute for supporting the initiative if this means getting audiences to think more about how feminine perspectives and relationships are missing from so many movies. I'd like it more if they were highlighting the shocking paucity of female directors working today, down, according to a 2012 report, to only 5% of active directors in Hollywood, a 2% reduction on 2010, but you can't win 'em all.

5 However, I'm not so sure if I feel so supportive of television channel Viasat Film. Their idea of promoting Tejle and Co's Bechdel test-initiative is to have a 'Super Sunday', showing surefire-ratings earner *The Hunger Games* (fair enough), the loathsome Margaret Thatcher biopic whitewash *The Iron Lady*, and Oliver Stone's violent drug dealer drama *Savages*, not exactly a woman-centric film even if it does technically pass the Bechdel test. Maybe any publicity is good publicity — but really? Is that the best they could do?

6 Judging by the comments beneath the original article in the *Guardian*, this kind of affirmative-action programming still has the power to get people's knickers in a serious twist, provoking howls of fury about the 'nanny state' (the Swedish government is not making this a law, guys — it's just a few cinemas creating publicity) and how flawed the test is if it

'fails' films like the *Lord of the Rings* cycle or *The Shawshank Redemption* or, oh God the pity, Clint Eastwood and Jeff Bridges 70s buddy movie *Thunderbolt and Lightfoot.*

7   Personally, I too have reservations about the validity of Bechdel test, if we're going to take it so seriously, because it would 'fail' some of the best films I've seen this year at festivals like the London film festival. Jonathan Glazer's magnificent *Under the Skin* probably wouldn't come up to snuff, given Scarlett Johansson's character is practically the only woman in it, and yet it's a film deeply concerned with female power and agency that in its sly metaphoric way says way more about gender than, say, *The Iron Lady.* Nicole Holofcener's acclaimed bittersweet examination of a love-triangle *Enough Said* might fail on the grounds that the two women in it mostly talk about men. Even the relentlessly slushy but effective *Saving Mr Banks,* which stars Emma Thompson as children's author P. L. Travers locking horns with Tom Hanks' Walt Disney over adapting *Mary Poppins,* would also fail, even though it features one of the stronger female protagonists of the year.

Adapted from an article on the *Guardian* film blog, November 2013

Question

7   Both writers consider the application of the Bechdel test to films. Identify the key areas on which they agree, and those on which they disagree. In your answer, you should refer in detail to both passages.   5

You may answer this question in continuous prose or in a series of developed bullet points.

For answers see page 237.

You may have noticed that some of the types of questions you have learned about in this chapter did not appear in this final practice task. The examiners always ask the questions they feel passages deserve, and not every sort of question will come up every time. However you still need to know how to answer every question type, because you don't know when they will come up.

You will need lots of practice of this task before your exam. This book can only help you begin that process. You've seen some examples of what the questions in this exam might be like. Now it's up to you to get as much practice as possible. There are past papers that you can find online, or buy, or that your teacher will have in school. And remember, always:

ANSWER WHAT THE QUESTION ASKS YOU!

CHAPTER 4 The Critical Reading Exam

Critical reading means being able to demonstrate your understanding of texts you have studied in class.

You will be tested on this by sitting an exam (sometimes called the Question Paper) in May of your Higher year.

The exam is broken down into two parts:

- In **SECTION 1** you will read an extract from **a Scottish text** you have studied in class, and answer **questions**. There are **20** marks available for answering these questions.
- In **SECTION 2** you write **one critical essay** about a text you have studied in class. This text can be Drama, Prose, Poetry, Film and Television Drama or Language Study. This essay will be given a mark out of **20**.

The entire exam is only **1 hour and 30 minutes** long. That's not long for everything you have to do, so you need to be thoroughly prepared before you go into the exam.

You need to know your texts very well. You need practice in exam technique. This chapter will help you to do both these things.

How to use this chapter

The chapter will begin by teaching you in detail about two Scottish poems. Then you will learn about the Scottish text questions. These will be based on the two poems in this book. The last part of the chapter will be about critical essay writing. Again, any examples or models will mostly be based on the two poems.

 Warning

The poems you will explore are on the list of Scottish texts at the time when this book is being written. BUT, this list may change from time to time. Before you launch into learning everything there is to know about these poems, get your teacher to check if they are still on the list. You might need to study different poems for your exam.

Two poems by Don Paterson

The Scottish text options include prose (both short stories and novels) as well as poems. There are also several plays on the Scottish text list. It just isn't possible in a book of this size to cover all the potential texts. Other books published by Hodder Gibson, especially those by Carolyn Cunningham and Willie McGuire, can provide more guidance. We're going to look at poems because these are the shortest types of text, and the easiest therefore to fit in this book. Poems are also ideal for this book because the Scottish text question asks you to compare one part of a writer's work to another. By looking at two poems, we can make this sort of comparison.

Don Paterson

The poems are both by a writer called Don Paterson.

Don Paterson was born in Dundee in 1963. He moved to London in 1984 to work as a musician, and began writing poetry around that time. His first book of poems was published in 1993. He has won many awards and honours for his poetry. He teaches at the University of St Andrews and also works for a poetry publisher.

There are six Paterson poems on the set text list. The two that we will study have been chosen because of their similarities, which will help later when we look at the Scottish set text question. They are both about real life experiences, and were both published in 2003 in his collection *Landing Light*.

Both poems will be printed in this book, but you need to have copies for yourself, on paper. This way you can underline, highlight and make notes so that you are engaging and interacting with the poems.

Both poems are also written in the same, specific, form. They are both sonnets. So, before we read them, it's a good idea to spend a little time finding out about the sonnet form.

The sonnet form

A sonnet should have 14 lines, and these lines are usually ten syllables long. Most sonnets rhyme. (If you're not sure how to use letters to describe a rhyme scheme, check with your teacher.) One sonnet rhyme scheme goes like this:

ABAB CDCD EFEF GG

This is called the Shakespearian sonnet, because he wrote so many of them. In this kind of sonnet, there is usually a turn, called the **volta**, between the eighth and ninth lines of the sonnet. This is where there is a change of mood, or tone, or a move to a different part of the argument or idea of the poem. The eight lines before the volta are called the **octet**; the six lines after the volta are called the **sestet**. Shakespearian sonnets end with a pair of rhymed lines, the last two lines of the sestet. This is called a rhyming **couplet** and often works as a kind of summing up or punchline.

Here's Shakespeare's sonnet number 12:

> When I do count the clock that tells the time,
> And see the brave day sunk in hideous night;
> When I behold the violet past prime,
> And sable curls, all silver'd o'er with white;
> When lofty trees I see barren of leaves,   5
> Which erst from heat did canopy the herd,
> And summer's green all girded up in sheaves,
> Borne on the bier with white and bristly beard;
> Then of thy beauty do I question make,
> That thou among the wastes of time must go,   10
> Since sweets and beauties do themselves forsake,
> And die as fast as they see others grow;
> And nothing 'gainst Time's scythe can make defence
> Save breed, to brave him when he takes thee hence.

Active learning

This is quite a tricky piece of writing to understand. Work with a partner or a small group.

- Look at the octet, before the volta. Shakespeare gives lots of different examples. What do they all have in common? Therefore, what is the octet of this sonnet about?
- Now look at the sestet, after the volta. What does the speaker find himself worrying about in lines 9–12?
- What conclusion does he come to in the closing couplet?

There are other rhyme schemes too. The Petrarchan sonnet form (named after an Italian poet) goes:

ABBA ABBA CDE CDE   or   ABBA ABBA CD CD CD

and you may also find sonnets rhyming:

AABB CCDD EEFF GG   or   ABBA CDDC EFFE GG

In fact the sonnet form can be very flexible. This next one was written by Percy Bysshe Shelley in 1817:

Ozymandias

I met a traveller from an antique land	
Who said: 'Two vast and trunkless legs of stone	
Stand in the desert. Near them on the sand,	
Half sunk, a shattered visage lies, whose frown	
And wrinkled lip and sneer of cold command	5
Tell that its sculptor well those passions read	
Which yet survive, stamped on these lifeless things,	
The hand that mocked them and the heart that fed.	
And on the pedestal these words appear:	
"My name is Ozymandias, King of Kings:	10
Look on my works, ye mighty, and despair!"	
Nothing beside remains. Round the decay	
Of that colossal wreck, boundless and bare,	
The lone and level sands stretch far away'.	

Active learning

Work with a partner or a small group.

- What is the rhyme scheme of Shelley's sonnet?
- Look at the octet, before the volta. What is the speaker describing?
- Now look at the sestet, after the volta. What is the message of this sonnet?

Although the sonnets above are both quite old, many writers still use this form. 'Prayer' by Carol Ann Duffy and 'Poem' ('And if it snowed …') by Simon Armitage are good examples of modern sonnets.

Don Paterson seems to find sonnets fascinating. As well as writing his own, including the two we are about to study, he's written a book of commentary on Shakespeare's sonnets, and has edited a collection called *101 Sonnets*, which contains poems by many writers from the last few hundred years.

'Waking with Russell'

Getting in

Before you read the poem, think about these two questions:

1 Have you ever had to look after a baby? What happened?
2 Has there been a moment in your life so far that you would say was a turning point, a time when you somehow changed?

These are quite personal questions, and you don't have to share your answers if you don't want to.

Meeting the text

You are about to read the sonnet. It's a good idea if you have a copy of it on paper, so you can annotate the poem. As you read it, work out the answers to these questions:

1 Who are the characters in this poem, and what are they doing?
2 Only one, very small, thing actually **happens** in this poem. What happens?
3 As you read the poem, mark letters at the end of the lines to help you work out the rhyme scheme. **Hint:** In this poem the rhymes are not the very exact *cat, mat, rat, fat, splat, drat* sort. If you think of the rhymes as softer sound matches, a way of making words chime and harmonise with each other, you'll find this easier to do.

Waking with Russell

Whatever the difference is, it all began
the day we woke up face-to-face like lovers
and his four-day-old smile dawned on him again,
possessed him, till it would not fall or waver;
and I pitched back not my old hard-pressed grin   5
but his own smile, or one I'd rediscovered.
Dear son, I was mezzo del cammin
and the true path was as lost to me as ever
when you cut in front and lit it as you ran.
See how the true gift never leaves the giver: 10
returned and redelivered, it rolled on
until the smile poured through us like a river.
How fine, I thought, this waking amongst men!
I kissed your mouth and pledged myself forever.

Thinking through

Share your answers to the 'Meeting the text' questions you were given at the start of the poem.

 ## Let's get to work

As we study this poem we'll look especially at how Paterson's techniques, including his use of the features of sonnet form, allow him to show the importance of a tiny moment in life. We'll work through the poem step by step, with teaching and commentary. Throughout this, there will be short questions for you to answer and key techniques will be picked out in bold.

The title

In some ways, this is very clear. It tells us about the situation in the poem. Someone has woken up. Someone else — Russell — is there. But, we don't know yet who Russell is.

Lines 1–6

These first few lines clarify some of the things we've been wondering about. The speaker says that he and Russell woke up, 'face-to-face, like lovers'. That **simile** using 'like' immediately tells us that they are not lovers: we are dealing with some other kind of relationship. Once line 3 describes Russell's 'four-day-old smile,' we realise he is a new-born baby. From here we can make a good guess that the speaker is Russell's father, as the most likely person to wake up with a tiny baby is that baby's parent, and as we know this writer is male.

The poem opens with **uncertainty**, as Paterson says, 'Whatever the difference is'. He knows he is different, he's not sure yet in what way. This intrigues the reader too: the difference between what and what, we wonder.

At this stage, Paterson is **writing about his son**.

1 Which words tell us this?

Paterson uses **ambiguity**, when words may have two or more possible meanings. We don't get told which meaning is preferable, so we have to keep holding them both in our heads at once. He tells us Russell's smile 'dawned on him again'.

This could mean that his smile comes to him, almost like a surprise or a realisation, like when we say that an idea has 'dawned on' us.

OR

It could be a reminder, through the use of the word 'dawned', that this is an early morning poem.

OR

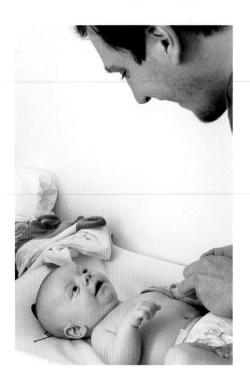

As we often use 'dawn' as a metaphor for new beginnings and fresh starts, it could be a way of saying that this moment marked a new beginning in the speaker's life.

This line also tells us a little about Russell's nature.

2   What does the **word choice** of 'again' tell us about the kind of person he is already, though still so young?

The **word choice** of 'possessed' is important too.

3   What are the connotations of this word? What does it suggest about the effect of the smile on the baby?

Now think about how the poem, which you've read already, finishes. You should see that, by the end, Paterson is totally possessed by Russell, taken over and changed by love for his son.

'Possessed,' is just one of several very **active and expressive verbs** in this poem. 'Pitched back' is another.

4   From your knowledge of language, give two other verbs that have the same meaning and connotations as 'pitched back'.

This section of the poem is full of **rejection of negatives**.

5   Explain how we could say that each of the verbs 'fall' and 'waver' is negative.

Russell's smile 'would not fall or waver'. It is strong and undefeatable.

As well as rejecting these negative verbs, Paterson also rejects his 'old, hard-pressed grin'.

6   What does the **word choice** of 'hard-pressed' suggest about his old grin?

This section of the poem ends with Paterson saying he had 'rediscovered' his smile. Seeing his baby son smile at him has brought back something in him that was lost, or gone, or forgotten. He has been rejuvenated and refreshed.

The volta

You learned earlier that most sonnets have a **volta**, a turn in their plot, idea or mood, between lines 8 and 9. In this sonnet, the volta comes earlier, between lines 6 and 7.

How can we tell this is the volta? Because there is a change in the way the poem is told. It goes from being a sonnet about his son, to being a sonnet **addressed to** Russell.

7 Which phrase tells us he is speaking to his son?
8 Which individual words in lines 7 to 14 also tell us he is writing to Russell?

The fact that this poem has an **early volta** is part of its message and meaning. The second part of the poem is bigger than the first. The poet's new self, he hopes, will last longer than his old self. The early volta is a kind of optimism in the poem. And, for his baby son, life is all ahead of him, in the future. Four-day-old Russell has (almost) no past.

Lines 7–12

This section opens with an **Italian phrase** 'mezzo del cammin'. This literally means 'in the middle of the path'. However, it is usually used more metaphorically, to mean being halfway through life. This is because the phrase was used in the first line of a very famous fourteenth-century poem called 'The Inferno', in which the poet Dante describes a journey through Hell. Paterson is making an **allusion** to this other poem — a reference that he hopes his readers will spot and understand.

We could almost say that 'mezzo del cammin' is meant to suggest a mid-life crisis. But, for Paterson, that crisis isn't followed by a journey into Hell. Instead, it is critical in the sense of being critically and massively important. He doesn't head downwards into Hell; his life takes an upward turn instead.

9 What do the words 'as ever' tell us about his life before he became a parent?

This section of the poem starts to tell us how Russell has changed the writer's life. Look at lines 8 and 9:

> 'and the true path was as lost to me as ever
> when you cut in front and lit it as you ran'

Those two **active, expressive verbs**, 'cut' and 'lit' make the four-day-old baby sound unusually powerful and assertive, and the lines give us a picture of how the boy made his father's life clearer and less confusing.

There are some important **sound effects** in this part of the poem. First, Paterson uses perfect end rhyme, when words at the end of lines have a very exact sound match. We see this in his use of 'giver' and 'river'.

Secondly, he uses the technique of **half rhyme**, which is when the final consonants of words match. We see this in the *-t* endings of 'cut', 'lit', and 'gift'.

Third, he uses **assonance**, which is when the vowel sounds of different words match. We find this in the repeated short *-i* sounds in the words 'in', 'lit', 'it', 'gift' and 'giver'.

Fourthly, the poet uses **alliteration**, when words close to each other begin with the same sound. There's alliteration of the *g-* sound in 'gift' and 'giver'; there's alliteration of the *r-* sound in 'returned', 'redelivered', 'rolled' and 'river'.

The *r-* sound in the words mentioned above is also present in the middle of 'returned' and 'redelivered', and at the end of 'river'. This *r-* sound is one that we make by trilling our tongues against the upper gum — an action that is sometimes called 'rolling the r'. Linguists (people who specialise in the study of how languages work and are spoken) call this a **rhotic** sound. So, in this part of the poem where he tells us about a smile uncontrollably rolling over and through him and his son, the writer uses lots of rolling *r-* sounds. He gives the same power and momentum to his sounds as to his idea, so that the sounds support the ideas.

All of these sound effect techniques have the effect of grabbing the reader's attention, and making us truly concentrate on the poet's words.

10 Which two words in lines 9–12 each use three sound effect techniques: rhyme, assonance and alliteration?
11 Why do you think Paterson has done so much to draw our attention to these particular words?

In lines 11 and 12 we see father and son smiling and smiling back at each other. He uses another **simile** here.

12 Quote the simile.

This gives us the idea that the smile is unstoppable, that it sweeps them up and carries them along.

These lines also use more of those **powerful and expressive verbs**.

13 What are they?

Lines 13 and 14

This is the closing **couplet** of the poem. Although the two lines don't rhyme with each other, as the poem continues with its simple A, B, A, B rhyme scheme, they do form a strong conclusion.

Paterson tells us what he thought: 'How fine … this waking amongst men!'

14 What is the effect of the exclamation mark?

He's only talking about a four-day-old baby, but he describes himself and his son with the **word choice** 'men'. This makes the two of them seem like equals. It also another very optimistic note in the poem — it looks ahead to Russell's adult life, even though he is new-born.

'Waking' is **ambiguous** because it's both **literal** and **metaphorical**. It tells us he really woke with his baby son, but he also woke up to life again.

The last line contains another example of powerful **word choice**, 'pledged'.

15 What does this word suggest?

This poem is about a simple, tiny event. Someone's baby smiled at him, and he smiled back. A bad poet could have written a very bad, sickly-sweet, sentimental poem about this. Paterson, a brilliant poet, writes a powerful and optimistic one.

> ### *Active learning*
>
> Now that you have read and worked through the poem, you should be able to understand it.
>
> **First**, draw a line down the centre of your page. Call one side BEFORE and the other side AFTER. On the first side, write down what you know about the poet's life before he became a father. On the second side, write down what we know about his life after becoming a father.
>
> **Next**, in just one or two sentences, write a statement of the message of this poem. What is Paterson telling us?

Technique revision

Now that you've worked your way through the material about 'Waking with Russell' you should know the poem, and its techniques, very well. Here's a revision task.

Later in this chapter, when we look at critical essay writing, you'll learn how to use the **PEE** structure to build paragraphs in your essays. This stands for making a **Point** about something the writer is doing or a technique the writer uses; giving **Evidence** (preferably by quoting) from the text; and finally **Explaining** the **Effect** on the reader.

Active learning

Take a large piece of paper. Mark it up into a grid like the one below. For every technique, fill in a quotation from the poem, and explain the effect it has on the reader. Some boxes have been filled in for you.

Point — a technique	Evidence — quotation	Explanation of effect
title	*Waking with Russell*	Intrigues the reader by making some things clear but leaving us puzzled about others
word choice	*again*	Tells us Russell often smiles, reveals his cheerful character

You can carry on the rest of the table yourself. You'll need a big bit of paper, maybe two, as you need to add the following techniques:

- Deal separately with each of these two similes:
  like lovers, like a river.
- Deal separately with each of these examples of word choice:
  whatever, possessed, hard-pressed, as ever, men, pledged.
- Deal separately with each of these sound effect techniques:
  rhyme, alliteration, assonance, half rhyme, use of rhotic *r*.
- Deal separately with each of these expressive verbs:
  possessed, pitched, cut, lit, poured, rolled.
- Deal separately with each of these ambiguities:
  dawned, waking.
- use of !
- volta
- rejection of negatives
- early position of volta
- allusion
- couplet

You'll find another of these revision exercises at the end of the work on the next Paterson poem in this book. The task won't be so fully explained again; you'll just get a list of the techniques to revise, but you can look back to this page to remind you what to do. It's time now to go on to our second Paterson sonnet.

'The Thread'

Getting in

Before you read the poem, think about these questions:

1 Have your parents ever told you about what happened around the time of your birth? What do you know about the start of your life?
2 What outdoor games can you remember playing as a child?

Meeting the text

You are about to read another sonnet about Paterson's family life. Again, it's a good idea if you have copy of it on paper, so you can annotate the poem.

> ### The Thread
>
> Jamie made his landing in the world
> so hard he ploughed straight back into the earth.
> They caught him by the thread of his one breath
> and pulled him up. They don't know how it held.
> And so today I thank what higher will   5
> brought us to here, to you and me and Russ,
> the great twin-engined swaying wingspan of us
> roaring down the back of Kirrie Hill
>
> and your two-year-old lungs somehow out-revving
> every engine in the universe.   10
> *All that trouble just to turn up dead*
> was all I thought that long week. Now the thread
> is holding all of us: look at our tiny house,
> son, the white dot of your mother waving.

As you read it for the first time, work out the answers to these questions:

1 Who are the characters in this poem, and what are they doing now?
2 The poem also deals with a past time. What happened then?
3 Look at the layout on the page. What key difference do you see between this poem and the previous one?

4   Again, as you read the poem, mark letters at the end of the lines to help you work out the rhyme scheme. **Hint**: it's different, and a bit more complex, than the rhyme scheme of 'Waking with Russell'.

Thinking through

Share your answers to the 'Meeting the text' questions you were given at the start of the poem.

Let's get to work

As we study this poem we'll look especially at how Paterson's techniques, including features of sonnet form, allow him to contrast two very different times in his life. We'll work through the poem step by step, with teaching and commentary. Once again, there will be short questions for you to answer and key techniques will be picked out in bold. Throughout all of this, we'll see how this poem can be compared to 'Waking with Russell', which we looked at earlier.

The title

As with the previous poem, this title intrigues us. The fact that it is called 'the' thread, not 'a' thread shows that this is something definite and certain for the writer, but it isn't certain yet for us. We immediately wonder, 'What thread?'

Lines 1–8

As with the first poem we read, Paterson starts by talking about his son, telling us how 'Jamie made his landing in the world'. The name detail immediately makes the poem feel realistic. We're reading about a different boy this time, Jamie rather than the earlier Russell, and the description of the poet and his boys as 'twin-engined' in line 7 tells us the children are twins.

In the first three lines we see the beginning of two **extended metaphors** that run throughout the poem: the metaphor of a thread, and of an aeroplane. There is a third metaphor too, of ploughing.

1   Explain how line 1 begins the aeroplane metaphor that runs through the poem.

Line 2 says Jamie landed, 'so hard he ploughed straight back into the earth.' This suggests his birth was not so much a landing as a plane crash, a time of danger to life, as a plough tears up the earth and turns the soil over. The words 'into the earth' further tell us how near to death the boy was, as they hint at the idea of a body being buried in a grave. We could also say that this makes 'The Thread' what we might call an 'earthy' poem — a realistic one.

The other **metaphor** is introduced in lines 3 and 4: 'They caught him by the thread of his one breath/and pulled him up.'

2   Who do you think 'they' were?
3   What does the use of the word 'thread' tell you about the Jamie's health and strength when he was born?

We often say that things which are uncertain or at risk are 'hanging by a thread'. Paterson is making an **allusion** to that phrase to let us see how fragile his son's life was. Even now, he is not sure how the boy survived.

4   Quote the words which tells us this. Why is the length of the sentence important?

The **verbs** here are significant. 'Caught' and 'pulled' both suggest quick, alert, and active intervention. The medical staff had to work urgently and skilfully to save Jamie.

The writer, thinking about it today, thanks 'what higher will/brought us here'. Jamie's survival seems like a miracle, something that cannot just be explained by good medical care. The line isn't explicitly religious, but it suggests that human expertise alone was not enough to save the boy, and the vague 'what' ties in with 'they don't know' above.

There's a change at this point in the poem. Lines 1 to 4 have been about Jamie, but now Paterson speaks to him.

5   Which words in lines 5 to 8 show he is now speaking to his son?

This **change of address**, from speaking **about** his son to speaking **to** him, reassures the reader that the poem has a happy outcome: the boy is alive and is there to be spoken to.

The **extended metaphor** of the plane reappears here, but is expanded. In line 1, Jamie seemed to be a little aircraft, all by himself. Now he is part, along with his father and twin brother, of, 'the great twin-engined swaying wingspan of us/roaring down the back of Kirrie Hill'. The boy who almost died is alive and a vital part of a vibrant family.

The **word choice** in these lines emphasises Jamie's strength. The plane is 'great'. Its movement is described with the **active, expressive verbs** 'swaying' and 'roaring'. The fact that it is 'twin-engined' doesn't just tell us that the brothers are twins, but that the formerly weak Jamie is now every bit as fit and strong as Russell. The father, plus the twin who was always healthy, and the twin who nearly died, now make up one strong, male unit: 'you and me and Russ'.

The **metaphor** of the boys as engines also shows us how important the boys are to him. They are the force that brings drive and power to his life.

This section of the poem uses a number of sound effect techniques. Firstly, Paterson uses **assonance**, when vowel sounds within words sound alike.

6   Which words in lines 2, 3 and 4 have assonance?

He also uses **internal rhyme**, when words within a line of poetry rhyme with each other.

7   Which words in line 6 rhyme with each other?

This use of assonance, and of internal rhyme, is going on inside a poem where there is already an overall scheme of rhyming words at the end words of the lines. So, the poem is full of sounds that chime with each other.

8   These sound matches pull the poem together: they make it into a tight unit in which all the parts relate to each other and work together to create a pleasing whole. How does this relate to the picture of the father and twin sons running down the hill?

In line 8, the poet describes the 'wingspan' shape they make as they run downhill. The **word choice** here ties in with the extended metaphor of the plane, but it does something else too. It suggests the boys are under their father's wing, with connotations of protection and care.

Those last words, 'Kirrie Hill' refer to Kirriemuir, a small town in Angus, where Paterson lived. By using the local nickname for it, he brings more **realism** into the poem, and the phrase again has **assonance**.

The volta

The writer plays a bit of a trick on us here. We know that this poem is a sonnet, and it seems to be laid out to clearly divide the first eight lines, the octet, from the last six, the sestet. There's a gap, a kind of stanza break, between lines 8 and 9. It looks like a very clearly signposted volta. But it's not.

9   Read lines 5 to 10. Explain how we know that there is not, in fact, a volta between lines 8 and 9.
10 This sonnet does have a **turning point**. Where does it actually fall? In as much detail as you can, explain how you know that that is the turning point.

So why does Paterson place his turning point so much earlier than the usual volta position, creating this **early volta**? Perhaps to show us that, for Jamie, the turning point between life and death came very early on, in the first few days of life.

Lines 9–14

In these lines we see a **contrast** between Jamie now, and Jamie at the time of birth. There's **hyperbole** — writer's exaggeration — in the description of the boy, 'somehow out-revving/every engine in the universe.'

11 How do these lines continue the extended metaphor of the plane?

12 With which line from the earlier part of the poem do these lines make a strong contrast?

13 How does the use of 'somehow' in line 9 refer back to line 4?

Although we are now in the present, Paterson cannot help remembering the past, and the first few days of Jamie's life, because that time was just too stressful and worrying for him to be able to forget it. This is another reason why we know the sonnet doesn't have a neat volta: even in the happy present he remembers the past, so past and present keep mixing together throughout the poem.

14 Why do you think line 11 is in italics when the rest of the poem is in plain text?

The writer of this book has known pupils who read the poem and really thought Jamie had died. Those pupils do need to read a little more carefully, but the fact they made that mistake shows how powerful that line is. It is short, blunt, matter-of-fact, and on first reading seems too tragic for us to want to argue with.

The writer tells us that this 'was all I thought that long week.' But, we know that can't be true. Think back to the first poem. The boys are twins. 'Waking With Russell' is about Russell's 'four-day-old smile.' So, there was at least one moment in that week when Paterson was able to forget his worries about Jamie, to enjoy waking with, and smiling at, Russell.

That doesn't mean the writer is lying to us. In fact, with this **apparent untruth**, he's telling us something very deeply true. When we face a terrible crisis, it seems to take over and dominate all our thoughts. When life is full of danger and the threat of tragedy, it's easy to think that there is nothing else but danger and tragedy. In this case, we have the twin poems to remind us that when one twin boy was hovering between life and death, the other had a smile that changed his father's life.

We return to the **metaphor** of the thread.

15 Quote the line that tells us how strong Jamie now is.

Father and sons are running towards home from the top of Kirrie Hill, so their house looks 'tiny'. However this **word choice** of 'tiny' also implies that Jamie is huge, and again reminds us how fit and strong he is now.

The last line of the poem mentions the one remaining member of the family, the boys' mother. She is described **metaphorically**, as a 'white dot'. This ties in with the plane metaphor. She is the little dot of white light that guides the plane home, the landing light. (The book in which these two poems first appeared was called *Landing Light*.) So, although the boys' mother isn't mentioned until this final line, the poem presents the whole family as a unit, in which each member is necessary to the others: Paterson is the body of the plane, the boys are the engines, their mother is the light that guides them home. The poem that began with a crash landing ends with a safe landing.

Technique revision

Now that you've worked your way through all the work on 'The Thread' you should know the poem very well. Now revise your knowledge of Paterson's techniques.

Active learning

You're going to carry out the same exercise that you did at the end of the 'Waking with Russell' work. (Look back to it now if you need to be more fully reminded of the instructions.) Take a large piece of paper and mark it up into a **PEE** grid. For every technique, fill in a quotation from the poem, and explain the effect it has on the reader. For a grid about 'The Thread' you need to work with the following techniques:

- Deal separately with each of these extended metaphors:
  the plane, the thread.
- Deal separately with each of these metaphors:
  ploughing, engines, white dot.
- Deal separately with each of these verbs:
  caught, pulled, swaying, roaring,
- Deal separately with each of these items of word choice:
  great, twin-engined, wingspan, tiny.
- end-of-line rhymes
- the overall use of rhyme and other sound effects
- realistic detail
- use of italics
- change of address

- turning point
- assonance
- title
- hyperbole
- allusion

- mixing of past and present
- internal rhyme
- contrast
- apparent untruth
- false volta

That's the end of our work on these two sonnets. They work well together. Each shows the impact that becoming a father has had on the writer; each shows his love for his sons. Although one sonnet is entirely about Russell, and the other is mainly about Jamie, together they show his fatherly love for both boys. Sonnets traditionally express romantic love, but these explore the love a parent feels for children.

There are four other Paterson poems on the Higher list. You will need to study them **all** if you hope to use them for the Scottish set text question. Remember your teacher should double check if these poems are still on the set list at the time when you are using this book!

If Don Paterson has been taken off the Scottish text list by the time you take this course, you could still study 'Waking with Russell' and 'The Thread' as texts for the critical essay. If you do that, your Scottish set texts will need to come from a different genre, not poetry but either prose or drama.

The Scottish set text questions

Because we have just spent so much time looking at two of the set Scottish poems, it makes sense to look at this part of the exam now. The Scottish set text questions are in the first section of your Critical Reading exam paper.

What you will be assessed on

In this part of the exam you will read an extract — or in the case of poetry, perhaps a whole poem — from a Scottish text you have previously studied in school and then answer some questions.

There will be several questions focussing on the extract, or poem, itself. These questions will usually be worth 2, 3 or 4 marks. There will be a total of 10 marks' worth of questions.

The last question will be a far bigger one, worth 10 marks. It will test your broader knowledge of the rest of a novel or play, or of other short stories or poems by the same writer.

Active learning

You're going to try some questions on the first Paterson poem you studied. Your teacher may want you to work on your own, or perhaps with a partner or in a group. Start by turning back to 'Waking with Russell' and reading it again. Then try each question. If you are working with someone else, do make sure you still write down your answers as you would in an exam. Here are the questions:

1 The poem comes to a turning point after line 6. With reference to at least two techniques, explain how this turning point is made clear to the reader.   4

2 With reference to lines 7 and 8, explain what the speaker means when he describes himself as 'mezzo del cammin' (line 7).   2

3 Evaluate the effectiveness of lines 13 and 14 as a conclusion to the poem. You should deal with ideas and/or language.   2

Give your answers to your teacher to mark. It's best if you don't try the next task until you know how well you got on with this one.

For answers see page 239.

Active learning

You're now going to try some questions on the second Paterson poem you studied, 'The Thread'.

This time you should definitely work on your own. Start by turning back to 'The Thread' and reading it again. Then try each question, writing down your answers as you would in an exam.

1 By referring to one example from lines 1 to 4, analyse how the writer uses a metaphor to clarify one of the main concerns of the poem. **2**

2 By referring closely to at least two examples from lines 3 to 10, show how the language of the poem conveys the idea of uncertainty. **4**

3 With reference to at least two examples taken from throughout the poem, analyse how the writer conveys the contrast between Jamie now and at the time of his birth. **4**

Give your answers to your teacher to mark. Don't go on to the next task until you know how well you got on with this one.

For answers see page 240.

As we saw already, the last question will be a far bigger one, worth 10 marks. This question will get you comparing the extract, or the poem, to the rest of the work you've studied. For example:

- If your Scottish text is a play or novel, and the extract focussed on one character, you might be asked to look at how that character develops over the course of the text.
- If your Scottish text is a play or novel, and the extract focussed on a particular theme, you might be asked how that theme is explored and developed in the rest of the text.
- If you have studied poetry, the final question may ask you how something the writer does in the poem printed in the exam paper, such as exploring a particular theme, or using a particular technique, compares to other poetry you have studied by the same writer.

These are just some of the possibilities for that last question. As always, the best advice is:

ANSWER THE QUESTION YOU ARE BEING ASKED!

Before we go on to look at the final, 10-mark, question, the one that gets you to place this poem in the wider context of Paterson's other work, there's something you need to do.

Active learning

Work with a partner or a small group. Get a large sheet of paper and give it the heading **Similarities**. Compare the two poems and use the sheet to create a record or poster of your discoveries. The first two have been done for you.

SIMILARITIES

- each poem is about one of the writer's twin sons

- each is a sonnet

Carry on finding more answers in your group. If you push yourself to think of the content of the poems, their themes and ideas, the techniques Paterson uses, and also the ways in which he uses these techniques, you should be able to get at least ten similarities.

That task was designed to get you comparing the two poems we've looked at, as this is what you will be expected to do in the final, 10-mark question on your set Scottish text.

Active learning

You are going to work with your partner or group again. You will see a specimen final question.

This question is worth 10 marks and therefore needs a much bigger answer than the questions you tried earlier, the ones that referred only to one particular poem.

Here's the question:

- Discuss how Paterson uses contrast in 'Waking with Russell' and at least one other poem to highlight the poems' main concerns. **10**

Here are some tips to help you answer it:

- You can earn up to 2 marks for identifying features that two or more Paterson poems have in common.
- You can earn up to another 2 marks for any references you make to the poem printed in your exam paper — in this case 'Waking with Russell'.
- There are up to 6 marks available for discussing similar references in at least one other poem by the same poet.

In the exam you can, if you wish, tackle this as a kind of mini essay, a set of linked points. But, it's perfectly all right if you give a set of bullet-pointed answers that fit together to form a complete response to the question. On this occasion, as you're working with others, you can answer in a series of bullets.

Work together to answer the question. When you have written your answer, give it to your teacher to mark.

For answers see page 241.

Active learning

Here's another possible 10-mark final question. This time you are going to try it on your own. Before you try it, re-read the advice given above about how to tackle the question and how the marker will reward your work.

Here's the question:

- Referring closely to 'The Thread' and at least one other poem, discuss how the poet develops the idea of the impact that fatherhood has had upon his life. **10**

For answers see page 242.

That's the end of our work on the Scottish set text question. You will need lots of practice of this task before your exam. This book can only help you begin that process and can only give you an example of what the Scottish set text questions might be like. You can, and should, also use past papers to help you.

The critical essay

You've written critical essays before, for your National 5 exam. You should already understand what you are being asked to do. Remember:

- A critical essay **is not** a chance for you to write everything you know about a text.
- It **is not** a chance to explain your favourite things about a text.
- It **is not** a chance to tell the marker about the bits you understand best, or find easiest to explain.
- It **is not** an invitation to write a commentary on the whole text from start to end.

A Higher critical essay is a kind of test. It tests your ability to **select** from your knowledge of a text, and to use that selected knowledge to meet the demands of a **specific** task or question.

What you will be assessed on

In this part of the exam you will be given a choice of questions. These questions will be divided into five sections. Each section contains questions about a different genre. These are:

- drama
- prose (which will be subdivided into fiction and non-fiction)
- poetry
- film and television drama
- language study

There will be **three** questions for each genre. (In the prose section there will be three questions each for fiction and non-fiction prose.) These questions will not name any specific texts. Instead, they will be quite broad and general questions that are likely to suit many texts from that genre.

Remember, the genre you choose to write about in your essay cannot be the same one you choose for your Scottish set text question. For example, if your chosen Scottish writer is Don Paterson, your critical essay cannot be about poetry.

You will have about 45 minutes to write the essay in, and it will be marked out of 20.

The examiners will be looking at four different areas of your essay-writing skill: **knowledge and understanding; analysis; evaluation** and **technical accuracy**.

- **Knowledge and understanding** means how well you can show that you understand and know the text you have studied. It also includes how well you use evidence from the text to write an essay that clearly answers the question you have been asked.
- **Analysis** means being able to examine and explain the way the writer writes: the techniques he or she uses and the effects created by these.
- **Evaluation** means having a personal response to and a personal opinion about what you have read. You will be able to show what you have gained from the text.
- **Technical accuracy** is how clearly you put across your ideas. This includes your spelling, grammar, sentence structure, paragraphing and punctuation. It also means that your essay will be clearly understandable at first reading.

As you work through this chapter you will learn to produce essays that display all these skills.

The next few pages will teach you how to do this. As we have studied two Paterson poems, we will make quite a lot of references to poetry essays, but the techniques you will learn should help you to write about any kind of text that you have studied this year. Whichever texts you have studied in class, you will need to know everything there is to know about them, so you can pick the right details from that knowledge to use in the exam.

Choosing an essay

At the top of the essay section of the exam you'll find a general instruction like this:

Attempt ONE question from the following genres — Drama, Prose, Poetry, Film and Television Drama, or Language.

You may use a Scottish text but NOT the one used in Section 1.

Your essay must be on a different genre from that chosen in Section 1.

You should spend approximately 45 minutes on this Section.

Pay attention to this. You **must** make sure you don't write on either the same text or the same genre as you do in the Scottish text section of the exam. (You are allowed to write about a text that is printed, in whole or in extract form, in the exam paper, as long as it's **not** the one you answered on in that earlier Scottish text section.)

In the first few minutes of your exam you need to weigh up your choices quickly but carefully, so that you can do your best work overall and earn as many marks as possible.

How will you choose the best question? To begin to work this out, we need to look at the way the individual questions are worded.

All the essays tasks follow the same pattern. They are set out in two paragraphs. For example:

> **Choose a poem which features a relationship.**
>
> **Discuss how the poet's presentation of this relationship adds to your understanding of the central concerns of the poem.**

To choose which essay to write, you're going to look at just the **first** paragraph of the essay task.

As soon as you see these words, you need to run through a quick mental checklist. Let's assume you go into the exam having studied Don Paterson. You can ask yourself:

> *Have I studied any poems?*

To which the answer would be:

> *Yes.*

So, you **might** be able to write this essay. Now it's time to focus in even tighter on that first paragraph and look at **what kind of poem** the examiners want you to write about. So now you need to ask yourself:

> *Do any of the poems I've studied feature a relationship?*

This essay question turns out to be quite a good one, because you get two quite positive answers:

> *Both 'Waking with Russell' and 'The Thread' feature Paterson's relationship with his sons.*

It's time to narrow down your choice. To help you do this, take another look at the words in **the second paragraph** of the task. This paragraph is where the examiners tell you how they actually want you to tackle the essay. The words of the second paragraph give you instructions that you must follow. If you don't obey the instructions in paragraph two of the task, you aren't answering the essay question and you will certainly not pass.

For this essay, these words in paragraph 2 are important:

> **… how the poet's presentation of this relationship adds to your understanding of the central concerns of the poem.**

Now you can narrow down your options by asking yourself:

> *Does one of these poems more clearly use the writer's relationship with his son to help me understand the central concerns of the poem?*

We can see now that it is perhaps easier to write this essay about 'Waking with Russell', than about 'The Thread'. In 'Waking with Russell' we can see how the relationship with his baby son is used to highlight the central concern of the poem, which is how much the writer has been changed.

At this stage you could decide to write your critical essay on Don Paterson's 'Waking with Russell', or you could carry on looking through the exam paper until you find a different essay that appeals to you even more.

The good news is that finding an essay question is not meant to be difficult. The examiners try very hard to make the questions quite open and general. In any set of three questions about a particular genre of writing, it should nearly always be possible for you to find at least one task that fits a text you have studied in that genre.

Active learning

To show you what I mean about the questions being quite open and general, take a look at this set of three poetry questions that appeared together. You'll recognise one of them:

- Choose a poem in which the poet explores one of the following emotions: grief, happiness, love, alienation. Discuss how the poet's exploration of the emotion has deepened your understanding of it.
- Choose two poems which deal with the same theme. Discuss how the theme is explored in each poem and explain which poem you believe offers a more memorable exploration of the theme.
- Choose a poem which features a relationship. Discuss how the poet's presentation of this relationship adds to your understanding of the central concern(s) of the poem.

Now answer these questions:

1 You already know that task 12 fits 'Waking with Russell'. Now decide whether tasks 10 and 11 fit either 'Waking with Russell' or 'The Thread'.

2 If you have studied other poems for Higher, do any of these questions fit those poems?

3 If you studied poetry for National 5, think back to those texts. Do any of these three questions fit those poems?

Before we leave the idea of choosing your essay, remember, if Paterson is the only author you've studied for Scottish set text, you can't do your critical essay on him too. And, remember your essay question must come from a different genre than your Scottish set text.

Writing your introduction

The first paragraph you write in the essay will be your introduction. Whenever you write a critical essay, the same three things should appear in the opening sentence:

- the title of the text you read
- the name of the author
- a clear indication of what you will be writing about

As we've already seen, the first paragraph of the essay task helps you to choose which task you are going to do. Once you have chosen an essay to tackle, that same first paragraph of the task instructions is also useful for something else. It helps you to write the introduction to your essay. To do this, you are going to **recycle** many of the words from that paragraph.

Let's assume that you have chosen to do the essay task we looked at in detail earlier, and that you are going to write about 'Waking with Russell'. Here's the first paragraph from the essay task we saw earlier on. Look at the words printed in bold type.

Choose a poem which features a relationship.

You can recycle some of those words in the first sentence of your essay. The words you recycle will help you to give a clear indication of what you will be writing about. You still need to add the title and author to these to have a complete first sentence, which would end up looking like this:

One poem which features a relationship is 'Waking with Russell' by Don Paterson.

If you feel like being a bit more stylish, you could try an opening like this:

Don Paterson's sonnet 'Waking with Russell' features a relationship, in this case the one between father and son.

Active learning

Look again at the opening paragraphs from the other two questions in that set of three essay tasks you saw earlier.

- Choose a poem in which the poet explores one of the following emotions: grief, happiness, love, alienation.
- Choose two poems which deal with the same theme.

First, turn each one of the suitable openings into a basic opening sentence of an essay. The first example above will help you.

Now look at the opening paragraphs again and use them to help you write more stylish opening sentences for these essays.

After the opening sentence, it's a good idea to continue your introduction by writing a **short** summary of your text. Any teacher can choose to teach his or her class any texts that they enjoy, and that they think their class will like. This means that you may end up writing your critical essay about a text that the exam marker has never read, or maybe even never heard of. Writing a **short** summary will give the marker a little bit of context and background, making it easier for him or her to understand comments you make about that text in your essay.

Warning

Take care! You'll have noticed two bold type reminders that you should be writing a **short** summary. The summary itself does not earn you any marks. It just helps you and the exam marker to get your heads clear. You must not waste precious exam time by waffling.

To let you see what I mean by a **short** summary, here's one for 'The Thread'.

In this poem the narrator — who seems to be the poet himself — considers the change in his son Jamie. The boy, very ill at the time of his birth, is now shown to be a fit and healthy toddler.

130

That summary is just 39 words long. It should be easily possible to summarise most texts in fewer than 50 words.

Active learning

First complete these two tasks.

1 Write a brief summary of 'Waking with Russell'.

2 If you have studied other literature or media texts in your Higher course yet, write a brief summary for each of them.

Now swap your summaries with another pupil.

Read and mark each other's work. Try to make each other's summaries as brief, clear and efficient as possible.

The main body of your essay

Once you've written the introduction and summary, it's time for the main body of your essay. This main body will be made up of several paragraphs — four or five will be enough.

We've already looked very carefully at the fact that the first paragraph of the essay instructions tells you what sort of text to write about. The second paragraph of the essay instructions tells you **what you are actually going to do** in your essay. Remember, if you don't do what that second paragraph tells you to do then you aren't answering the question and you will never pass the essay. Here is the whole of one of those questions we saw on page 128:

- Choose two poems which deal with the same theme. Discuss how the theme is explored in each poem and explain which poem you believe offers a more memorable exploration of the theme.

If you look at this instruction carefully, you will see that in this essay you have two main things to do:

1 **Discuss how** the theme is explored in each poem
2 **Explain which** poem you believe offers a more memorable exploration of the theme.

In fact many of the critical essays you will find in the exam will give you two things to do.

Active learning

You are going to see some essay questions in full. These questions will come from a variety of genres, not just poetry. From each second paragraph, pick out the two things you have to do in the main body of the essay.

Choose a **play** in which the conflict between two characters is an important feature.

Briefly explain the nature of this conflict and discuss how the dramatist's presentation of this feature enhances your understanding of the play as a whole.

I have to ...

Then I have to ...

Choose a **novel** or **short story** in which there is a disturbing or violent incident.

Explain briefly what happens during this incident and discuss to what extent the disturbing or violent nature of the incident is important to your understanding of the text as a whole.

I have to ...

Then I have to ...

Choose a work of **biography** or **autobiography** in which the writer's description of an emotional experience creates a powerful impression.

Briefly explain the emotional experience and then discuss how the writer's description of this experience creates this powerful impression.

I have to ...

Then I have to ...

Choose a piece of **journalism** in which the writer persuades his or her reader to a point of view by effective use of language.

Briefly explain the writer's point of view, and then discuss how the writer's use of language is effective in persuading the reader.

I have to ...

Then I have to ...

Choose a **film** or **television drama** in which a central character is in difficulty.

Briefly explain what the difficulty is, and then discuss how the film or programme makers' presentation of the character's difficulties enhances your understanding of a central concern of the text.

I have to …

Then I have to …

Not every critical essay task gives you two things to do. For example, you may find one like this:

> Choose a novel or short story in which a central character is presented as a menacing or threatening presence.
>
> Discuss how the writer's presentation of this character adds to your understanding of the text as a whole.

In this task you don't have two different things to do, you just have to look at how the writer's presentation of this character adds to your understanding of the text as a whole. The important thing you must always do is read the question to find out clearly and exactly what you have to do and what you have to write about.

So, now that you know what you are supposed to do, how are you going to do it? Let's take a look at an essay task that would be good for 'The Thread'. Here's the question in full.

> Choose a poem in which aspects of structure (such as verse form, rhyme, metre, repetition, climax, contrast, narrative development …) play a significant role.
>
> Show how the poet uses **at least two** structural features to enhance your appreciation of the poem as a whole.

A good way to tackle this essay is to start by working out which structural features are important in 'The Thread'. The question helpfully gives you a list of suggestions. Did you notice that the list ends in …? That means there might be other structural features that are not on that list, but that are relevant to 'The Thread'.

Here are some structural features that are relevant to this poem:

- use of sonnet form
- contrast
- position of stanza break
- rhyme

If you wrote one paragraph for each of these, you'd have four paragraphs in the main body as your essay. As you write these paragraphs:

- every one of the main body paragraphs must help you to do what your chosen task tells you to do.
- every one of the main body paragraphs must use evidence from the text.

Active learning

Here's an example of a paragraph which does the two things mentioned above. Read it carefully and decide:

1 Which words in the paragraph show that this pupil is trying to stick to the chosen task?

2 Which words in the paragraph show the pupil is using evidence from the text?

One feature of the structure of this poem is its use of contrast. We see this particularly when Paterson contrasts his son's breathing at birth, which he describes as:

> 'the thread of his one breath'

with the way the same boy breathes now:

> 'your two-year-old lungs somehow out-revving
>
> every engine in the universe'

At birth, Jamie was so near death that he had only 'one' breath, not the many that are needed for life, and that breath was so thin and fragile as to be merely threadlike. This metaphor reminds us of the expression 'hanging by a thread', meaning utterly unstable, and reinforces for us how near Jamie came to death. In contrast to this 'one' breath, Jamie's toddler lungs are now stronger than 'every' engine, and not just every engine in the world but every single one 'in the universe'. This use of hyperbole emphasises his current strength and health, and enhances the reader's appreciation of the poem by showing us the complete and joyful change in Paterson's young son — a transformation the poet celebrates by writing this poem.

Did you manage to answer the questions?

Check the answers on page 242.

Did you notice how this pupil set out the quotations? They are indented — moved away a little from the left hand side of the page — to make them stand out. But, you don't need to skip a line above or below the quotation. You are not starting a new paragraph: the quotation is part of the paragraph. The pupil also used quotation marks ' ' around the quoted words.

Let's focus a bit more carefully on how to write the paragraphs in the main body of your essay. There are two things you can do in these paragraphs so that they will be well written and will help you to achieve the task you've chosen.

1 Beginning the paragraph with a **topic sentence**.
2 Using the PEE structure.

Topic sentences

Topic sentences are called this for two reasons:

1 Firstly, they tie in with the topic of your essay.
2 Secondly, they let the reader understand the topic of the paragraph you're on.

Using a topic sentence at the start of the paragraph sets you off in the right direction.

Active learning

You're going to see again the essay tasks you examined on page 132. Over the page, you'll see a list of sentences. Each one is a topic sentence from one of the essays. Can you decide which essay each topic sentence belongs to?

Here are the essay topics:

1 Choose a play in which the conflict between two characters is an important feature.

Briefly explain the nature of this conflict and discuss how the dramatist's presentation of this feature enhances your understanding of the play as a whole.

2 Choose a novel or short story in which there is a disturbing or violent incident.

Explain briefly what happens during this incident and discuss to what extent the disturbing or violent nature of the incident is important to your understanding of the text as a whole.

3 Choose a work of **biography** or **autobiography** in which the writer's description of an emotional experience creates a powerful impression.

Briefly explain the emotional experience and then discuss how the writer's description of this experience creates this powerful impression.

4 Choose a film or television drama in which a central character is in difficulty.

Briefly explain what the difficulty is, and then discuss how the film or programme makers' presentation of the character's difficulties enhances your understanding of a central concern of the text.

Here are the topic sentences. Can you match each one to the right essay topic? It doesn't matter if you don't know the text the topic sentence is about; you are just looking at how well it ties in with the essay question.

a One way in which Orwell's description creates a powerful impression is in his choice of language to describe the elephant when he first sees it.

b One way in which Moffat presents Sherlock's difficulties is by having Moriarty seem to appear everywhere that Sherlock goes.

c This disturbing incident is used by Spark to deepen her characterisation of Miss Brodie as being highly manipulative.

d Shakespeare shows us that conflict can affect not only those characters who are at odds with each other, but also has consequences for those around them.

Did you notice that the first two topic sentences begin with, 'One way in which …' plus the name of the author? This is a perfectly satisfactory way to start a paragraph, and it will help you be clear to the marker and keep things clear in your head.

However you should also have noticed that the third and fourth topic sentences were more individual and more distinctive. Just as you saw on page 129, when we were learning about writing essay introductions, there's a basic way to do this, and a more stylish way. Once you feel you've mastered the basics, you should be looking for ways to impress the marker with your style and flair.

The PEE Structure

The PEE structure helps you to remember what goes in each paragraph.

- **P** — tells you to make a **P**oint about the writer's technique. In other words, mention something you can see the writer deliberately doing.
- **E** — tells you to give **E**vidence: this will nearly always be by quoting from the text, though it may sometimes be easier to give evidence by referring to something in the text.
- **E** — tells you to **E**xplain the **E**ffect of this, to show what the writer is doing to us, the readers.

The **P** part of this is also the topic sentence of the paragraph, so there's a bit of an overlap between the idea of using a topic sentence, and the idea of following the PEE structure.

Active learning

Copy the following paragraph into your notebook. It's deliberately not about a poem you are likely to study for Higher, so that you really have to think about how the pupil is organising the paragraph. Once you've copied it out, do these three things:

1 Underline the **P** part with a straight line.

2 Underline the **E for Evidence** part with a wiggly or jagged line.

3 Draw a box round the **E for Explanation** part.

One way in which Morgan makes his ideas memorable is by saying the same thing in three ways at once. He tells us that when faced with the guitar, the baby, and the chihuahua:

'Monsters of the year

go blank, are scattered back,

can't bear this march of three.'

If the 'monsters' go 'blank' then they must have no ideas and nothing to say for themselves. If they are 'scattered' then they are separated and no longer any kind of force. If they 'can't bear' then they are powerless compared to the three who 'march' in an organised and powerful way. The overall repetition of the fact that the 'monsters' can no longer cope shows how powerful the three simple things are.

Did you notice the three parts of the PEE structure? You should also have spotted that the pupil is writing in **present tense**. You should do this whenever you write about what you have read.

Active learning

Read the essay extract again. Pick out all the verbs that show that the pupil is writing in present tense.

Writing about techniques

On the exam paper, above each set of essay tasks, you will see a paragraph of advice. The wording of this paragraph follows a pattern.

Active learning

To get you to spot the pattern of this paragraph in the essay instructions, you're going to see the advice for two different types of essay. The first one is for poetry essays; the second one is for prose fiction essays. Read the two paragraphs and then answer the two questions below.

Answers to questions on **poetry** should refer to the text and to such relevant features as: word choice, tone, imagery, structure, content, rhythm, rhyme, theme, sound, ideas …

Answers to questions on **prose fiction** should refer to the text and such relevant features as: characterisation, setting, language, key incident(s), climax, turning point, plot, structure, narrative technique, theme, ideas, description …

1 Which words are always used at the **start** of the advice above the essay tasks?

2 What do you always see at the **end** of the advice above the essay tasks? What do you think this means?

What this paragraph of advice does is just remind you to write about some of the techniques the author uses, or some of the things that made that text worth studying in the first place. Remember that **a technique is anything a writer deliberately chooses to do**. While some techniques have particular names, like those listed in the paragraphs above, anything a writer does on purpose to have an effect on the reader is a technique.

It doesn't even actually matter which techniques and features you write about. You don't have to write about the ones named in the paragraph, because the three dots at the end of that paragraph allow you to write about whichever techniques and features you believe are important for the text and task you have chosen. What does matter is that you should deal with the writer's techniques, because the question has told you to do so, and because the markers will be looking for this in your essay.

For example, suppose you were writing an essay on 'Waking With Russell'. Depending on which essay you chose, you could pick any of the following techniques and features that we looked at as we studied the poem, none of which are on the list in the box in the exam paper:

similes	alliteration	assonance		half rhyme	rhotic *r*
rhyme	verbs	ambiguity		use of !	allusion
volta	couplet	rejection of negatives			

You can also write about the technique of word choice, which **is** named in the advice box above the poetry questions on the exam paper.

The way that you write about techniques is all tied in with that important **PEE** structure. The **P** part, remember, is where you make a **P**oint to introduce the technique. The first **E** part has you quoting **E**vidence of that technique being used by the author. When you get to the second **E** part of the structure you are **E**xplaining how the writer creates an **E**ffect, how he or she achieves what he or she set out to.

There are words and phrases you can use to show that you are dealing with the writer's techniques.

The following words and phrases describe **what the writer does**, or **what part of the text does**. They will help you to show that you are **analysing** the author's work.

has connotations of	suggests	shows	
creates	mirrors	establishes	underlines
reinforces	emphasises	highlights	
foreshadows	exemplifies	explains	
demonstrates	echoes	reveals	hints

The following words and phrases describe **how the reader feels**, or **how the text affects us** as we read. They will help you to show that you are **evaluating** the author's work, and the way that it has an effect upon us.

thought-provoking	inspiring	horrifying
hard-hitting	stimulating	pivotal moment
key idea(s)	fast-paced	effective
gripping	skilful(ly)	perceptive
moving	profound	striking
important	intelligent	thoughtful

Active learning

Work with a group. Read the wording of this essay task, which is suitable for getting you to write about 'Waking With Russell':

Choose a poem in which the poet explores one of the following emotions: grief, happiness, love, alienation.

Discuss how the poet's exploration of the emotion has deepened your understanding of it.

First, think of at least three ways in which Paterson explores the emotion of love so as to deepen our understanding of this emotion.

Then compare your own group's answers to this with those from the rest of the class.

Next agree on the best answers for building paragraphs for the essay. You need to end up with as many good ideas as the number of groups in the class.

Now work just with your own group again. Take one of the paragraph ideas your class agreed on. Write it up into a paragraph for this essay. Remember to:

- use quotations from the text and to indent the words that you quote
- make sure you start with a topic sentence and that that topic sentence works as the **P** part of the **PEE** structure in your paragraph
- use some of the key words and phrases from the boxes on page 139

Last, read your paragraphs aloud in class or give them to your teacher for marking.

The conclusion

After your introduction, summary and main body, you need to finish off your essay with a conclusion. The conclusion ought to do two things:

1 sum up and round off what you have written
2 give your personal response

Summing up just means reminding the examiner what you have written about. It should be only one sentence long and could sound something like this:

Clearly, Paterson's exploration of his love for his baby son allows him to present the reader with a developed understanding of this emotion.

Giving your personal response takes a little more thought. Earlier in your school career your personal responses were probably a bit like this:

> I liked the poem because it has a happy ending. I would recommend it to other pupils to read.

You have to do something a little more complicated now because, at Higher level, your personal response, just like everything else in your essay, should fit your chosen task, as well as fitting the text you are writing about.

This task was about how Paterson explores the emotion of love in such a way that he deepens out understanding of it. Your personal response should say something about how well you think he does this. You could say whether you think his ideas are clear. Here's one example of how a pupil tackled it — you're going to see her whole final paragraph.

> Clearly, Paterson's exploration of his love for his baby son allows him to present the reader with a developed understanding of this emotion. He makes it absolutely obvious that love has the power to transform, and that it nourishes both parties. In fact he shows that the best love is mutual, and makes no distinction between the lover and the beloved.

So, that's it. You know how to write an essay. If you've worked through this chapter you found out step by step how to tackle this part of the exam. Before you go into the exam, your teacher will give you lots of chances to practise essay writing in class.

Active learning

You're going to see the whole of the wording for an essay task that suits the Paterson poems.

First of all, above the essay choices for poetry, the exam paper has this wording:

Answers to questions on **poetry** should refer to the text and to such relevant features as: word choice, tone, imagery, structure, content, rhythm, theme, sound, ideas …

Then you see this essay task:

Choose two poems which deal with the same theme.

Discuss how the theme is explored in each poem and explain which poem you believe offers a more memorable exploration of the theme.

Now, using all the advice from this chapter and everything you have learned, write this essay. Remember you need to have:

- an introduction
- about four or five main body paragraphs beginning with good topic sentences and using the **PEE** pattern
- a short summary

Hint: This question gives you two things to do, and gets you to think about two poems. Spend a few minutes working out how you are going to divide the five body paragraphs of your essay to cover everything you are asked to do.

- a conclusion in which you summarise the essay and give your personal response.

Check over your essay and then hand it in to your teacher for marking. Don't just check your content, look at your language too: your spelling, grammar, paragraphing, punctuation and expression.

Essay writing in the exam

During the Higher course you will get lots of chances to write essays about the texts you study. At first your teacher may support you in some of the following ways:

- giving you a plan to follow
- making a plan with the class
- letting you plan in groups or pairs
- letting you use your texts and notes while you write the essay
- giving you as long as you need to finish the essay
- letting you take the essay home to finish it

However by the time you get to the exam you need to be able to quickly choose, plan and write your essay, all in 45 minutes. Three things will help you with this.

First, remember, the questions are planned to be open and general. The examiners aren't trying to catch you out, they're trying to offer you a variety of opportunities to show off what you have learned.

Second, you need to know your texts really well before you go in to the exam, and you need to know all your notes and materials about those texts. That way you can pick out the right material to use to answer the essay question you have chosen.

Think of it like this. There's probably all sorts of different equipment in your kitchen. If you know what you're going to cook, and you know what you're about to do, you can pick out the right items. Baking cupcakes needs very different utensils to making a lasagne.

Similarly, the information you use to write an essay about how the author makes you feel sympathy for a character might not be the same information you would use to write an essay about how the writer deals with a particular theme or issue.

Third, you need to make a quick plan in the exam before you write your essay. It can be a list of the five key ideas you want to base your main body paragraphs on, or a mind map or spider plan with a leg for each main body paragraph, but however you do it you need to know what you are going to say to answer the question.

Sometimes, pupils go into the exam and panic. No matter how scared you are, don't be tempted to write about the Film and Television Drama option if you haven't been taught that in class. Even if you are Scotland's biggest *Doctor Who* fan, don't write about what you haven't been trained to write about. The same applies to the language section.

There might well be a question in there about teenage slang, and you may be a slangy teenager, but don't try to write about it if you haven't been taught it.

Another danger in the exam is that you might write the essay you want to write, and not the one the examiners want. It's really important to learn essay skills — and that's what this whole chapter has been about — but there's no point trying to learn a particular essay off by heart, even if it's one you got a good mark for in class. You can only write about what the examiners want on that day.

CHAPTER 5 The Writing Portfolio

To pass Higher English, you need to pass the Analysis and Evaluation and the Creation and Production Units. These are covered in the first two chapters of this book. You also need to pass the course assessment. One part of this course assessment is called the Question Paper — an exam that you will sit. This is covered in Chapters 3 and 4. The other part of the course assessment is the Writing Portfolio, which you will learn about in this chapter.

Your Portfolio is worth 30 marks, which also makes it 30% of your total mark for Higher. You will produce **two** pieces of writing, each marked out of 15. These pieces will come from different genres. The Portfolio will then be sent away to the SQA to be marked.

You will complete your Portfolio by building on skills you have already developed earlier in school, particularly in the National 5 course and in the Higher Creation and Production Unit.

It may take you most of your Higher year to get the Portfolio together. You may wish to try the different sorts of writing taught here at different times, and to produce a number of different first drafts before you decide, with help from your teacher, which two are best and should be redrafted for the Portfolio. You should not need to redraft any piece more than twice.

What you will be assessed on

In both of your pieces, the discursive and the creative, the markers will be looking at four particular areas of your writing skill: your **content**, your **use of language**, your **accuracy** and your **ability to achieve your intended purpose**.

Your piece should have the right **content**. This means that you will stick to your chosen **purpose** and write something that fits your chosen audience. You will be skilled at writing in your chosen genre.

Style includes being able to use the conventions of your chosen genre effectively. Your word choice and expression will be varied and effective. The structure of your piece will help it to achieve its **purpose**.

Technical accuracy is how well you use the English language. This includes your paragraphing, spelling, grammar and punctuation, which should all be consistently accurate, with very few errors. Your writing should communicate clearly and immediately with the reader.

There are also more particular assessment guidelines for each genre of writing. You will find these in the sections of this chapter that deal with those genres.

Combined assessment

The work you do on your Portfolio may help you to pass one of the units as well.

- It might be possible to use this work as evidence of writing for the Creation and Production Unit.
- The research you do to prepare for your discursive writing might also be useful in preparing for an individual presentation, or some other kind of talk.

Your teacher will make sure that you have covered all the skills each unit asks for.

 Warning

The next few pages are going to contain lots of information about the course requirements for writing. Don't panic. You don't have to try to memorise all of this. As you read it over, just make sure you understand everything. You can check back to these pages at any time to make sure that you are following the rules and guidelines properly.

What you can write

Your Portfolio should contain two pieces in two different genres. One piece should be what the SQA calls '**creative**', which actually means that you can produce any one of these types of writing to fulfil the requirements for this genre:

- a personal essay
- a reflective essay
- an imaginative piece

Later in this chapter you will learn more about the two of these styles, personal writing and imaginative fiction.

The second Portfolio piece should be what the SQA calls '**discursive**', which actually means that you can produce any one of these types of writing to fulfil the requirements for this genre:

- an argumentative essay
- a persuasive essay
- a report for a specified purpose

Later in this chapter you will learn about the first two of these styles, persuasive and argumentative.

Length

Your Portfolio pieces should each be no more than 1300 words long. (Footnotes are not counted as part of this total.) This does not mean you have to write 1299 words to please the marker. A shorter piece can still get a very high mark, if it is well-written and fulfills its purpose, However if your piece is a lot shorter it may not be the sort of developed work that Higher markers want to see. If your piece is too long, you will penalise yourself, because the marker will just stop reading.

Your title, any footnotes, and any bibliography or list of sources are not counted. If your piece contains quotations these are regarded as part of the word count.

Authenticity

Because your Portfolio is worth 30% of your marks, quite a sizeable chunk of the entire Higher course, it's vital that the SQA can be sure that every pupil is working in the same way and under the same conditions, so that marking can be fair. Your Portfolio has to be your own work, and at Higher level you are not allowed to have too much support or detailed input from your teacher.

You will work on your Portfolio under what the SQA calls 'some supervision and control'. This is a way of saying that your teacher should always be able to know that the work is entirely your own. There are various ways your teacher can be sure of this: you might be asked to keep a checklist of your work, and will certainly be asked for a list of sources you consult. Most schools will also ask you to write first drafts in class, and you will definitely have to do this if you are also using this writing as evidence for the Creation and Production Unit.

What you can do	What you can't do
Be given teaching that extends your knowledge, understanding and appreciation of a range of genres	Rely heavily on ideas or wording that you found in a printed or electronic source
Use printed or electronic sources to find background information or ideas	**What your teacher can't do**
Use a dictionary, spell-checker or thesaurus	Give you detailed advice about how to re-structure or re-word your first draft
Discuss your topic and/or ideas with your teacher as part of your planning	Pick out and correct mistakes in your expression or your technical accuracy
Be given written comments on your first draft, and discuss that draft with your teacher	Tell you that you must write about a certain genre or topic that he or she has chosen
Be given broad suggestions for how to improve your first draft	Give you detailed notes, or a specific plan, or a model so detailed that you wouldn't be coming up with your own structure

This might all sound very detailed and strict. Remember you can check back at these rules at any point in your work, and remember that their overall purpose is to get you to do what you should want to do anyway — to use your own ideas to write your own piece that shows your own interests and abilities.

Sources

You'll probably need to refer to outside sources as your write your discursive piece. These must be acknowledged.

- If you have used a newspaper or magazine article you must name the writer and give the publication date.
- If you use information from the internet you must give the name of the site and the specific page address.
- If you quote from a book you should give the title and publication date.
- Any quotations should be inside quotation marks.
- You **absolutely cannot, ever**, copy and paste, or retype, exact wording from a website or from anywhere else and pass it off as your own work.

Drafting and redrafting

All real writing is drafted and redrafted. However, because your Higher Portfolio is a test of how well you can write, and to make sure that everyone is being tested fairly, you should not keep endlessly polishing your work.

Your teacher should keep a note of your title and ideas, your plan, your first draft and a copy of your final version. Doing so is part of the 'supervision and control' mentioned earlier.

Your teacher can write comments and suggestions on your first draft, and can discuss these with you, but cannot mark mistakes in detail. It's up to you to be able to correct these. You should not normally have more than two goes at writing any particular piece.

You will need to sign a declaration to say that your Portfolio is your own work. The two pieces that you send away should be produced under conditions that help to ensure that the work is your own. In practice, the easiest way to do this is to write your first draft of each piece in class. Your teacher will compare that draft to any later versions to make sure that the work, as it improves and develops, is without a doubt still your own.

Presentation

It is possible to send in neatly handwritten work, but ideally your Portfolio pieces should be word-processed, and printed in black ink on just one side of the paper. If you are typing your work, use a clear standard font of 12 point size. Your text should be justified — it should have a straight margin on the left. Margins should be 2 centimetres wide all round the page and you should use double line spacing, with a double return for new paragraphs. The poor marker may have several hundred pieces to read and all these guidelines make your work clear and easy to follow.

Well done! You've made it through pages of rules and guidelines. Did you understand it all as you read it? Remember that you can refer back to these pages at any time. In fact you should keep coming back to these pages and double checking that you are following the rules.

Now that we've got through all this, let's move on to the fun part, the writing itself.

At the start of the chapter we saw that the SQA wants you to write in two different main genres, **creative** and **discursive**, and that these break down into various types. There isn't space in this book to deal with every possible genre of writing, but we will look at the four that most pupils are most likely to want to write: **prose fiction** and **personal writing** from the creative genre; and **argumentative** and **persuasive** writing from the discursive genre.

Prose fiction

There are many different forms of imaginative writing, including poetry, description and all sorts of script for stage and screen. However most Higher pupils who tackle imaginative writing do this by creating a piece of prose fiction.

The wide genre of prose fiction includes all short stories and all novels. However we can often tell that the fiction we are reading belongs to a more particular genre. For example, Terry Pratchett and J. R. R. Tolkien's books belong in the fantasy genre. Hilary Mantel and Philippa Gregory both write historical novels. Each genre has its own rules and conventions (the way things usually happen) and these can be very helpful for writers.

Work with a partner or small group. Make a list of all the fiction genres you can think of.
Next, share your answers with the whole class and build up a bigger list.

In this chapter, we are going to find out about one particular fiction genre — **the detective novel**. You may have heard of Ian Rankin, Anne Cleeves, Val McDermid, Jo Nesbo and Henning Mankell who write in this genre. The makers of television programmes love this genre too.

Going deeper

The rest of this part of the chapter is going to be about writing detective fiction. It will prepare you to write the first chapter of a detective novel as a possible portfolio piece.

If you choose to do this, the chapter will give you examples, advice, and support. But, you might choose to do something different:

- You might research the conventions of a different fiction genre, and write an opening chapter in that genre instead.
- You might write a short story that fits a particular, different, genre, rather than writing an opening chapter.
- You might use the classic structure of a short story, building up action from an initiating incident towards a climax and final resolution. (If your school has the book *National 4 & 5 English* by Jane Cooper, you can read much more about this in the chapter on the National 5 writing portfolio. All the advice is there, although as a Higher pupil you would need to write a more sophisticated story.)

Work with a partner or small group.

- Make a list of all the crime writers you can think of.
- Now list all the television programmes you can think of that are about crime or detection.

Next, share your answers with the whole class and build up a bigger list.

Don't panic. You're not going to be asked to write a whole novel. You're just going to write the first chapter.

Active learning

Work with a partner or small group. Make a list of answers to this question:

What do you think a writer needs to do in the first chapter of a novel? (Don't think specifically about detective novels for the moment, just list what you think every novel writer should do at the start of their book.)

Next, share your answers with the whole class and build up a bigger list.

Active learning

Work again with your partner or small group. Make a list of answers to this question:

What particular things do you think a writer needs to do in the first chapter of a detective novel?

Next, share your answers with the whole class and build up a bigger list.

Read the following text. It's just the first two pages of a book, not the whole chapter.

Beware of the Dogwalkers

'We should just round up all the dogwalkers.'

'Ma'am?'

'The dogwalkers. Haven't you noticed it's always them who finds one of these? Very suspicious if you ask me.'

'Quite, Ma'am. Anyway, what would you like me to do?' Perhaps this was just the DCI's little joke. It was P.C. Harry Stevens' first murder, but he'd heard that officers who saw this kind of thing all the time developed a sort of black humour, a coping mechanism.

'Bring me the dogwalker,' said DCI Heather Barnes wearily. 'Just the one dogwalker. The one who found her.'

'Certainly Ma'am.' Stevens began scrambling up the slope away from the burn and towards the footpath at the top where a shaky-looking middle-aged woman was sitting on a fallen log. She was clutching her spaniel as if it might bring her some comfort — unlikely as the dog was too busy yapping at the growing crowd. How could a crowd form in a place like this? Stevens liked cities, bars, and shops. To him this pathway at the edge of a village might as well have been the Gobi desert, but a crowd was forming nonetheless. Already he could see three other uniforms, two bio-suited members of the MO's team and a local television news crew. News crews were bad news.

Barnes knew this too. 'And get rid of that camera crew!' Stevens heard her yell as he approached the dog lady.

The body was lying, as in Heather's memory they always seemed to, half buried. The dog had scurried through the leaves in its excitement and she couldn't be sure how much it might have disturbed the scene. The MO's men should be able to tell her. 'I'm sorry,' she said to the dead girl. 'I will find out who did this.' It was what she always said to the dead.

At the top of the slope Harry Stevens was wishing he felt more authoritative. 'I must ask you to step back and cease filming. You'll have an opportunity to ask the DCI any questions you like at a proper briefing later.' The few minutes he'd spent with the dead girl seemed to have made him smaller and quieter and the news crew weren't really paying him much attention.

'Just a couple minutes. Yeah? Local colour? Early reactions?' The reporter was wearing a slightly too shiny suit under his slightly too red anorak. His wellingtons worried Stevens most of all. The man was keen. Any minute now he might head off down the slope towards the boss.

Impatient at last with waiting for the walker to be brought to her, Heather Barnes was on her way back up the slope, having left the body with the men in the white suits. She made straight for the reporter. 'Mr Morton. You have an amazing instinct for these sorry scenes.'

'Just doing my job, Heather. People have a right to know when there's a maniac on the loose.'

'MISTER Morton,' she said firmly. 'We are at the very early stages of what will be a complex investigation …'

'So you're saying you won't be able to find this guy quickly?'

'I'm saying,' she said through gritted teeth, 'that it is far too early for you to be using words like loose and maniac, or even assuming that we are looking for a guy.'

'So you have no leads whatsoever? Viewers will find that very disturbing.'

'A discovery has been made Mr Morton. At this stage I am unprepared to say more.'

'But it's a girl isn't it?' persisted the reporter. 'And it looks from up here as if she's been murdered.'

Heather had had enough. 'Mr Morton you are not helping. In fact you are actually stopping me at this moment from doing my job at all. I need to interview the woman who found the body.'

'So you're at least prepared to confirm that the girl's dead then? Not just sleeping?'

'Enough, Morton.'

As she walked off, the reporter turned to his cameraman. 'Anything we can use?'

'Not much. But I did get a little sound clip earlier on when I was setting up the levels. Something odd that DCI said to her PC. You should take a listen.'

Active learning

Do you want to add anything to your list of what you think a detective novelist needs to do in his or her first chapter?

Now read the rest of Chapter 1 of *Beware of the Dogwalkers*.

Heather was in the incident room when she saw that night's news. It started well. The staged press conference was clear and brisk. She could see herself putting across the facts: a dead body, that of a woman probably in her late teens, had been found by a local person. Early indications were that the victim had been lying there for less than twelve hours. Residents were asked to report anything that might be significant to the investigation. Police were especially hoping to hear from anyone who was worried about a missing friend or relative as this might help to identify the deceased.

All of that was fine. The next item was more of a problem. A number of animal welfare groups, the Kennel Club and the local chapter of the Association of Professional Dogwalkers and Petsitters had all joined together to issue a strongly-worded statement. They utterly condemned the suggestion that the killer might have been a dogwalker.

This called for an exceptionally strong coffee. The pot that held the proper stuff was empty, as usual. Nowhere in the serious crime manual did it say who was in charge of the coffee pot, so it was always empty. Heather reached into her desk drawer and found a jar with about half an inch of granules solidified at the bottom. Poking them with a fork — there was no sign of a spoon either — did no good. Sighing, Heather tipped boiling water straight from the kettle into the jar, screwed the lid on, and was shaking it vigorously when the Super strode in.

'Now Heather!'

'Sir?'

'The wife's furious. I've just had her on the phone. She can't believe what you said about dogwalkers. You know how fond she is of wee Angus and Rosie.'

'With respect, Sir …'

'DCI Barnes, people only say that when they're about to say something very disrespectful, and you know that I hold my dear wife in the highest regard.'

'Yes Sir, and I'm sure you're very fond of her dogs too, but wouldn't it be more appropriate for your wife to be furious about the fact that someone has been killed?'

'Just so Heather. Anything in that jar for me?' The Super, having delivered his message and done his domestic duty, was now back to his usual avuncular self.

'Not really, Sir, not unless you like tar with your shortbread.'

'Better come to my office then. I've got a pot of Colombian on the go.'

Superintendent Bruce Henderson's office was legendary. His dog-loving wife, Olive, was famed for keeping him far under her thumb, but she was a lovely home baker. Bruce's office was both a haven from her iron rule, and a source of delicious aromas that sometimes reached as far as the holding cells. Heather accepted a mug of Colombian, a brownie, and a small cheese scone. Apparently Olive was practising for the Women's Guild annual bake off.

'So what do we have Heather?'

'Pretty much what you heard me say at the news conference, Sir. There's a dead girl but we don't know who she is. No ID, no match to any current missing person's report. MO's team think she was killed somewhere else and dumped there shortly after she died. We didn't tell them that.'

'Anything else you didn't tell them? Do you know how she died?'

'Blunt force trauma to the head. Hit two or three times but the first blow was probably enough to kill her.'

'That's good.' Henderson took a deep bite from his brownie. A walnut piece dropped onto his napkin. 'So what can we do about the dog thing?'

Heather sighed. 'I didn't know they were listening, Sir. I was down the bottom of the slope with Harry Stevens. He was looking a bit green. His first body you see. I thought a wee joke might help. Bloody directional microphones.'

'Absolutely. But we'll have to do something, just to calm them down and get the attention back on the real story. We've no clues and we need the public to help, not to be told by that idiot Morton that we're about to round up all the pet owners.'

'I suppose I could make a statement. Say how much we appreciate the fact that the dog-walking community have always helped us with our enquiries.'

Henderson sucked in his teeth, his current mouthful of coffee, and a number of deliciously chocolaty crumbs. 'I don't think that's quite the way to put it. Isn't helping us with our enquiries what people do when we arrest them — because we've got a strong suspicion that they actually might have killed someone and dumped the body?'

'Yes Sir.'

'Yes Heather. I think some kind of gesture might be called for.'

★ ★ ★ ★ ★

She felt stupid. The force's media team had suggested she'd 'play more sympathetically with the public' if she wasn't alone when filmed. 'I won't be alone,' she'd insisted. 'I'll have two west highland terriers, that idiot Peter Morton and his fat cameraman. Plus I've just been told to expect some guy who used to present Blue Peter and a team from the dog channel!'

But they'd made her take Harry Stevens too. He'd been sent home to put on something that wasn't uniform, but it was obvious to everyone that the whole thing was staged. Heather's office suit looked wrong on the footpath and wrong beside Harry's designer jeans. Angus and Rosie clearly had no respect for her authority and were winding themselves around her ankles. Olive Henderson had handed them over with a long list of instructions and a stern look and was now hovering just out of shot.

They'd chosen a neutral location of course, a country park. All the footpaths radiated from what had once been a rich Victorian's country lodge and was now a nature interpretation centre and ranger station.

They'd been walking for about ten minutes when the path they were on turned towards a burn and the ground grew wet and slimy. Morton and his cameraman, slithering along behind them, were not happy. 'Slow down can't you? I'm sure we've got enough footage now.'

'But Peter,' she grinned, 'I think we're far enough from the road to let these wee guys off their leads.' Bending down she unhooked the two little white dogs, who darted off immediately in quite opposite directions.

Within moments she'd lost sight of Angus in the undergrowth by the water. She gave Stevens a look.

'Yes Ma'am.'

He was back horribly soon. 'Ma'am, I think you'd better come and take a look.'

The film crew caught up with them just as Heather was reaching for her mobile.

Active learning

Discuss the answers to these questions:

- What has the writer done in this first chapter to make you want to read on into Chapter 2?
- What do you think the police have found at the end of this chapter?
- What do you think is going to happen in Chapter 2?
- What do you think is going to happen in the rest of the novel?

You should have noticed that the writer is doing more than just setting the plot — the crime story — in motion. She's also establishing characters, and letting us see the relationships between them. Because the story mostly sticks to Heather's point of view, we can tell that she is the main character, and is someone we are supposed to like and sympathise with. We see that she has a difficult relationship with the reporter, but a mostly good one with her own boss, Superintendent Henderson, and that she and the uniformed PC, Stevens, aren't quite used to working together yet.

People often ask writers where they get their ideas from. The writer of *Beware of the Dogwalkers* got the idea from a country walk, when she realised that she was in the kind of place where dogwalkers always seemed to find bodies. You might be worried that you'll have trouble coming up with an idea of your own, especially when so many other people have written detective novels before you. To prove that ideas can come from anywhere, it's time to play a game.

Active learning

Close your book. This game will only work if you don't know what comes next. As long as your teacher has a copy of the book and can tell everyone in the class what to do, it'll work out fine. Go on, close your book.

The only person reading this now should be the teacher. This exercise uses randomly chosen words to set up the plot of a story in which there is a suspicious death. The use of random words in this is actually very structured, so it's important that you take your pupils through this task in order, and that they follow the instructions carefully.

First put your pupils in to pairs and get them to choose two random words. It works best if the words they choose are nouns. Make sure every pair has time to choose their two nouns before you explain the next step.

Then explain the following: The two words they have chosen are to be used to create the scene or setting of a crime story. (For example, if they chose the words *tiger* and *stain*, the set-up could be that a man was found dead just outside the tiger cage in a zoo with a strange green stain on his shirt.)

Give them a few minutes to work their scenario out. At this stage they do not have to decide exactly how the victim died.

Next get your pairs of pupils to choose a further three random nouns. Give them plenty of time to do this before you go on to the final step.

Now tell them that these words are the clues. They must now use these words to construct a reasonable hypothesis, using these clues to explain how the suspicious death took place and who might have done it. (For example if the second set of words went *rhino, corn, chicken*, the explanation could be that the man was on his way to take a bucket of corn to the chickens when he was charged by an escaped rhino. The green stain came from a pen in his pocket that burst when he was crushed by the charging beast.

Last, get your pupils to share their answers with the class, first of all saying what their words were, then explaining what scenarios or solutions they came up with. Finally, tell them they can open their books again!

I hope you can see that ideas can come from anywhere, and that the oddest things can sometimes get you going on a story. Let's look a little more specifically now at one particular element of your chapter — the crime scene.

You'll find one of these in the first few pages of nearly every detective novel, or before the first advert break in any television crime drama. Certain elements — what we might call genre markers — come up again and again:

- the senior detective arrives to find other police force staff already at work
- the senior detective usually has a more junior colleague
- the place setting is described to create atmosphere
- there is a detailed, possibly gruesome, description of the victim's body
- a police doctor or pathologist is at work
- the detective starts noticing clues, asking questions and drawing conclusions

As you read the following two crime scenes, look for the above elements.

The first crime scene comes from one of Ian Rankin's Edinburgh-set novels about Inspector John Rebus. During the Edinburgh Festival, something nasty has been found under the Royal Mile.

'You know where we are?' the constable asked.

'Mary King's Close,' said Rebus. Not that he'd ever been down here, not exactly. But he'd been in similar old buried streets beneath the High Street. He knew of Mary King's Close.

There were ducts and pipes, runs of electric cable. Signs of renovation were all around. Rebus pointed to an arc lamp. 'Can we plug that in?'

The constable thought they could. Rebus looked round. At the end of the hallway he could see a wooden toilet, its seat raised. The next door along led to a long vaulted room, the walls whitewashed, the floor earthen.

'That's the wine shop,' the constable said. 'The butcher's is next door.'

So it was. In its ceiling were a great many iron hooks, short and blackened but obviously used at one time for hanging up meat.

Meat still hung from one of them.

It was the lifeless body of a young man. His hair was dark and slick, stuck to his forehead and neck. His hands had been tied and the rope slipped over a hook, so that he hung stretched with his knuckles near the ceiling and his toes barely touching the ground. His ankles had been tied together too. There was blood everywhere, a fact made all too plain as the arc lamp suddenly came on, sweeping light and shadows across the walls and roof. There was the faint smell of decay, but no flies, thank God. Dr Galloway swallowed hard. Rebus tried to steady his own heart.

Though it was against regulations he leaned forward and touched the young man's hair. It was still slightly damp. He'd probably died on Friday night and was meant to hang here over the weekend, time enough for any trail, any clues, to grow as cold as his bones.

'What do you reckon, sir?'

'Gunshots.' Rebus looked to where the blood had sprayed the wall. 'Something high velocity. Head, elbows, knees and ankles. He's been six-packed.'

From *Mortal Causes* by Ian Rankin

This second crime scene is deliberately bizarre. In this novel, nursery rhyme characters are real people, mostly living quiet lives in the suburbs. Should any 'nurseries' become involved in crime, either as victims or suspects, Detective Inspector Jack Spratt and his Nursery Crime Division investigate them. In the following extract, Humpty Dumpty has suffered a fatal fall.

The yard was shaped as an oblong, fifteen feet wide and about thirty feet long, surrounded by a high brick wall with crumbling mortar. Most of the yard was filled with junk — broken bicycles, old furniture, a mattress or two. But at one end, where the dustbins were spilling their rubbish on the ground, large pieces of eggshell told of a recent and violent death. Jack knew who the victim was immediately, and had suspected that something like this might happen for a number of years. Humpty Dumpty. The fall guy. If this wasn't under the jurisdiction of the Nursery Crime Division, Jack didn't know what was. Mrs Singh, the pathologist was kneeling next to the shattered remains dictating notes into a tape recorder. She waved a greeting to him as he walked over but did not stop what she was doing. She indicated to a photographer areas of particular interest to her, the flash going off occasionally and looking inordinately bright in the dull closeness of the yard.

Humpty's ovoid body had fragmented almost completely and was scattered among the dustbins and rubbish at the far end of the yard. The previous night's heavy rain had washed away his liquid centre, but even so there was still enough to give off an unmistakable eggy smell. Jack noted a thin and hairless leg — still with a shoe and sock — attached to a small area of eggshell draped with tattered sheets of translucent membrane. The biggest piece of shell contained Humpty's large features and was jammed between two dustbins. His face was a pale white except for the nose, which was covered in unsightly red gin blossoms. One of the eyes was open, revealing a milky-white unseeing eye, and a crack ran across his face. He had been wearing a tuxedo with a cravat or a cummerbund — it was impossible to say which. The trauma was quite severe and to an untrained eye his body might have been dismissed as a heap of broken eggshell and a bundle of damp clothing.

Jack kneeled down to get a closer look. 'Do we know why he's all dressed up?'

Mary consulted her notebook.

From *The Big Over Easy* by Jasper Fforde

Active learning

Discuss the following questions with a partner, a group, or the class:

- Did the writers use all the genre markers you expected?
- Did the writers use any ideas or techniques that surprised you?
- Which did you prefer, and why?

Active learning

At this stage, it's a good idea to also watch at least the first 20 minutes of a television detective drama. There's almost certainly something suitable on television this week, or your teacher might show something to your whole class. You should watch until you get at least as far as a 'scene of the crime' moment like those above.

We're going to leave the detective novel on one side for a little while, and look at some more general writing skills that will help to bring your chapter to life.

First, we're going to look at a skill that's often summed up in the words: **show, don't tell.** To make that clear, have a look at the following sentences.

I came into the room. I saw Alan. I greeted him and sat down in a chair.

Now look at these sentences.

I stormed into the room. I glared at Alan. I grunted at him and flung myself into a chair.

How does the speaker feel about Alan? Angry of course. But notice, he never **tells** us, 'I felt angry with Alan.' Instead, by changing the simple verbs like *came, saw, greeted* and *sat* into more expressive ones like *stormed, glared, grunted* and *flung*, the narrator **shows** us the emotion.

Active learning

Go back to the first basic set of three sentences beginning, 'I came into the room ...' Rewrite them to show the following emotions:

- The narrator is afraid of Alan.
- The narrator finds Alan very attractive.
- The narrator is surprised to find Alan there.

As you can see, the difference between showing and telling often comes from choosing interesting vocabulary. By using the right words to put across how characters move, act, appear, or speak, we can show what they are like, or how they are feeling.

Active learning

Copy and complete the following table. It'll help you create a bank of words and phrases.

	How might the character speak?	What might their face look like?	How might the character move?
angry			stamping slamming storming grabbing
sad	stuttering sighing moaning		
happy			
scared		white faced eyes wide mouth tight	

Active learning

One more task on showing, not telling. This one will take us back towards the detective novel.

Write a paragraph to describe, in as much detail as possible, a desk in a police station. The way you describe the desk, the things you put on it, and how everything has been set out, should start to show the life and character of the detective who works at that desk. For example if there are photographs of children on the desk, we can guess that the detective is probably a parent. Lots of dirty coffee cups and an empty painkiller box suggest one kind of person, a nearly-empty desk with a ticked 'to do' list on it suggest quite another.

Don't use any characters, action or speech in your writing, just description. When you've written your piece, swap with a partner and see what you can work out about each other's detectives.

Looking at a real example

You are going to see a piece of detective fiction produced by a real pupil. First of all just read through the piece of writing. You may wish to do this aloud around the class, or you might want to read it on your own.

Chapter 1 – Rock-A-Bye-Baby

When the phone rings before dawn, it rarely brings good news. When that phone belongs to a Detective Inspector, it never brings good news.

Leah Stark grunted a greeting. Less than five minutes later she had pulled herself out of bed, dressed and was rushing out the door, leaving her husband sleepy and confused.

It was a bitterly cold morning. Leah stepped out of the car and hurried over to her workmate. He was behind the local supermarket, where the dumpsters sat and deliveries were dropped off.

'Morning Leah,' smiled Detective Sergeant Toby Smith. They had worked together on many cases.

'Hey Toby. What's going on?' Leah asked as he led her over to the dumpsters. All she had been told over the phone was that there had been an 'incident' behind the supermarket.

Toby stopped between two dumpsters and pointed. 'That's what's going on.'

Leah sucked in a breath as she crouched down. A woman, probably in her mid twenties, was huddled on the ground, her arms clutching a blanket. Her head was bent, and her chin sagged onto her chest, leaving her dark hair falling over her face. Frost had formed on top of her head and shoulders. Inside the blanket, a hand enclosed in a tiny mitten could just be seen. Leah had to fight against her maternal instinct as she looked at the little hand. She stood up, her fists clenched at her sides. She struggled to keep her face from betraying her emotions as she asked 'Any idea what happened?'

Toby shook his head, 'We're not sure yet. Pathologist's on his way, but nobody's touched the bodies or even had a good look at the mother's face. The most obvious explanation would be that they froze overnight. Temperatures were below zero.'

Leah bit her lip, thinking of her own little girl, still safely tucked in her bed. She was about to comment on how horrible the situation felt, knowing Toby would understand, when they were joined by the pathologist. Jim Roberts was well into his fifties and had been in his profession nearly thirty years, much longer than either of them. His silver hair looked like the frost on the ground.

'Somebody want to fill me in?' Jim asked, looking at them through his half moon glasses.

'Unidentified female, still holding her baby. Looks like they froze, but nobody's had a good look at either of them. Store worker found them this morning when he was preparing for the shop to open. He's inside at the moment, very shaken. Absolutely crapped himself when he came across them. He's only seventeen. Leah and me will go talk to him while you do your thing out here.'

Toby tugged on Leah's arm and half-dragged her into the supermarket through the back door. 'Sorry, Leah, but I couldn't feel my toes anymore. Been here longer than you have. Still, the manager's letting us use his office. I bet it's really warm in there.'

Leah rolled her eyes and opened the door to the office. It was extremely tidy, not a sheet of paper out of place. The bin didn't even have anything in it. She guessed that this was probably because the store hadn't opened yet and everywhere was still sparkling clean from last night's cleaners. A boy sat on a plastic chair, looking very out of place. In contrast to the scarily tidy surroundings, he had very scruffy hair, rather dirty hands and a shirt that was only half tucked in.

'I didn't do it, I swear!' the boy cried, almost as soon as Toby and Leah walked through the door. His eyes darted around their faces, looking for any sign that they were there to arrest him.

'Relax, would you? We just want to take a statement from you. Nobody's blaming you for anything. Just tell us what happened this morning.' Leah tried to smile encouragingly at him.

The boy swallowed and looked at her, his pale blue eyes still searching her face. His braces glinted as he began to answer her, talking very quickly. 'I came in this morning, stocked some of the shelves, went to chuck out the old packaging and then I saw her. Them. They were just curled up there, not moving or anything. I totally freaked out and called you lot. Didn't realise I'd end up getting involved, but I didn't touch her, or the body, or move the buckets or anything. My name's Andy, by the way. Andy Nichols.'

Leah smiled at him again as Toby said 'Thanks Andy.' It'll just be a couple more questions, then you can go home. We checked with your boss, he's OK if you want to go home early.'

Andy swallowed again, his Adam's apple bobbing visibly in his skinny neck. 'Boy,' he said, looking a little shocked, 'I always wanted a half day. Didn't know I had to find a dead person before it would happen.'

* * * * *

Jim Roberts knelt down and touched the woman's hand. It refused to move, clutching the baby tightly even in death. Rigor had almost completely set in but, given the extreme temperature, that put her death at around five hours ago, in the small hours of the morning. That fitted in with Toby's theory that they had frozen.

Jim pushed the woman's hair aside. There, on her neck, was an angry looking purple line, clearly from some kind ligature. He sighed. The investigation had just changed from a tragically wasteful death into a murder case. He gently prised her eyelids apart, and had his ideas confirmed. In the whites of her eyes, there were little pinpricks of blood. Petechial haemorrhaging, consistent with asphyxiation. The poor girl. He couldn't think of any reason anybody would do this to her. And to leave her here so her baby froze too…

Jim worked her elbow just enough until the rigor broke with a pop. He did the same to the other arm and lifted the baby, still wrapped in its many blankets. He peered inside the bundle, hoping against hope that the infant would not show the same signs of strangulation as the poor mother.

He pushed the blanket away from the baby's face.

'Mary, mother of God,' he murmured quietly. He pulled his phone from his pocket.

* * * * *

Leah and Toby were still gently questioning Andy, trying to press him for information, but it was hopeless. The boy had no idea what had happened. He was shocked and upset and clearly just wanted to go home. Leah heard the sirens first. She looked out the window and watched with some confusion as an ambulance pulled into the yard. Surely it was a bit too late for all that?

Her silent question was answered as Jim Roberts burst through the door to the office.

'What the…,' Toby started, but Jim cut him off.

'Did anybody think to check for a pulse?'

'No…we just assumed…it was so cold last night…,' Leah stammered, hope beginning to rise in her.

'Idiots!' Jim shrieked, 'You completely useless turds! You had no other way to be sure!'

Andy stared at the older man, his mouth open.

Jim closed his eyes and pinched the bridge of his nose, trying desperately to regain some composure. He looked at Andy, Toby and finally settled his eyes on Leah. Quietly he said, 'The mother was murdered. She was strangled to death. But the baby…the baby is still alive.'

Active learning

Now that you have read the story once, you are going to analyse it in more detail. Consider these questions.

1 Did the writer use the genre markers you expected?

2 Did the writer do anything that surprised you?

3 Write a couple of sentences to show what made it a **good** piece of writing.

4 Suggest two things the writer could have done that would have made the story work **even better**.

Planning your own first chapter

You need to plan, in quite a lot of detail, two main aspects of your story. If you've planned stories in the past, what you probably did was plan the **plot** of your story, the events that would happen in it. We'll get round to that later. First you need to plan, and get to know, your main **character**. It's time to create your detective.

Active learning

Using the following list of questions and prompts, make a list of details that show that you know, and have carefully thought about, your main detective character.

- male or female?
- age?
- appearance?
- home/family situation?
- main personality traits?
- any unusual quirks, habits, hobbies?
- what is this person's background?
- what motivates them to do the job?
- does this person always stick to the rules?
- does your character work well with others, or prefer to go it alone?
- how does this person cope with the stresses of the job?

Once you answered all these questions, you should know your character well, and if you know them well, you can write well about them. **Be careful!** That doesn't mean that you will actually use all these details in your writing. After all you're only writing the first chapter of a novel. You should never end up writing something like:

> 'Heather, could never forget her first case. She hadn't been able to catch the killer and she'd never forgiven herself. Now she felt she owed it even more to every victim to find the killer.'

Writing that would be a horrible example of telling when you should be showing. Instead, knowing that a failed case is what motivates Heather, the author of *Beware of the Dogwalkers* writes:

> 'I'm sorry,' she said to the dead girl. 'I will find out who did this.' It was what she always said to the dead.

Once you know your **character**, it's time to start thinking about your **plot**.

Active learning

First of all, choose one of the following rough shapes for your chapter. Each has three steps, and each includes a crime scene.

Possible structure 1:

- Your detective arrives at the scene.
- The crime scene is examined and the detective gets information about the case from other characters.
- The story cuts to the detective following up some sort of lead.

Possible structure 2:

- Your detective arrives at the scene.
- The crime scene is examined and the detective gets information about the case from other characters.
- The detective leaves the scene with no real leads and facing a very baffling case. At the very end of the chapter, a clue or lead does come up.

Possible structure 3:

- The novel starts with somebody being attacked and killed. We may know who the victim is, but the identity of the attacker is not revealed.
- Your detective arrives at the crime scene.
- The crime scene is examined.

Possible structure 4:

- The novel starts with someone (perhaps a member of the public) finding a body.
- The novel cuts to your detective arriving at the crime scene.
- The crime scene is examined.

Possible structure 5:

- The novel starts with a description of a member of the public doing something quite normal.
- The novel cuts to your detective arriving at the crime scene.
- The crime scene is examined, and the reader now realises that the body being examined is that of the ordinary person they saw at the start of the chapter.

You should now have the very rough outline of the three main stages in your opening chapter and you should know your main detective character really well.

Active learning

Spend about half an hour planning your first chapter carefully, bearing in mind everything you've worked out so far. Your plan might use headings, might be a bullet pointed list, or might be a mind map or spider plan.

As you plan your chapter, think about whose point of view you will follow. A senior detective? A more junior officer? A witness or other member of the public?

Make sure your chapter is going to end in a way that makes the reader wish there was going to be a Chapter Two. You might use a full-scale cliffhanger, where you shock your reader into turning the page, or you might use a gentler hook like having your detective heading off somewhere so that we feel we want to go along too.

When your plan is finished, pair up with another pupil and explain your plans to each other. Don't be afraid to ask each other questions or to help your partner fix things that don't quite work yet.

Just before you write your story, here's some final advice:

1 Make sure you use dialogue in your chapter. If your characters don't speak to each other, they will never seem as if they are alive, and your story will feel completely flat and dull. Not only does speech give your story life, but the way characters speak and the words they use reveal lots about them.

2 British police detectives are known by their titles (Detective Constable, Detective Sergeant, Detective Inspector and Detective Chief Inspector, often abbreviated to DC, DS, DI, or DCI) and never just called 'Detective' as American characters would be. So, when you first introduce a character you would call them *PC Harry Stevens* or *DCI Heather Barnes*. After that you might call that person *Heather* if you want readers to sympathise with her or *Barnes* if you want her to feel like a more distant character.

3 British police tend to work in teams with a clear leader and a reasonably strong sense of rank. The head of a murder investigation

would be at least a DI, or even a DCI. Unlike the detectives you may have seen in American films or dramas, British police don't really have partners.

4 Detectives are in a police division called CID. They wear smart plain clothes. Uniformed police have different titles. It's likely that your crime scene would have a number of uniformed PCs at it, taking statements and securing the site.

It's now time to write your piece.

When you've written it, read your work over before you hand it in to your teacher. Think about the three areas the markers are looking at, content, style and technical accuracy, and ask yourself the following questions:

Content:

- Have I stuck to my purpose and written for my audience?
- Have I used the genre conventions?
- Does my writing show my creativity?
- Have I developed my ideas in some depth?

Style:

- Is my expression varied and confident?
- Does my style fit my chosen genre?
- Have I used structural devices like cliffhangers, flashbacks and cuts to give my work impact?
- Have I made the reader believe, and wish, that there could be a second chapter?

Technical accuracy:

- Are my spelling, grammar and punctuation all accurate?
- Is my work properly paragraphed?
- Can my work be clearly understood?

Once you have checked over your work, hand it in to your teacher. He or she will mark it and give you feedback and suggestions for ways to improve it for your Portfolio. If your teacher is also using this piece to assess your writing for the Creation and Production Unit, he or she should let you know whether you have passed the assessment standards for that unit.

Personal writing

In a piece of personal writing you will focus on a specific event or situation, and on your reaction to this. This is a genre of writing that many pupils do very well in. It is also one that you have probably worked on earlier in your school career.

Active learning

Your teacher needs to divide the class into two halves. Once you know which half you are in, your half needs to organise itself into small groups, with about three people in each group. Work in these groups for five minutes.

All the groups in one half of the class should list all the reasons why they think people do well at personal writing. All the groups in the other half of the class should list the particular features that we look for in a piece of personal writing.

Each group should share their answers with the rest of the class.

The SQA markers expect that your personal writing will focus on a specific event or events, or on a situation, and also on your reaction(s) to this. To let you see the kind of thing you are aiming for, and to give you an example to bear in mind as we work through the next few pages about skills for personal writing, read this piece by a Higher English pupil. This piece deals with fostering and adoption, which may be sensitive subjects for some readers. You may wish to read this at home rather than in class.

At first glance our family — mum, dad, daughter and son — appears as normal as any other but it is, in fact, quite different. My brother is adopted. It took a number of attempts before we were able to finalise this arrangement. Before my brother, Euan, there were two other foster brothers, Richard and Ian, who were unable to remain a part of our family life.

Richard came to us when he was six years old. Sadly, like many adoption cases, Richard had been mistreated. My first impression was of a distant child. Although he wasn't really part of our family, he wasn't not a part of it. He seemed more like the family pet than a brother but I accepted it all the same.

He adjusted surprisingly well considering: perhaps this was a result of his young age. Although Richard remained with us for four years I don't remember much about our relationship, but he was particularly close to my father who had always wanted a son. I can recall the silence in our house when his mother took him back, a silence broken by my father saying he'd always be welcome in our home.

Richard had, for some strange reason, believed it was his fault his mother had left him and so jumped at the chance to return to her. Six months later he was again rejected, thrown out of the house, his belongings sold and his bank account emptied — his mother kept all the proceeds. The offer of help that my father had given Richard could not be taken up — we had another 'brother' by then and Richard soon became little more than a memory.

As I look back on these events, I realise the influence and the pain that his mother had inflicted upon him. Because of these, Richard could never have allowed himself to become part of our family.

The other 'brother' was a boy called Ian who was nine when he came to us. Ian made the biggest impression on me in the three years he lived with us — I was older then and was able to remember more. Like Richard, Ian had been in care. Unlike Richard, this had been since he was two. It took some time to realise the full extent to which this 'care' had affected his life.

Suddenly I had the protection of an older brother. Wherever he went I followed, with the intensity of a besotted fan. For me, Ian was more than just a foster brother. We grew close as we shared our childhood and it was this that hurt so much when Ian left.

My mother said she could no longer cope with him because he was 'just an empty shell,' and showed no emotion. According to her, Ian hid a cold-hearted nature behind a mask of childhood innocence. I don't remember seeing this side of him at all. I look back on the day that he was taken away and I recall the tears that he cried. I think perhaps that Ian never truly realised how much he had until he was taken away. I imagine the pain my mother must have felt as she watched him go and realised that it was her who had decided his fate. If I sound bitter I don't mean to because I'm not, but I just think it was wrong to have given up so easily: perhaps it is because of this that there are so many foster children still in care while childless couples pursue some idea of a 'perfect' family.

When Ian left, our family drew into itself for a time, but my father still had his dream of having a boy and so, once again, we contacted the social services. This time we got a toddler, eighteen months old, called Euan. His young age was perhaps a blessing as it enabled him to adjust well. He doesn't remember anything now about his previous life, and so he isn't curious about his real parents, or about the reasons for his separation from them.

At first, because of the large age gap between us, it seemed like Euan was more my own child than a brother and I took an active part in teaching him to read and write and telling him what I knew about life. I remember certain events during his early childhood that a mother usually remembers, such as his first day at school and his first tooth falling out. I think that my position in the family as only child after Ian left gave me more responsibility, and it was this that contributed to the feeling of protectiveness when Euan came along.

I think that he has had a lot of pressure placed on him by my parents to be better than Ian and Richard and I believe that their expectations are too great for such a young child. The problems that Ian and Richard faced have nothing to do with Euan's life and it is in this sense that I believe the past should be forgotten and we should all look to the future.

As Euan has settled in to the family, I have begun to think about the role of the social services and the awe-inspiring power that they hold. They literally decide on the fate of the child in care. The social services have the power to make or break a family according to their whims while the child plays piggy in the middle. This often ends with the foster family, hurt and having been rejected once too often, giving up hope and watching as the social worker drives off down the road with their dream in the back seat.

Rejecting Ian was a cruel thing to do, especially to a child who had been in care all his life, and after reflecting I believe that it would have been handled differently had my parents been his real parents. I think that parents who have difficulties with foster children tend to give up easier than they would if it had actually been their own child and it is because of this that there are so many children languishing in care today.

It seems, now, that our family has come to the end of its emotional drama and the search for a little boy is over. It is through this search that I have become strangely older and wiser and I am able to stand back from my life, and look at how it has affected me and my family. I wonder, if my parents had realised what they would have to go through to fulfil their dream, would they still have pursued it?

However through all of this one thing remains true — a family is not the people with whom you are born but the relationships you form with them and how you, yourself, make it work. At times I feel nostalgic and wonder what happened to my other 'brothers'. Maybe one day I'll know.

We'll return to that piece as we work through this chapter. For the moment, just keep in mind that this is the kind of thing you are aiming to do.

Choosing what to write about

It shouldn't be too hard for you to choose a topic. After all you know yourself better than anyone else does. You are unique, interesting and well worth writing about.

And you do have to choose your own topic. Not only is your teacher not allowed to give you an exact subject to write about, in this case your teacher just can't. Only you have lived your life and you are the only person in the world who has had your particular set of experiences. You are the only person in history who ever had the exact set of family and friends that you have. Your brain is the only one in the entire universe to hold your set of memories, thoughts and feelings.

Active learning

Stop and think. Is there an experience you have had which matters to you very much, one that you'd like to write about in your personal essay? If you can think of such an experience, make a note of it now. If not, read the next section and follow the prompts.

Narrowing down your ideas

If you don't already have a subject in mind, then it may help you to think very quickly about a lot of different experiences you may have had, and see if any of them are suitable for a longer piece.

Active learning

Take the question 'What is the … thing that has ever happened to you?' and insert each of the seven options below in turn. Whenever one of the options applies to your life, write a couple of sentences to answer the prompt.

1 worst

2 hardest

3 happiest

4 saddest

5 most frightening

6 strangest

7 most confusing

Active learning

For those options below that apply to your life, write a couple of sentences to answer the prompt.

Which event or situation in life …

1 has most shaped you?

2 made you grow up or mature?

3 most changed your family?

4 was the biggest challenge for you?

5 was when you experienced great loss?

6 was when you experienced great success?

7 was when you experienced failure?

8 was when you had to take responsibility?

9 made you feel most isolated?

10 made you feel different to those around you?

11 made you feel you were being stereotyped?

12 showed you the best of people/someone?

13 showed you the worst of people/someone?

Active learning

Now you are going to think about these nine ways a person could make an impact on your life. Again, for those options below that apply to your life, write a couple of sentences to answer the prompt.

Which person …

1 has most influenced you?

2 has most helped you?

3 has most hurt you?

4 has least understood you?

5 do you miss most?

6 have you been in most conflict with?

7 have you had the most complicated relationship with?

8 have you had a very changeable relationship with?

9 are you most glad to be rid of?

Lastly, think about these possibly rather surprising ideas:

- What's the best mistake you ever made?
- What has been your most disastrous success?

Did you notice that every one of those more than 30 prompts and questions used the word 'you' or 'your'? That's because this really is a **personal** writing task. Whatever you write, including pieces where the original impetus comes from thinking about another person, the piece is about you, and you are writing it to reveal yourself, your thoughts and your personality.

You should now have many short paragraphs in front of you. Read them over. Is there one you could write about in depth in your personal essay? Remember you need not only to focus on an event or situation, but also to explore your reactions to it.

Although you won't be writing your essay for a while, it's a good idea to choose your topic now, so that as you work through the rest of this chapter you are doing it with your subject in mind.

There are other ways you might come up with topics. You could look through some photographs to see if that sparks anything off. If you keep a diary, have a look at that. If you have a Twitter account, look through past tweets. Are there recurring themes, or ideas that you keep coming back to? A good piece of personal writing doesn't have to be based on something huge: if you flip forward to page 186 you'll find an essay called *Class Room* which arose from a number of small incidents that got the writer thinking.

Good writing techniques

Thoughts and feelings

Your personal writing will really come to life when you include your thoughts and feelings. No one else knows these. Only you can tell the reader about them.

To show you what I mean, let's look at an example from a book called *Touching the Void*. The writer, Joe Simpson, was climbing in Peru when he broke his leg. In this extract his climbing partner is about to begin lowering the injured Simpson down the mountain on a rope.

> I lay on my chest immediately beneath Simon, and edged down until all my weight was on the rope. Initially I couldn't commit myself to letting my feet hang free of the snow. If it crumbled we would be falling instantaneously. Simon nodded at me and grinned. Encouraged by his confidence I lifted my feet and began to slide down. It worked!
>
> He let the rope out smoothly in a steady descent. I lay against the snow holding an axe in each hand ready to dig them in the moment I felt a fall begin. Occasionally the crampons on my right boot snagged in the snow and jarred my leg. I tried not to cry out but failed. I didn't want Simon to stop.
>
> In a surprisingly short time he did stop. I looked up and saw that he had receded far from me, and I could make out only his head and shoulders. He shouted something but I couldn't make it out until three sharp tugs explained it. I was astounded at the speed at

which I had descended 150 feet. Astounded and pleased as punch. I wanted to giggle. In a short time my mood had swung from despair to wild optimism, and death rushed back to being a vague possibility rather than the inevitable fact. The rope went slack as I hopped on to my good leg. I was acutely aware that while Simon was changing the knot over we were at our most vulnerable. If I fell, I would drop a whole rope's length before it came tight on to him, and he would be whipped off the mountain by the impact. I dug my axes in and stayed motionless.

Active learning

Simpson is obviously feeling a mixture of emotions, some positive, some negative. Copy and complete the following table to help you explore the emotions in the extract. You should be able to find a wide range of emotions.

Emotion	Evidence	Positive or negative
hesitation	'Initially I couldn't commit myself to letting my feet hang free of the snow.'	negative

Interestingly, people often write extremely well about hard experiences. If we go through sad, difficult or tragic events we are strongly aware of how we feel at the time. Sad situations affect and shape us. We have to keep working with and processing the memories, thoughts and feelings that go with these events. We are acutely aware of our reactions.

Active learning

Go back to the piece of personal writing about adoption that was printed on page 170. Pick out that writer's thoughts and feelings.

Details and description

Because your memories are important to you, when you bring them to mind they will be full of tiny details, things you noticed at the time. Many of these details might not be very important in themselves, but they are important in your writing because they bring that memory to life.

To let you see what I mean, here's a piece from the start of *Touching the Void*, before Joe Simpson breaks his leg.

I was lying in my sleeping bag, staring at the light filtering through the red and green fabric of the dome tent. Simon was snoring loudly, occasionally twitching in his dream world. We could have been anywhere. There is a peculiar anonymity about being in tents. Once the zip is closed and the outside world barred from sight, all sense of location disappears. The sounds of rustling, of fabric flapping in the wind, or of rainfall, the feel of hard lumps under the groundsheet, the smell of rancid socks and sweat — these are universals, as comforting as the warmth of a down sleeping bag.

I felt a homely affection for the warm security of the tent and reluctantly wormed out of my bag to face the prospect of lighting the stove. It had snowed a little during the night, and the grass crunched frostily under my feet as I padded over to the cooking rock. There was no sign of Richard stirring as I passed his tiny one-man tent, half collapsed and whitened with hoar-frost.

This short passage is stuffed with tiny details. Simpson manages to use nearly all of his senses to bring the description to life.

Active learning

First **list** your five senses. Then **re-read** the Joe Simpson passage above. Next, **note down** the details that fit each sense. Which sense has the writer not used in this extract?

It's easy to use your sense of sight as you describe what you remember in detail, but Simpson's example is a good reminder to bring in as many of our other senses as is appropriate.

Active learning

Now read this third extract from *Touching the Void*. Although Joe's accident hasn't happened yet, he and Simon have already had a difficult time, being caught in a storm just after reaching the summit of the mountain. They've spent the night in a cave Joe dug in the snow. As you read, make a list of the small details that make it seem vivid and convincing. Again, look for his use of different senses.

I had the stove burning away cheerfully by my side, and could look beyond it through a hole in the snow cave. The early morning sun etched the ridge lines with shadows and danced blue shadings down the edges of the mountain face. For the first time in the last four days the tense concentration in my body relaxed. The anxious struggles of the previous night had been forgotten.

It was cramped in the snow hole. Simon was still asleep, lying on his side close by me, facing away. His hips and shoulders pressed up against my side, and I could feel his body warmth seeping through my sleeping bag. I moved carefully to avoid waking him and felt myself smiling. I knew it would be a good day.

I dressed and geared up first, before climbing out of the cave. Simon was slow getting ready, and it wasn't until he joined me outside that I remembered his frostbite. My good humour vanished to be replaced by worry when he showed his fingers to me. One fingertip was blackened and three other fingers were white and wooden in appearance.

Did you notice that, as well as the descriptive detail you were looking for, Simpson again uses a mixture of positive and negative emotions in his writing?

Active learning

Go back to the piece about adoption on page 170. What are the details that bring it to life?

Using dialogue

Something else you can do with this genre of writing to bring it to life is to put speech into it. Just as dialogue makes stories vivid, it does the same for personal writing. Don't worry if you can't remember the exact words you and other people said, you can make up something which seems close enough.

In this extract from her book *The Reading Promise*, American writer Alice Ozma remembers how her father, a school librarian and single parent, tried to understand the subtleties of dressing for a high school prom.

'Does it have to be a 'gown'? Can't you just wear something you already own?'

'There's a dress code. Plus, I'll feel really weird if I'm underdressed. I'll stick out in a bad way.'

'What about a nice skirt, and a button-up shirt? Would that fall under the dress code maybe?'

Single fathers of girls have a lot of tricky issues to face. They deal with puberty, boys, and dating as best they can. I give them, and especially my father, enormous credit for this. My grandmother passed away when I was thirteen. My sister moved out when I was in middle school. My father was too proud to ask his sister for advice. So with relatively little female input, he found his way through the maze of teenage girlhood right beside me, learning to trust me and, eventually, the boys I chose to date. I am proud to say that most of the time, he fully understood what he was doing and made reasonable, logical decisions. I chalk some of this up to all the books we read about young girls. They were almost entirely fiction, but they were usually quite realistic and gave us both great insight into what 'normal' girls and 'normal' families did. Even with all of our reading though, some things still absolutely baffled my father. As my senior year of high school came to a close, I realised that prom was one of those things.

My father just didn't understand the hype.

'It's one night!' he kept repeating whenever he saw the list of things I needed to buy and do.

My list was actually quite modest, compared to most girls I knew: I wanted my hair done, only because I didn't know how to do it myself. I wanted a dress. So far, that was it. I didn't feel the need to bother with shopping for a purse, or jewellery, or even shoes. I was fine with hunting around my closet for something that would come close enough. But things kept popping up.

'Stephanie says I should get my nails done,' I mentioned over breakfast one morning shortly before the big night, 'but it seems like a waste of money. What do you think?'

'"Done"? What do you mean by "done"? Painted?'

'Well that's one option.'

'They're too stubbly. You chew on them like you've got the secret to eternal youth in your — what's the white part called? The tip?'

'I could get fake nails I guess.'

'Oh my goodness no. They look like cat claws, and when the teachers at school get them they make this awful clicking sound whenever they type. It's enough to drive a person batty.'

'I wasn't planning on typing very much at prom.'

He let air out of the corners of his mouth dramatically.

'Still,' he said. 'Who would even notice if you had them? In your prom photos, is anyone really going to look at your fingernails?'

Notice that the dialogue here does more than just bring the writing to life. It also shows us what the two characters, father and daughter, are like, and lets us see something of the relationship between them.

Active learning

First, just to show why it is better to use dialogue, try to rewrite the above piece so that we get all the same information, but without either of the characters speaking.

Now think about the piece that you are planning to write. Where could you use speech to bring it to life?

Using storytelling techniques

Earlier in this chapter, when you were preparing to write your piece of prose fiction, we looked at the technique of showing, not telling. This is just one of many storytelling techniques (and the dialogue that you just worked on above is another) that will help make your personal writing better.

Active learning

First, go round the class and give everybody a letter A or B. All the letter A pupils should re-read the piece of writing about adoption which was printed on page 170. All the letter B pupils should re-read the three extracts by Joe Simpson and the one by Alice Ozma (pages 175–180).

As you re-read your piece(s), look for and note down evidence of the writer using any of these techniques:

- dialogue
- showing not telling
- imagery
- starting at a moment of action
- flashback

- short sentence or paragraph for impact
- minor sentence
- jump cut to a different scene or action
- repetition
- use of incident or anecdote

Also, think of one technique you think your writer could have used but did not. When could he or she have used that technique? How would this have improved the piece of writing?

Now find someone with the other letter, who has read the other piece(s) — not someone who sits near you in class. Share what you found with each other.

Reactions

When you have worked on personal writing before, you probably concentrated most on bringing the experience to life. Your focus might have been quite narrow or egocentric — looking back at what the experience meant to you and to those close to you. Now that you're working at Higher level, your reactions and responses should go further. It might help if you think of the piece of writing like this:

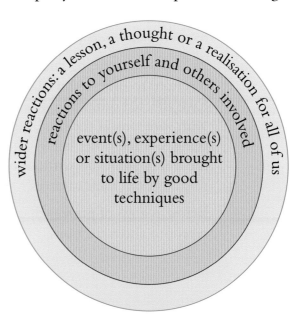

wider reactions: a lesson, a thought or a realisation for all of us

reactions to yourself and others involved

event(s), experience(s) or situation(s) brought to life by good techniques

Reactions to yourself and others

To do well in this task, you need to do something only mature and insightful writers are able to do: **examine yourself**. If you stand in front of a mirror you can examine yourself pretty thoroughly by looking at your reflection. Every spot and blemish will be visible, but you'll also be able to see all your good features and everything that you like about yourself — that you have poise and posture, that you have an intelligent face.

If you apply this idea to your writing it means that you might question and criticise yourself. On the other hand you might realise that you handled the situation well. You may realise that certain experiences have shaped you and made you into the person you are, just as growing up changes the way your face looks in the mirror.

Often events in our lives make much more sense once they are over and we are older and wiser. Perhaps when something happened to you it was a really terrible experience, but now you realise that you benefited from it in some way. Events may be confusing when they happen, but when you look back on them they may make more sense.

As well as examining and reacting to yourself, you can explore your reactions to others. You may be aware of how events and experiences have affected other people as well as you. It may be that you disagreed with someone at the time, but you now realise they did the right thing. On the other hand, when we are young we sometimes accept the things adults do without question, but as we grow up we are not so sure about their motives.

Below is a list of phrases that can be used to explore and share your reactions and reflections.

- Looking back …
- On reflection …
- With hindsight …
- In retrospect …
- Nowadays I feel/think/believe …
- If I could do this again …
- If this happened now …
- I learned …
- I realise …
- I understand …
- I should have …
- I could have …
- I wish I had …
- Because of this I am …
- Since this happened I …
- When I think back on this …
- Thinking about it now I feel …
- At the time I … but now I …
- If I could change things …
- It was a … thing to do because …
- I wish this had never happened because …
- Now that I've been through this …
- I grew through this experience because …
- This made me think about …
- This experience shaped me by . . .
- I'm glad this happened because …
- That's when I realised …

Although these phrases can be used to start sentences and paragraphs, your writing will actually be more subtle, and therefore better, if you don't use them quite so blatantly.

> **Despite the loss of her friendship, I grew through this experience because …**

is better than

> **I grew through this experience because, although I lost a friend I …**

and

> **I was unable to admit to anyone that I was in the wrong, but on reflection …**

is better than

> **On reflection, I realise I was in the wrong …**

Active learning

Go back to the subject that you thought of earlier, the topic you have chosen to write about. Spend some time making notes on your reactions to this. What lessons have your experiences taught you about yourself and those around you? How have these experiences shaped and changed you?

Reacting and responding more widely

When tackling this kind of task at Higher level, you should take your reactions and responses wider still. You need to show that your experiences have taught you something about life, about society, or about people in general, that you now have a lesson, a thought or a realisation for all of us.

Look at this extract from the piece you saw earlier. The writer, having described the effects these events had on her own family, begins considering the wider 'system':

As Euan has settled in to the family, I have begun to think about the role of the social services and the awe-inspiring power that they hold. They literally decide on the fate of the child in care. The social services have the power to make or break a family according to their whims while the child plays piggy in the middle. This often ends with the foster family, hurt and having been rejected once too often, giving up hope and watching as the social worker drives off down the road with their dream in the back seat.

Most of the writer's wider reaction and response comes near the end of the piece:

I think that parents who have difficulties with foster children tend to give up easier than they would if it had actually been their own child and it is because of this that there are so many children languishing in care today...

However through all of this one thing remains true — a family is not the people with whom you are born but the relationships you form with them and how you, yourself, make it work.

The writer considers how foster or adoptive families react to difficult children, and ends the piece by challenging us to rethink a definition of what a family might be.

Active learning

In your own words, sum up this writer's wider reaction and response. What did the writer learn?

Here's another extract from Joe Simpson's *Touching The Void*. Again this comes from the early part of the book. Joe and his climbing partner Simon have just reached the summit of a mountain in the Peruvian Andes called Siula Grande.

Active learning

As you read, look for and note down:

- any times when Simpson is examining himself
- any times when Simpson reacts or responds in a way that lets him take a wider look at human nature

We took the customary summit photos and ate some chocolate. I felt the usual anticlimax. What now? It was a vicious cycle. If you succeed with one dream, you come back to square one and it's not long before you're conjuring up another, slightly harder, a bit more ambitious. I didn't like the thought of where it might be leading me. As if, in some strange way, the very nature of the game was controlling me, taking me towards a logical but frightening conclusion. It always unsettled me, this moment of reaching the summit, this sudden stillness and quiet, which gave me time to wonder at what I was doing and sense a niggling doubt that perhaps I was inexorably losing control — was I here purely for pleasure or was it egotism? Did I really want to come back for more? But these moments were also good times, and I knew that the feelings would pass. Then I could excuse them as morbid pessimistic fears that had no sound basis.

Active learning

Go back to the subject that you thought of earlier, the topic you have chosen to write about. Spend some time making notes on how you could use this experience for wider reaction. What lessons have your experiences taught you about life, about society, or about people in general?

Looking at a real example

You are going to see another piece of personal writing by a pupil. Ideally you should have a photocopy of this piece, as that will help you with the later stage of this task.

At the start of this chapter you found out that, in personal writing, the SQA markers expect you to focus on an event or events or on a situation, and on your reactions to this. This piece, *Class Room*, is an example of a piece focusing on the writer's reaction to a number of apparently small but thought-provoking events.

First of all, just read through the piece.

Class Room

'You're so lucky Paula*, you can just get your Dad to pay for it.'

Aged eight, I watched my parents' marriage fall apart due to the stress caused by work and financial crises. Money was evil. However, I also watched them build their careers back up and turn into happier people. Money was the catalyst for this.

So, I have always been aware of money, but this comment by a classmate was the first time someone had directly flagged up the issue of my class. I couldn't help thinking that it was inappropriate. I don't think he meant to leave me feeling exasperated and irritated, but he did. It was his declaration of my supposed status. He was referring to my parent's financial situation, not mine. His preconception was an unjust remark; he had no idea about my father's job.

I had been categorised.

I began to wonder if I had always been aware of the divide between rich and poor — the divide between those who are financially comfortable and those who struggle. Have I been living in a bubble all my life? Perhaps I have, always aware but choosing to ignore it, ignoring the less fortunate.

When I think back to that boy's comment, I am reminded of a classroom – a microcosm of society in which people from different walks of life must interact with each other.

His assumption got me thinking: what is my own preconception of class? At this age, my exposure to society and the various types of people in it boils down to my experiences in school, in music groups and in swimming clubs.

For example, when I would meet up with other members of these clubs, in particular after the summer holidays, I would share the experiences I had on my holidays. I would tell my friends and teammates the adventures I had been on.

But in recent years I have restricted myself and held back on the stories I tell. I have become more aware of the many people who do not get the opportunity to do such things, go such places, and who are not as lucky as I am. This makes me wonder: did I ever think of the people who didn't go on holiday when I recalled my adventures each August when we were all back at school? Did I see them sitting quietly as they compared their lives to mine? Did I take into account that I was bragging — did I even realise I was bragging? Maybe they thought if they shared the stories of their summers they would be judged and frowned upon. Was I sensitive to their feelings? These moments now fill me with embarrassment, making me feel uneasy about my younger self and the ignorance I was lucky to enjoy.

Memories often resurface of people less fortunate than me, and I wonder how some of the less privileged people I have encountered in life are doing today. I remember one such scenario vividly. We were playing the 'stand up' game in school and my teacher called out various items — we had to stand up if we owned them. One day she used houses for the game: detached, semi-detached, terraced, bungalow and flat.

Now a flat of course is a perfectly common residence. However, in the context of that particular school, surrounded by wealth and luxury, a flat was not considered to be the norm. When 'flat' was called out, one boy stood up and the class started to giggle. He must have felt isolated, exposed and embarrassed.

Why did the teacher think this game was a good idea? Was she living in a naïve bubble? Why didn't she think ahead to the possible outcomes of this scenario? She encouraged a separation between the wealthy children and the boy. Just as I felt prejudged by the boy in my class who had categorised me into a comfortable class bracket, so too must have the boy who lived in a flat.

I live in Edinburgh — one of the UK's wealthiest cities. Everywhere I go I am reminded of my own social status and that of others. To reach the city centre from my house I travel through extremes. It baffles me that, just minutes down the road from an area of severe deprivation, I pass houses worth over a million pounds in one of the most desired postcodes in the nation. It makes me wonder how rich and poor live alongside each other and what one must think of the other. There is no happy medium — no group of 'less wealthy' but 'not so poor' houses to bridge the gap between the very rich and the poverty-stricken.

On a recent school trip I was forced to ask myself how much Edinburgh still lives in the past of its rich ancestors and poor forefathers. We were learning about the old buildings that make up our city. A trip to a house called Gladstone's Land on the Royal Mile allowed us to view these buildings first hand, and my eyes were drawn to a bell. I asked the guide what it was and he explained that the wealthy residents of

those houses would ring and their maids would have to emerge from the depths of the house and rush to tend their masters' needs.

It struck me that these bells still exist in modern society — not perhaps in the form in which they used to exist, but it is still a common occurrence to have maids and cleaners working in the homes of the wealthy. Even though we think we've come so far since the time of our ancestors, the social divide in the 21st century is still prominent. All we need to do is look around us; open our eyes on the bus; acknowledge the existence of the homeless on Princes Street or the range of backgrounds in our children's classrooms.

The divide between rich and poor is not only apparent — it is embedded within us. We are all programmed to decode our classmates or work mates and to subconsciously make snap assessments of their social standing and backgrounds.

I was irritated when this happened to me; I didn't like it. However, I too am a product of this socially aware society. I would like to say it is not a prerequisite that my friends come from a particular background; I would like to say my school helps to reinforce the value of diversity, yet I know we all still judge each other, and that we feel at our most comfortable surrounded by people who are actually quite a lot like us.

★names have been changed to protect the writer's privacy

Active learning

Now that you have read the piece of personal writing once, you are going to analyse it in more detail. The easiest way to do this is to have a photocopy of it in front of you. You'll also need pens and pencils. If you have a variety of colours, that's even better.

You'll need to use the following symbols:

1 Every time you find the writer sharing **thoughts** draw a **think cloud** beside this in the margin.

2 Every time you find the writer sharing **feelings** draw a **heart** beside this in the margin.

3 Every time you find the writer using **detail or description** draw an **eye** beside this in the margin.

4 Every time you find the writer using **dialogue** draw a **speech bubble** beside this in the margin.

5 Every time you find the writer using **a storytelling technique** draw an **open book** beside this in the margin. Write the name of the technique on the pages of the book.

6 Every time you find the writer **discussing or sharing her reactions**, write a **bold capital letter R** in the margin. If you think the writer is **reacting more widely**, put a capital **W** before the **R**.

7 Write a couple of sentences to explain what made it a **good** piece of writing.

8 Suggest two things the writer could have done that would have made the work **even better**.

This is a useful example piece. It shows that you can build a thoughtful essay from a number of smaller moments — that you don't have to have something huge happen to you before you can write about it.

Going deeper

By the way, if you'd like to look at one more example of a personal essay before you plan and write your own, read the essay *Shooting an Elephant* by George Orwell. (You'll find it easily on the internet, or your teacher may have a copy in school.) He uses all the skills of personal writing. He brings an incident to life in detail; tells us about his own reactions, thoughts and feelings at the time; reflects on his own behaviour and that of others around him; and thinks more widely about the nature of empires. All of this makes his piece an excellent example of personal writing.

Planning your personal piece

You've had a chance now to look at two long pieces of personal writing produced by Higher pupils, and at a number of shorter extracts from published books. Reading and examining all these pieces has shown you that you need to use all these genre features:

thoughts	feelings	detail and description
dialogue	storytelling techniques as appropriate	reactions to yourself and others
wider reactions		

It's time now for you to plan your piece. There are many ways you could do this. Some people make spider plans. Some people list their ideas. Some people write paragraph-by-paragraph plans. All of these ways are useful, and you should do whatever is best for you, and for the way your brain works. Here, however, is one possible plan you might want to use.

Active learning

You'll need a photocopy of the blank plan on the following page. You should have lots of ideas by now, so ask your teacher if you can have a copy in A3 size.

Use the prompts and shapes to help you plan your piece of personal writing. The shapes are those you used to annotate the piece entitled *Class Room*, but they are bigger this time so that you can write your ideas on them.

What event(s) or experience(s) are you going to write about?

Which storytelling techniques will you use, and at which points in your writing?

Reactions to self/others

Wider reaction

Active learning

Using your plan to help you, explain your ideas to another pupil.

Your teacher may also want to see and discuss your plan. Remember that he or she should keep a copy of that plan as evidence that your portfolio is your own work.

Active learning

It's now time to follow your plan and write your piece.

When you've written it, read your work over before you hand it in to your teacher. Think about the three areas the markers are looking at, content, style and technical accuracy, and ask yourself the following questions:

Content:

- Have I stuck to my purpose and written for my audience?
- Have I used the genre conventions for personal writing?
- Are my ideas, feelings and experiences expressed and explored maturely, with insight?
- Does my writing show my personality and individuality?

Style:

- Is my expression varied and confident?
- Does my style fit my chosen genre?
- Have I chosen a structure that helps me fulfill my purpose and put across my meaning?

Technical accuracy:

- Are my spelling, grammar and punctuation all accurate?
- Is my work properly paragraphed?
- Can my work be clearly understood?

Once you have checked over your work, hand it in to your teacher. He or she will mark it and give you feedback and suggestions for ways to improve it for your Portfolio. If your teacher is also using this piece to assess your writing for the Creation and Production Unit, he or she should let you know whether you have passed the assessment standards for that unit.

What we've done so far

So far in this chapter we have found out about the rules and guidelines for Higher writing. We found out about the genre that the SQA calls **creative writing**. This covers three sorts of piece:

- a personal essay
- a reflective essay
- an imaginative piece

and we learned in detail about the personal essay, and about one particular imaginative genre.

Now it's time to go on to the other major genre, which the SQA calls **discursive writing**. Remember that in your Portfolio, you need one piece from the Creative genre, and one from the Discursive.

Discursive writing

The second Portfolio piece should be what the SQA calls **discursive**, which actually means that you can produce any one of these types of writing to fulfil the requirements for this genre:

- a persuasive essay
- an argumentative essay
- a report for a specified purpose

We're going to work on the first two of these in detail.

In **argumentative** writing you explore an issue or topic. You will explore two (or more) points of view about this subject, and you will usually come to a conclusion at the end, while still allowing the reader to decide for him or her self.

In **persuasive** writing you start with a clear belief or strongly held point of view. In this kind of piece, you will try to use evidence and language to make the reader agree with you.

You can't really decide whether your piece will be argumentative or persuasive until you've chose a subject, so let's deal with that issue first.

Choosing a topic

Some topics come up again and again. Your teacher, and the SQA marker, have probably read all the arguments about **euthanasia, abortion** and **capital punishment** many times before, and will quickly notice if you miss out anything they expect to find, or if there is any important aspect of the argument which you don't explore carefully enough.

Unless you are truly an expert, or really feel that you have something striking and original to say, it might be best to steer clear of writing about these subjects. And, if you really want to tackle one of these issues, it's best to do it in a two-sided, argumentative way. Otherwise you risk sounding like an extremist.

Whether your writing ends up being argumentative or persuasive, you need to pick a topic about which people have strong opinions. It should also be a topic in which you have a genuine interest: your finished piece of writing should show real interest and engagement with the ideas or issues you are writing about, and should also show that you understand these well. You need to sustain and develop this over up to 1300 words. You'll only manage all of this if you pick a topic you care about.

So how do you choose a subject? You could:

- ask yourself which subjects you are interested in or care about: these will often be tied in to the things you choose to spend your time on
- visit your school library: some publishers produce special series of books where each book contains articles on one controversial subject. Without even reading the books themselves at this stage, just finding out which subjects they deal with might help you think of a topic
- watch television news programmes, read newspapers and use news websites
- ask your teacher which topics his or her pupils have written successfully about in the past

Active learning

You shouldn't go any further, or spend any time on research, until you know that your teacher thinks your topic is a good one. Once you have chosen a topic, write it down and give a note of it to your teacher.

If you know already which approach you want to take — two-sided argumentative or one-sided persuasive — write this down along with your subject. If you're not sure which approach to take yet, don't worry. It will become much clearer after you've done your detailed research.

Researching

Whether your piece of writing is one-sided or two-sided, and no matter how much you think you already know about the subject, you need to do some research. Everything you eventually write will be based on this and it's time well spent.

Your first port of call will probably be the internet. You could visit the websites of charities and pressure groups who have an interest in your topic. If, for example, you are writing about development issues you could visit the sites of organisations like Oxfam or Christian Aid.

Many newspapers have excellent websites. These can be very useful if your topic has been in the headlines recently, and often give real-life examples you can use. One very good site is www.guardian.co.uk which makes no charge and is easy to search.

You need to take far greater care with the online encyclopedia www.wikipedia.org because it is written by the people who use it. This means that though the contributors are genuinely interested in their subjects, some of what they write can be quite biased. You shouldn't use Wikipedia as your only source, and you should check anything you find there against other sources to make sure it is accurate.

If you don't know which sites you want to use, you'll need to begin by using a search engine such as Google. Try to use only one or two keywords for your search. The computer doesn't know what you are thinking, or why you are looking these words up, so be as precise as you can about what you want.

If you're using a phrase, put double quotation marks round it. Let's suppose you are writing an persuasive essay in which you contend that Formula 1 motor racing should not be regarded as a sport. Looking for "Formula One" will find web pages using that complete phrase. This might be just what you want to know:

> **One factor which surely suggests that Formula One is not a sport is that contestants take part sitting down.**

If you type the same two words without quotation marks you will get all the pages that have the word *formula* and the word *one* anywhere on the same page. This isn't so helpful:

> **One chemical formula used a particularly vile combination of noxious liquids.**

This is good time to go back to your school or local library and ask the staff for advice about the most suitable sources of information on your topic. One thing you will find there is an encyclopedia. These can be very good on established factual information, but as huge books like this take many years to write and put together, they are not great sources for material on current controversial topics. For that, you may be better going back to the internet.

Depending on your topic, you might also speak to people about their own experiences. If you are writing about the rights and wrongs of organic food and you know a farmer, speak to him. If you are arguing that young people nowadays are put under far too much pressure to achieve at school, ask a teacher what she thinks.

By the way, and just in case you think you don't, or in case you think your topic doesn't call for it, everyone needs to do research. Even the most personal persuasive essay will only persuade, will only convince the reader, if what you write is supported by facts, statistics, experiences and anecdotes.

Using your own words

There was one very important note of advice in the guidelines at the start of the chapter: you **absolutely cannot, ever**, copy and paste from a website or from anywhere else.

You are allowed to get ideas and information from sources, but you can't use someone else's words and pass them off as your own. This is called **plagiarism** and if the examiners think that you have cheated in this way the consequences can be very serious.

To help you avoid accidentally falling into plagiarism, here's a useful piece of advice to follow during the research stage:

Warning

It's OK to read, underline or highlight someone else's words, but **WHENEVER YOU MAKE A NOTE, DO THAT IN YOUR OWN WORDS**. It doesn't matter if you type the words, or handwrite them, **WHENEVER YOU PUT WORDS ON A PAGE, THEY SHOULD BE YOUR OWN**.

I hope all those bold and shouty capitals got the point across. The advice is only useful of course if you know how to put something into your own words. This skill is called **paraphrasing**. It's worth practising because it won't just be useful to you in your discursive writing. You also need to be able to do this to demonstrate your understanding of reading, both in the unit assessment, and in the Reading for Understanding, Analysis and Evaluation exam. In these tasks, lifting words straight from the text will mean you get no marks, even if you have found the right information.

There's a third reason for making sure that you can paraphrase all the ideas and information you find. You're not just avoiding plagiarism, and you're not just practising a skill you'll use elsewhere too. You're also making sure you understand what you have read. The best way to prove that you really grasp something is to be able to explain it yourself in a different way.

Look at this sentence found by a pupil who decided to research global climate change:

> The overwhelming consensus among climate change scientists is that human activities are responsible for much of the climate change we're seeing.

The pupil needed to put this in his own words, which he did like this:

> Those who research this subject believe our own actions are the main cause of the climate change we are experiencing. They are in almost complete agreement about this.

This pupil used a lot of different tactics as he paraphrased.

First, he changed some important words or expressions.

Active learning

You will see a list of expressions from the original sentence. What did he change each one in to?

- overwhelming consensus
- climate change scientists
- human activities

- responsible for
- much of the
- we're seeing

Second, he changed the number of sentences from one to two. Third, he put the two ideas in the original sentence the other way round. All of this shows that he has understood and can process the information.

What he didn't change was the phrase *climate change* itself. Because that is his subject, and that is what his whole essay is about, he can keep using those words.

Active learning

Here are five more extracts pupils found while researching different topics. Remembering the techniques above, paraphrase each extract. The subject of each extract is given for you at the start.

1 [The death penalty] Those who believe that deterrence justifies the execution of certain offenders bear the burden of proving that the death penalty is in fact a deterrent.

2 [Raising the legal age for buying alcohol] In the US, the age to drink legally is 21. However, it is naive to assume that there is no drinking problem. University students attend house parties where binge drinking is the norm. They lack the protection that would come from being in a bar or nightclub. In addition, attending such parties usually requires transport, which is a key reason why so many American students drink and drive.

3 [Having a curfew for teenagers] It is impossible to solve anti-social behaviour by using repression. If the British government enforces this law, rebellious teenagers will merely become convinced that society is actually against them.

4 [The pros and cons of same-sex schooling] Thirty years ago, the popular belief about same-sex education was that it upheld out-dated stereotypes about gender, such as women should study nursing and men should study engineering. Experts at that time believed that coeducation dispelled those gender myths.

5 [Whether footballers are overpaid] Football has become an industry, and its employees — the players — have taken their places alongside the world's elite of movie and rock stars. Across the planet, football has slowly grown to become the world's biggest and most widely followed sport. It is only natural, therefore, that some of the huge profit that the football league makes each year finds its way into the hands of its key assets: the players.

Citing your sources

Another of the authenticity guidelines we saw at the start of the chapter was about being able to show where your information came from. As you research, take a note of all these things. You will need to list them in a **bibliography** at the end of your essay:

- the writer and publication date of newspaper or magazine articles
- the website name and specific page address for any information found on the internet
- the title and publication date of any books referred to

Active learning

If you haven't already discussed with your teacher whether your essay will be two-sided argumentative or one-sided persuasive, now is the time to do so. Read over your notes, and consider what approach you are going to take. These prompts should help you decide:

- If you find your topic interesting, but you're genuinely not sure what your stance on it is, or if you think it's a highly complex issue without an easy answer, you should go for the argumentative approach.
- If you've developed a genuine opinion on the subject, and if you think you can put it across in a way that makes you sound engaged and committed without seeming to be a raving zealot, go for the argumentative approach.
- If the best writing style for you is to be measured and formal, then you should probably go for argumentative writing.
- If you know that you can write in a lively and witty way, you could try persuasive writing.
- Finally, more weighty subjects suit the argumentative genre better, while odder, less serious or more quirky subjects can benefit from a persuasive approach.

Using your research to support opinions

Once you have collected your information, you should try to find a way to make each fact or idea you have found support an opinion. Facts can be proved. They are true and nobody can argue against them.

> **Pizza is made by placing cheese, tomato sauce and perhaps other toppings on a bread base.**

Opinions are more personal. They are what people think, and different people can have different opinions about the same thing.

> **Never mind the calendar, central heating and public sanitation, the best thing Italy ever gave the world was pizza.**

In **persuasive** writing, organise the facts to support what you believe. In **argumentative** writing, organise them to support the two different sides of the argument.

Here's an example from pupil who is writing persuasively about his belief that footballers are overpaid.

FACT/EXAMPLE FROM RESEARCH

The typical Premiership footballer earns £60,000 a week. The salary for a newly qualified police constable is less than £20,000 a year.

HOW DOES THIS SUPPORT MY OPINION?

The fact that some footballers can earn over 150 times as much as police officers, who do a valuable and dangerous job, shows they are overpaid.

Look through the notes you gathered during your research. Remember, these should be in your own words by now. Organise your material as shown above, picking out the useful facts and working out how each one could be used to support an opinion.

A good writer will be able to 'spin' facts to support their opinion. Two newspapers could have two very different opening sentences at the start of their front-page stories.

> A tram scheme that will turn the city centre into a building site and cause years of traffic chaos was revealed today.

> A tram scheme that will provide rapid, low-carbon public transport and cut journey times across the city was revealed today.

They're both reporting the same story, but they have spun the facts to suit their opinion.

Being able to bend facts towards the direction you want to go is especially useful in persuasive writing when you are trying to make your readers agree with you.

Planning two-sided, argumentative pieces

In these essays you should show that you understand the arguments on both sides. At the end you can give your opinion, and your readers can decide on theirs.

There are two ways you can structure these essays. We'll look very quickly first at the simple structure. It would be more impressive though if you used the complex structure, and we'll go into that in more detail. The **simple structure** works like this:

Step 1 A one paragraph introduction to the topic:

> **Although Britain abolished the death penalty in the 1960s, there are frequent pleas for its re-introduction, usually after the details of some grisly multiple murder are splashed across the tabloids.**

Step 2 A link sentence, explaining which side of the argument you will begin with.

> **Those who advocate the return of capital punishment have many firmly-held beliefs.**

Step 3 Now take all of the points on one side of the argument. Each point should be in a separate paragraph, and these points should be backed up with facts, observations or personal experiences. Use **topic sentences** and the **PEE structure**. (You will find out more about these soon.) Start with the strongest, most convincing arguments and work your way down to the weaker ones. You should aim to have at least three or four paragraphs on the first side of the argument.

Step 4 Write a link sentence showing that you are about to switch to the other side of the argument.

> **Those on the other side of the argument are just as passionate in their belief that there would be no benefit in executing even our most notorious criminals.**

Step 5 Now do the same on this side of the argument as you did at Step 3 above, working again from the stronger points down to weaker ones.

Step 6 Finally, in your conclusion, briefly sum up what you have written. Now say which side you agree with and why. Show which arguments convinced you, or refer to an experience in your life or the life of someone you know which has convinced you that a particular side is right. You may wish to leave the reader with something to think about.

> **It is clear that both sides have strong arguments. Having examined them I feel that on the whole we will not create a better Britain by killing our criminals. Any system that says it is wrong to kill people, but then tries to prove that by killing, is misguided and wrong.**

By the way, the example comes from an essay on the death penalty because the topic is on that short list of overworked topics earlier in the chapter, and is a topic you probably should not actually be writing about yourself.

The **more complex structure** for two-sided pieces makes you look more skilled at handling your material. It works like this:

The introduction and conclusion are the same as they are in a simply-structured essay. However, in the main body of the essay, you begin with the strongest argument from one side of the argument. Then, in the next paragraph, you work through a point on the opposite side that contradicts what you have just written about. Each of these paragraphs will use **topic sentences** and the **PEE structure** which will be explained later in this chapter.

To illustrate this, let's imagine an essay on another of those overworked and therefore banned topics, euthanasia. Here's a point from the pro-euthanasia side of the argument:

> **Perhaps the strongest argument for allowing terminally ill patients to choose to die is that this will prevent great suffering. Not only**

can people in the final stages of a long illness experience terrible pain, they may also suffer the indignity of being unable to take care of their own most basic needs. The right to die could spare them all of this.

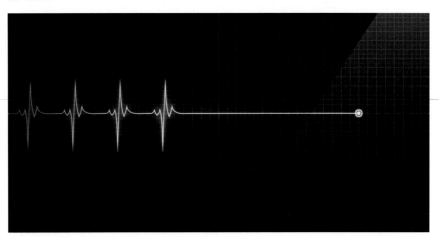

Now here's the answering point from the anti-euthanasia side.

However this assumes that dying patients are somehow not being properly cared for. This is not true. Modern advances in pain control mean that even the last days of life can be made comfortable, allowing patients to spend longer with their loved ones. Many say that we should not demand the right to choose when we die, but the right to die with dignity.

Then take the second strongest point from the first side of the argument. Explain it, and then challenge it by making another point from the opposite side to contradict it. Keep going, following this pattern.

You may find that some of your points cannot be paired up in this way. You can deal with them just before you start your conclusion. All the remaining points can be rolled into two short paragraphs, one for the ideas which support one side of the argument, for example:

There are other valid reasons why many people think that we should allow the ill to choose when to end their lives …

and the other for the evidence that concludes the other side of the argument, for example:

Those who are against this also have further important points to make …

Once again, the example comes from an essay on euthanasia because that topic is on our short list of overworked subjects, and is a topic you probably should not actually be writing about yourself.

Active learning

If you know that you are going to write an argumentative essay, decide now which of the two structures would be best for you to use.

Structuring persuasive writing

Organising this kind of piece is very similar, but simpler. In persuasive writing you don't have to switch from one part of the argument to the other, because you are always trying to defend your own point of view.

Step 1 A one-paragraph introduction to the topic. Make clear straight away what you believe about the subject. Use your wit and passion to grab the reader's attention from the start.

> **Our supermarkets, corner shops, even our petrol stations are filling with brightly-coloured celebrity magazines. We seem to have become so used to them that we never question their place in our lives. However I firmly believe Britain would be a better place if we gathered up every copy of *Heat, Hello, OK, Grazia* and all their shiny little clones and dumped them in a recycling facility. Somewhere offshore. The mid-Atlantic should do it.**

Step 2 Using the points you've planned, set out your argument. Each point should be in a separate paragraph, and these points should be backed up with facts, observations or personal experiences. Use **topic sentences** and the **PEE structure** whenever you can. (You will find out more about these soon.) Start with the strongest, most convincing arguments and work your way down to the weaker ones.

> **What's most striking about these magazines is their overwhelming similarity. The same faces crop up week after week, and a trawl of any given week's offerings will throw up (and that vomit reference is deliberate) perhaps five or six versions of the same story about the same botoxed fembot having boozy second thoughts during her tacky, Sahara-themed hen night. With so few characters to go round, and so little of interest to say about them, do we really need more than a dozen weekly magazines all trying and failing to say it?**

Although you are always defending your own position in this kind of writing, your argument will be stronger if you can show that you understood the other side's position and can disprove it.

> **Some readers will defend these tatty comics, and the creatures they tirelessly report on, by saying that they bring celebrities down to**

Earth. What *Heat, Grazia, More, OK* and the others do for us is show that celebrities are nothing different. They are just like little old us. But they aren't. In real life divorce is a heartbreak not easily cured by taking a dozen friends on a get-over-him holiday in the Maldives. When real people lose or gain half a stone in weight they buy a new pair of jeans. They do not get papped in their bikini and splashed across the front page. Real women do not marry three times before their thirtieth birthday and get a different paper to pay for every tasteless set of nuptials.

Step 3 You may find that some of your points are not strong enough to be dealt with in their own separate paragraph. If you still feel they are valuable and want to use them, then you can deal with them just before you start your conclusion. All the remaining points can be rolled into one short paragraph:

As if all of this is not enough, we also have to remember …

Step 4 Finally, in your conclusion, briefly sum up what you have written. End with a strong, clear statement that shows again why you believe you are right. You may also want to challenge the reader to think or respond.

Sweeping the celebrity magazines from the shelves would make the world a better place. We'd fill our minds with higher thoughts, we'd have a much clearer view of what normal adult behaviour looks like, and we might even read more books. Do you really need to know how much a television presenter weighs?

Structuring your paragraphs

As well as structuring and ordering your whole essay, you need to have a clear structure in each paragraph. The best way to do this is to use **topic sentences**, and **the PEE pattern**. You should also be using these when writing critical essays about the literature you've read, but they apply just as much here.

Topic sentences

A topic sentence is called this for two reasons.

1 It refers to the topic of the essay.
2 It introduces the topic of its paragraph.

The topic sentence is usually the first in the paragraph. Look at the following paragraph from our writer on the death penalty. The topic sentence has been underlined. The words that tie that sentence in to the topic of the whole essay are in bold.

Some wish to see the **death penalty reintroduced** as a punishment for murder because they see it as a way of making the punishment fit the crime. If someone is guilty of taking a life, they argue, that person should then forfeit his own life. Any other punishment is too merciful, too lenient in the harsh light of what the criminal has done. This argument is strongly advocated by some Christian commentators as they believe it fits the Biblical principle of 'an eye for an eye'.

Using PEE

If you are writing an argumentative essay, then within each paragraph of your essay, apart from the introduction and conclusion, you should try to use the **PEE** structure. You may not be able to use this structure quite so often in persuasive writing, but should still do so whenever you can. It goes like this:

- P − Make a **POINT** that is relevant to the topic of your essay. This point is the topic sentence at the start of the paragraph.

  One reason why celebrity magazines should be terminated is because this would actually make the lives of celebrities better and happier.

- E − Give **EVIDENCE** to back up the point you are making. This should be either a fact you found out during your research, something you have noticed, or something you have experienced yourself.

  A flick through just three of these, all published in the last week, revealed a total of 32 photographs which had obviously been taken by paparazzi photographers without the subject's permission, and at times clearly without even their knowledge.

- E − **EXPLAIN** this. If you are writing to persuade, show how it adds to your argument. If you are doing a piece of discursive writing, show how the point and evidence contribute to this side of the topic.

  It can do no good for anyone's mental health to know that they are being constantly stalked, and that even to put the bin out or nip to the shops for a pint of milk is regarded as an invitation to invade their privacy.

Direction markers

Certain words and phrases signal the direction of the argument in a piece of discursive writing, or emphasise the writer's point of view in persuasive writing. Most of these words and phrases appear at the start of a paragraph or sentence.

Active learning

You may wish to work with a partner or small group. Look at these four headings:

- These expressions move the argument forwards.
- These expressions let the argument change direction.
- These expressions allow the writer to sum up.
- These expressions show the writer is sure he is right.

Now look at the expressions below. Each one fits best under one of those headings. Get a piece of A4 paper and divide it into four large boxes. Put each heading at the top of a different box. Underneath the heading, list the expressions that fit there. Check any new words with a dictionary as you go.

nonetheless	rather	in contrast	instead
without a doubt	undeniably	surely	definitely
thus	otherwise	moreover	yet
nevertheless	finally	on the contrary	obviously
likewise	conversely	on the other hand	whereas
unquestionably	therefore	however	next
despite	similarly	in spite of	absolutely
at the same time	without question	and	alternatively
in retrospect	without doubt	significantly	but
in conclusion	first(ly)	accordingly	although
also	in brief	second(ly)	indubitably
in addition	furthermore	as a result	equally
consequently	third(ly)	because	
on the whole	to sum up	to balance this	
what is more	in other words	certainly	

Finally, still working with your partner, see how many words or phrases you can think of to add to each list.

Some other useful words

If you want to refer to another argument so you can knock it down, two useful words are **claim** and **allege**. They hint that you do not believe something the other side says.

> The footballer **claims** to be a dedicated family man and a devoted father to his two young sons.

> Her enemies **allege** that she reached her current position after unusually fast promotion through the company, a firm in which she has a very close relationship with the chairman, Sir Antony Blackadder. She however **claims** that Blackadder merely recognised her potential and mentored her to help her fulfil it.

What is the writer suggesting about the footballer and the businesswoman mentioned above?

Some words are useful if you can't prove something for sure. These words are also useful for suggestions and rumours. These words include **reported, rumoured, believed, could, likely, would, reported**, and **may point to**. For example, here's a piece of gossip that may have very few provable facts behind it:

> It is **believed** that troubled television presenter Sonia Summers **could** again be struggling with the addiction problems originally **reported** earlier this year. It is **rumoured** that her use of alcohol and painkillers **could have** risen once again to the worrying heights that allegedly led her to seek treatment in January. It is **likely** that television bosses, who pay her £1 million a year to present 'A Healthy Mind In A Healthy Body' **would be** very unhappy if she were facing such issues. The television star's close friends are **reported** to be very concerned. Summers's unexplained non-appearance on last week's episode of 'Weekly Come Prancing' **may point to** continuing problems with substance misuse.

Some particular techniques for persuasive writing

Persuasive writing tends to use certain techniques. Some of the most common are:

- **repetition** of words or phrases
- dramatic-sounding **short sentences**
- including the reader by using **'we' and related words**
- asking **rhetorical questions** — which do not need an answer but make the reader think
- using what's called '**the rule of three**' — doing something three times over. This might be three examples, three rhetorical questions, three uses of the same word or phrase, and so on.
- use of an anecdote or personal experience to justify why the writer holds a certain opinion.

- an appeal to the reader's emotions, or emotive language which stirs up the reader's feelings
- offering the reader a **vision** of success or achievement

Active learning

Read the following text. It is by the food writer and television presenter Hugh Fearnley-Whittingstall. From the starting point of a conversation with his young son, he takes the perhaps unexpected stance of persuading people that it's better for animals if we are NOT vegetarian. As you read the piece, look for examples of each technique being used.

Vegetarians With Teeth

'How do you know stegosaurus is a vegetarian?' asked Oscar.

'You can tell from his teeth,' I said, feigning confidence in my hazy paleontological recollection. 'Dinosaur experts think they weren't the right teeth for eating meat.'

'But Ned's got the right teeth for eating meat, and he's a vegetarian too,' said Oscar.

Good point, I thought.

'Well, Ned has a choice, because he's a human being. Animals either are vegetarians, or they're not.'

'I'm a shoe-man bean. Does that mean I can choice?'

'Yes,' I said.

'Well, I'm going to choice to eat meat then.'

'Why's that?' I asked.

'Because I like it.'

'Me too,' I said.

What I didn't say to Oscar is that I have been thinking a fair bit recently about the whole vegetarian/carnivore thing. Why exactly do I eat meat? I don't think it's particularly good for me (partial as I am to the fattier cuts). I abhor the way most of it is produced. And, much as I enjoy eating it, I don't imagine life without it would be completely unbearable. So you see, I am not an untroubled carnivore. So why haven't I become a vegetarian?

Well, I guess there's my image to think of. Connoisseur of obscure body parts. Enthusiastic muncher of small furry animals. But honestly, I'd give it all up — even the bacon — if I was properly convinced it was the right thing to do. Recently, I've been considering the matter in some depth for a book I'm working on. Soon I hope to have resolved the matter to the satisfaction of my own conscience — one way or another.

But in the meantime, there's one thing I'd like a bit of help with. And perhaps there's a vegetarian out there who can oblige. (Or more likely, a vegan, because what vegans understand, to their credit, is that the dairy industry is the meat industry — or at least the beef industry.)

My questions are these: what would the vegetarian Utopia look like? And would anyone seriously want to live there? How would vegetarians set about dismantling the mixed farming system? What would happen to all the farm animals?

One possible response is that because killing animals is simply wrong, a moral absolute, questions like mine are irrelevant (as well as irritating). But that really isn't good enough. Because if enough of us were genuinely persuaded of the wrongness of killing animals for food (which is presumably what vegetarians would like to happen) we could then choose democratically to live in a meat-free society and these questions would become very real.

Would vegetarians be in favour of the mass slaughter of farm animals, to accelerate the arable revolution? And if so, would the carnivorous minority be allowed a last supper of the slaughtered corpses? Presumably the answer is 'no' on both counts.

More likely, the WPTVB (Working Party for the Transition to a Vegetarian Britain) will favour a gradual scaling down of stocking, to a point where small populations of a wide range of breeds are managed, by man, in 'Tame Life Parks'. Here they are well looked after and preserved for their educational and historic interest. Meanwhile the countryside is turned over to the cultivation of fruit and vegetables — grown, of course, without the aid of animal manures, and therefore with the input of huge quantities of chemical fertilisers.

But the matter cannot quite rest there. What happens when the sheep and cows get a bit long in the tooth? Or short in the tooth, as is the problem with ageing livestock. They can't feed properly, and quickly lose condition. In the absence of predators to finish them off, they will die a lingering and stressful death. Will the vegetarians allow human, and humane, intervention? Can we 'put them out of their misery'? And, incidentally, do we incinerate their carcasses? Feed them to our pets? To the worms? Or, as a sop, to those appalling carnivores, for an occasional 'treat'?

I guess what it boils down to is this. All animals must live some kind of life, and die some kind of death. And having died, they will be eaten, whether it's by a maggot, a crow, or a person.

The carnivore's position, and mine until you persuade me otherwise, is that the best, most morally acceptable way to co-exist with our dependent, domesticated livestock is to take care of them when they are alive, ensure that they have a quick and, in relative terms at least, stress-free death. And then eat them.

I accept entirely that, through industrial farming practice, we are guilty of a gross abuse of our responsibility of care, and a treatment of farm animals that is often morally without defence. But surely reform, and not abstinence, is the answer?

If you're a sheep, the question of who ends up eating you when you're dead is the very least of your worries. And, in the long run, you'd probably rather be a sheep than a stegosaurus.

Active learning

Now try this: First, share your answers with the rest of the class. Next, give examples of any other techniques you found Fearnley-Whittingstall using to make his argument effective.

Active learning

It's time to plan your piece. (You may already have done quite a lot of planning after the research phase if you organised your material into what the facts were, and how each fact could be used to support an argument.) Look back at all the material you gathered from your research. Double check that you did put everything you found into your own words.

Following all the advice this chapter has given you, prepare a paragraph plan for your piece. Think about these things:

- What will you do to grab your readers' attention in the introduction?
- For each body paragraph, make sure you know:
    - what your topic sentence will be
    - what evidence you are going to use
    - how your evidence backs up the idea in your topic sentence
- How will you give impact to your conclusion?

Remember you have a choice of simpler or more complex structures if you are writing an argumentative essay.

It's now time to write your piece. Don't forget the bibliography of your sources at the end.

When you've written it, read your work over before you hand it in to your teacher. Think about the three areas the markers are looking at, content, style and technical accuracy, and ask yourself the following questions:

Content:

- Have I stuck to my purpose and written for my audience?
- Do I clearly understand my topic and have I shown that I am engaged with it?
- Is there evidence that I have researched the subject?
- Does my writing have a clear line of thought?

Style:

- Is my expression varied and confident?
- Does my style fit my chosen genre, allowing me to argue, persuade, or discuss, as appropriate to my task?
- Have I chosen a structure that helps me fulfil my purpose and put across my meaning?

Technical accuracy:

- Are my spelling, grammar and punctuation all accurate?
- Is my work properly paragraphed?
- Can my work be clearly understood?

Once you have checked over your work, hand it in to your teacher. He or she will mark it and give you feedback and suggestions for ways to improve it for your Portfolio. If your teacher is also using this piece to assess your writing for the Creation and Production Unit, he or she should let you know whether you have passed the assessment standards for that unit.

CHAPTER 6 Answers

Chapter 1

Answers to *First Date Fashion* on page 7

Supporting details:

1 You don't need to follow the latest fashions.
2 Don't dress too outlandishly.
3 Be the best version of yourself
4 Wear something that makes you feel confident.
5 Don't be too formal.
6 Don't wear shoes that might hurt.
7 Buy one new accessory for your outfit.

Answers to *Routine* on page 7

Main idea:

Quotation or gloss of: 'Routine is both a blessing and a curse.'

Supporting details:

Blessing

Gloss of: 'Without it, the working world would collapse, along with much of the rest of daily life: you'd never keep the house clean, or get the kids to school on time.' (Pupils may express this as one idea, or break it down into a number of smaller details.)

Curse

Gloss of: 'Each passing year converts some of [our] experience into automatic routine which we hardly note at all…' 'Life becomes calcified, until "the days and weeks smooth themselves out … and the years grow hollow and collapse."' e.g. We stop noticing life/life becomes dull.

Gloss of: 'Too much routine isn't merely boring; it also contributes to the ubiquitous sense of the years whizzing by as you get older, because so little takes place that's new and therefore memorable.' e.g. life becomes unmemorable.

Answers to *School Uniform* on page 8

Purpose: to argue in favour of formal, good quality school uniform: supported by reference to textual evidence.

Audience: the general reader/parents/school pupils: supported by reference to textual evidence.

Main idea 1: Quotation or gloss of: 'Good uniforms confer dignity.'

Supported by gloss of:

1 'They give the wearer a chance to take themselves seriously and to convey to others that they ought to be treated with respect.' e.g. wearers will respect themselves and expect others to respect them too.
2 'The benefit of being able to look at yourself in a mirror and say, "Yeah, I do look smart", of allowing yourself to think, "Perhaps I'm not thick after all."' e.g. wearers will feel that they look good and are intelligent.
3 'I regularly walk past students at the successful Mossbourne academy in east London, wearing grey blazers and ties, who, in the very act of wearing such a uniform, are transcending their circumstances.' e.g. good quality uniform lifts pupils above their environment.
4 'It's precisely because uniforms are presented to you to wear, without choice, that a sense of freedom in other areas is unleashed.' e.g. because pupils do not have to think about what they wear, they are free to think about other things.
5 'Uniforms don't cause the wearer to disappear: conversely, the better it is, the more chance you have to assert yourself within its limits. It doesn't stultify identity, it bolsters it.' e.g. good quality uniform gives pupils a positive identity.
6 '… treat themselves as people worth respecting' e.g. good quality uniform promotes self respect.

Main idea 2: Quotation or gloss of: 'Bad uniforms … diminish everyone.' Supported by gloss of:

1 'Poor quality school uniforms, in particular, embody a school ethos that expects little of its students or their parents.' e.g. bad or cheap uniform shows the school has low expectations of its pupils.
2 'These are most often the uniforms worn by children in largely working-class schools, ostensibly because they're "more practical" — cheaper for parents and easier to enforce. The less obvious inference is that students may as well prepare for a lifetime of wearing "practical" clothes.' e.g. bad or cheap uniform suggests these pupils will only ever do low-status jobs.
3 'You cannot learn to the best of your ability in a chaotic environment — whether at home, at school, or both.' e.g. pupils only learn well in settled environments.

4 'The same goes for uniform: if a code is only half-enforced, it reinforces the notion that you, your aims and by extension, your community, are not worth taking seriously.' e.g. if schools don't enforce a proper uniform, they are saying they do not value their pupils.

Answers to *Haute Homemade* on page 12

Standard 1.1 Purpose and Audience

In order to meet this standard and to pass the unit test for Reading, candidates would be required to answer both question 9 and question 10 correctly.

9 Identify one main purpose of this article. Explain your answer with close reference to the text.

The candidate should identify and explain the purpose of the article, supporting this with evidence in the form of quotation from or close reference to the text. There should be explanation of this evidence and not merely reference/quotation.

Possible purposes include:

- to complain
- to argue
- to condemn
- perhaps also to entertain

As it is possible to identify a number of possible purposes, including potentially many more than those given above, it is the citation and explanation of evidence that is crucial here.

10 Identify at least one possible audience for this article and explain your answer with close reference to the text.

Candidates should correctly identify at least one possible audience, supporting this with evidence in the form of quotation from or close reference to the text. There should be explanation of this evidence and not merely reference/quotation.

Possible audiences include:

- people who enjoy home cooking
- people who enjoy reading recipes/watching cookery programmes (e.g. *Masterchef*)
- the general reader (as this article comes from a newspaper)

As it is possibly to identify a number of possible audiences, including potentially many more than those given above, it is the citation and explanation of evidence that is crucial here.

Standard 1.2 Main Ideas and Supporting Details

In order to meet this standard and to pass the unit test for reading, candidates would be required to get at least two of the following four questions right.

3   Read lines 22–26 ('Who, in their right mind … what's the point?')
    What are the writer's main arguments against making this dish?
    Answer **in your own words** as far as possible.

Candidates should give at least two arguments against making this dish.

Possible answers include:

- it takes 4 hours to cook
- freezing time is also required
- the dish also has to be plated up
- it will take only a few minutes to eat the finished dish
- the overall effort required is therefore pointless

4   Read lines 27–35 ('Home cooking, as a term … narcissistic
    creations.') Explain at least **two** ways that the idea that 'Home
    cooking … has got above itself,' in the opening sentence is
    developed in the rest of the paragraph. You should answer **in your
    own words** as far as possible.

Candidates should give at least two ways in which the idea is developed.

Possible answers include:

- gloss of 'time consuming'
- gloss of 'stressful'
- gloss of 'expensive'
- you have to make things (e.g. pastry/bread/pasta) that most people
  usually buy
- it encourages out-dated behaviour (gloss of 'turning back the clock')
- it is vain/self obsessed (gloss of 'narcissistic')

5   Read lines 42–45 ('A bit of chicken … arranged beside the
    chicken.') What impression is given of this plate of food and how is
    this impression created?

Candidates should give at least one plausible impression of this dish.
This impression must be supported by at least one quotation from or
reference to the text. This evidence should be explained, not merely
quoted/referred to.

Impression: mean/small/not very filling or satisfying/not much of it

Evidence: reference to and explanation of:

- a 'bit' of chicken
- 'nil by mouth' e.g. suggests no food at all
- 'sprigettes' e.g. too small even to be sprigs (which are, themselves,
  very small pieces)
- 'four slices' e.g. small number, idea of counting implies meanness
- 'one' implies meanness
- 'just' emphasises meanness
- repetition of 'one, just one' emphasises meanness

6 How do the comments by the writer's friend in lines 56 to 59 ('I feel like I have to … everyone helping themselves.') illustrate the problems of cooking haute homemade? Answer **in your own words** as far as possible.

Candidates should refer to at least one of the friend's comments and explain how this comment illustrates the problems. e.g.

- 'I feel like I have to take the day off' — illustrates length of time required/extent to which this sort of cooking interferes with or does not fit in to normal life
- 'The thing is, I like putting … ' — illustrates that we are being encouraged to cook in a way that does not suit us/that is contrary to how we would like to cook/eat

Standard 1.3 Knowledge and Understanding of Language

In order to meet this standard and to pass the unit test for reading, candidates would be required to get at least two of the following four questions right.

1 Read line 1 ('I have had … have said it.') What tone does the writer establish in this opening line and how is this tone created?

Candidates should correctly identify a tone, supporting this with evidence in the form of quotation from or close reference to the text. There should be explanation of this evidence and not merely reference/quotation.

Tone: firm/definite/determined/tone of rejection/tone of refusal

Established by: quotation of/ref. to + explanation

- repetition of 'I' and 'I have' shows certainty/self-assurance
- 'will not' suggests refusal
- short sentences create impact
- repetition of short sentences creates impact
- 'There' (at start of sentence) emphasises statement/sums up her position

2 Read lines 18–21 ('Then I saw … old-fashioned undergarment.') How does the writer's word choice create a negative impression of the dish? You should examine at least **two** examples of word choice in your answer.

Candidates should quote at least two examples of word choice and explore the effects/connotations of the quoted word choice.

Possible answers include:

- 'sputum' suggests something coughed up/illness/disgusting/ unpleasant/unhygienic etc.
- 'slug' suggests inedible/ugly/does not belong on plate etc.

- 'structure' sounds mechanical/engineered/unnatural/inedible
- 'undergarment' implies something not to be eaten

7   Read lines 62–69. ('These are a must … not much going on in your life.') How does the writer's language undermine the description of the dish as 'peasant'? You should refer to at least **two** examples of language in your answer.

Candidates should quote or refer to at least two examples of language and explore how these undermine the idea implied by 'peasant'. Candidates are likely to indicate that 'peasant' suggests simplicity. This understanding may be implicit rather than explicit in their answers.

Possible answers include:

- the dish has been 'made more impressive' + explanation
- it is both 'poached' and 'roasted' suggesting complex/time-consuming/number of processes
- 'take a while' suggests time-consuming
- 'vinegar pearls' is oxymoron/unlikely/sounds impossible and therefore suggests difficulty/complex process
- 'Harper's Bazaar' is a glossy/fashion magazine which is at odds with the idea of 'peasant'
- 'takes three hours' suggests difficulty/complex process
- writer questions the use of 'whip', suggesting difficulty/complex process

8   Read lines 70–76. ('If you do master … jelly around it.') How does the writer's language create a contrast between the two different ways of presenting butter?

Candidates must show an understanding of both sides of the contrast. At least one feature of language should be referred to to support each side of the contrast.

First way: informal/quick/simple/haphazard etc. Supported by quotation of/reference to:

- 'a bit'
- 'squish'

Second way: effortful/unlikely/ridiculous/unnatural etc. Supported by quotation of/reference to:

- 'render' — implies effort
- 'smoking' — seems unlikely/unnatural for butter
- 'individual edible Saturns' - seems unlikely/impossible/ridiculous/grandiose
- 'smoking … moulding … lowering' — list of verbs/actions suggests complex/time-consuming/troublesome

Answers to *Frankenstein* on page 15

Standard 1.1 Purpose and Audience

In order to meet this standard and to pass the unit test for reading, candidates would be required to answer both question 8 and question 9 correctly.

8 Identify one main purpose of this novel. Explain your answer with close reference to the text.

The candidate should identify and explain the purpose of the novel, supporting this with evidence in the form of quotation from or close reference to the text. There should be explanation of this evidence and not merely reference/quotation.

Possible purposes include:

- to entertain
- to horrify, shock or frighten
- to explore an idea, e.g.
  - Can man create life?
  - What are the consequences of mankind 'playing God'?
  - What are the limits and/or dangers of scientific progress?

As it is possible to identify a number of possible purposes, including potentially many more than those given above, it is the citation and explanation of evidence that is crucial here.

9 Identify at least one possible audience for this novel and explain your answer with close reference to the text.

Candidates should correctly identify at least one possible audience, supporting this with evidence in the form of quotation from or close reference to the text. There should be explanation of this evidence and not merely reference/quotation.

Possible audiences include:

- readers who have followed Victor's progress in the novel so far and wish to see how his endeavours turn out
- readers who have heard of Frankenstein's monster/have seen a Frankenstein film (and now want to read the original source novel)
- readers who enjoy classic fiction
- readers who enjoy horror/gothic/science/speculative fiction
- readers interested in the idea of whether man can/should try to create life
- readers who enjoy fiction that deals with ideas/moral issues such as those that Victor confronts here.

As it is possible to identify a number of possible audiences, including potentially many more than those given above, it is the citation and explanation of evidence that is crucial here.

Standard 1.2 Main Ideas and Supporting Details

In order to meet this standard and to pass the unit test for reading, candidates would be required to get at least two of the following four questions right.

2   Read lines 10–19. ('How can I describe … straight black lips.') Explain, **using your own words** as far as possible, what makes the creature a 'catastrophe'? (line 10)

Candidates should give at least two reasons, using their own words as far as possible.

Possible reasons include:

- the yellow colour of his skin
- that the creature's skin barely covers his body
- gloss of 'watery' eyes
- his eyes are pale
- gloss of 'shrivelled complexion'
- gloss of 'straight black lips'

3   Read lines 21–24. ('I had worked … far exceeded moderation …') How is the reader made aware of Victor's determination to make the creature? You should answer **in your own words** as far as possible.

Candidates should give at least two details in evidence, using their own words as far as possible.

Possible answers include:

- we are told he worked 'hard'
- he worked for 'nearly two years'
- it was his 'sole purpose'
- he had 'deprived myself of rest and health'
- he had 'desired it with ardour'
- his desire to achieve this 'far exceeded moderation'

5   Read lines 26–53. ('Unable to endure … so miserably given life.') **Using your own words** as far as possible, briefly summarise how Victor spends the night. You should make at least **four** points.

Candidates should make four of the following points:
- he paced up and down in his bedroom
- he eventually fell asleep
- he had a bizarre dream/nightmare
- he woke up (in horror)
- the creature came into his room
- Victor rushed downstairs
- he spent the rest of the night walking up and down outside/in the courtyard

7a Read lines 67–75. ('Morning, dismal and wet … black and comfortless sky.') By referring to at least **two** details from the text, show how Victor's fear is conveyed.

Candidates should give at least two ways in which his fear is conveyed.

Possible answers include:

- he has not slept
- he quickly walks the streets
- he seems to be trying to avoid the creature
- every time he turns a corner he is afraid he will see the creature
- he does not dare return to his apartment
- he stays outside despite the rain

Standard 1.3 Knowledge and Understanding of Language

In order to meet this standard and to pass the unit test for reading, candidates would be required to get at least two of the following four questions right.

1 Read lines 1–9. ('It was on a dreary night … motion agitated its limbs.') By referring to at least **two** examples, show how Mary Shelley's word choice suggests an unsuccessful outcome of Victor's efforts.

Candidates should quote at least two examples of word choice and examine the connotations of what they quote.

Possible answers include:

- 'anxiety' suggests nervousness/fear
- 'agony' suggest pain/suffering
- 'lifeless' suggests death
- 'thing' suggests inanimate/inhuman
- 'dismally' suggests depressing
- 'nearly burnt out' suggests dying, growing weaker
- 'half-extinguished' suggests growing weaker
- 'dull' suggests disappointing/lifeless
- 'yellow' suggests sickly/jaundiced/unnatural
- 'convulsive' suggests spasmodic/seizure
- 'agitated' suggests spasmodic/seizure/not under control of self

4 Read lines 26–31. ('Unable to endure … moments of forgetfulness.') How does the context assist you in understanding the meaning of the word 'lassitude' as used in line 29?

Candidates should both give the meaning of the word and then provide evidence from the context.

Meaning — tiredness

Context evidence — he flings himself down on the bed (after pacing up and down)

6 Read lines 48–53. ('I took refuge … so miserably given life.') How does the description of the creature as a 'demoniacal corpse' convey Victor's attitude towards the creature?

Candidates should show an understanding of both 'demoniacal' and 'corpse'. Their identification of Victor's attitude to the creature may be merely implicit but should be discernible.

- 'demoniacal' suggests Hellish/Satanic/evil/inhuman
- 'corpse' suggests death

7b Read lines 67–75. ('Morning, dismal and wet … black and comfortless sky.') How does the image of an 'asylum' as used in line 70 help you to understand Victor's experience that night?

Candidates should give either one of the following two analyses:

EITHER Just as an asylum is a place of refuge/safety, so Victor has spent the night (in the courtyard) hiding away from the creature.

OR Just as an asylum is a place where the insane are sent, so Victor, driven mad by what he has done, spent the night in the courtyard.

Chapter 2

Answers to questions about register on page 43

A mise en scène, representation, institutional factors — film studies
B jurisprudence, precedent, duty of care — law
C enjambment, assonance, rhyme scheme — poetry
D bond, hedge fund, annuity — finance
E grind, carving, wipe out, 360 — snowboarding
F fold, sauté, ballotine — cookery

Chapter 3

Answers to understanding questions on page 66

1 Re-read paragraph 1. According to the writer, what is the difference between the original meaning of *nostalgia*, and what we now understand this word to mean?

2

Expected response	Additional guidance
Candidates should show an understanding of the original meaning of the term, and of its current understood meaning. 1 mark for each point from the 'Additional guidance' column. 0 marks for quotation alone — there should be at least some attempt at paraphrase.	Possible answers include: • original meaning: gloss of 'a yearning for … a specific time and place' • current understanding: gloss of 'in a general, sentimental way'

2   Re-read paragraph 3. Explain the two different ways in which the use of modern technology may have affected our feelings of nostalgia.   2

Expected response	Additional guidance
Candidates should show an understanding of the two different ways in which technology may affect nostalgia. 1 mark for each point from the 'Additional guidance' column. 0 marks for quotation alone — there should be at least some attempt at paraphrase.	Possible answers include: • It makes us feel closer (to home/to those we miss): gloss of 'the illusion of closeness' • It upsets us by reminding us what we are missing: gloss of 'sadden the caller by reminding them sharply of what they have left behind'

3   Re-read paragraph 6. How does the remainder of the paragraph elaborate upon the idea that there is 'a poor brake on the migratory urge'?   2

Expected response	Additional guidance
Candidates should provide evidence from the paragraph to show an understanding that many people plan to migrate or are open to the idea of migration. 1 mark for each point from the 'Additional guidance' column. 0 marks for quotation alone — there should be at least some attempt at paraphrase but markers should not expect paraphrase of statistical information.	Possible answers include: • gloss of '630 million adults or 14% of the world's population would move abroad permanently if they had the chance' • gloss of 'another 1.1 billion would move temporarily for better-paid work'

Answers to context questions on page 67

4   Look back at the paragraph on page 66 again. Using the formula given above, show how the context helps you to understand the meaning of the word 'malady' as it is used here.   2

Expected response	Additional guidance
Candidates should show an understanding of the meaning of the term, and be able to demonstrate how this may be derived from the context. 1 mark for each point from the 'Additional guidance' column: meaning + context.	Possible answers include: • meaning: sickness/illness • context: reference to 'sickness'/'mental and physical'

5 How does the context of the paragraph help you to understand the word 'mercenaries' as it is used there? 2

Expected response	Additional guidance
Candidates should show an understanding of the meaning of the term, and be able to demonstrate how this may be derived from the context. 1 mark for each point from the 'Additional guidance' column: meaning + context.	Possible answers include: • meaning: soldiers fighting for another country (not their own) • context: reference to 'in foreign armies'

Answers to word choice questions on page 72

1 Re-read paragraph 1. Explain how the writer's word choice conveys the strength of competition between web companies for users' attention. 4

Expected response	Additional guidance
Candidates should analyse how the writer's word choice conveys the competition between web companies. Marks will depend on the quality of comment. 2 marks may be awarded for reference plus detailed/insightful comment; 1 mark for reference plus more basic comment; 0 marks for reference alone. Possible answers shown in the 'Additional guidance' column.	Possible answers include: • 'better' suggests trying to out-do each other • 'rivals' suggests they are in competition • 'however' suggests they will do anything to attract user's clicks • 'doesn't care' suggests all means of attracting user attention are allowable • 'survive' suggests almost vicious, to-the-death competition between web companies • 'hyper-competitive' suggests exaggerated, over-the-top rivalry

2 Re-read paragraph 2. Explain how the writer's word choice in the rest of the paragraph supports his statement that 'this war for your attention isn't confined only to Facebook or Twitter or Pinterest, or to the purveyors of celebrity gossip or porn.' 3

Expected response	Additional guidance
Candidates should analyse how the writer's word choice supports his statement. Marks will depend on the quality of comment. 2 marks may be awarded for reference plus detailed/insightful comment; 1 mark for reference plus more basic comment; 0 marks for reference alone. Possible answers shown in the 'Additional guidance' column.	Possible answers include: • 'higher-minded' suggests better quality/more intelligent/more serious publications also want users' attention • 'institutions' suggests important/established/serious bodies also want users' attention • 'even' suggests level of surprise that such bodies are competing for user attention • 'never mind' suggests it is not just the web companies we expect, but other more unexpected ones, that compete for user attention

3 Re-read the first sentence of paragraph 4 ('There's a slightly depressing view … in the brain.') What is implied about the nature of the rewards users get for their use of the web, and how does the writer's word choice suggest this?   4

Expected response	Additional guidance
Candidates should first state what is implied about the rewards users get for web use, and go on to analyse how the writer's word choice implies this.	Possible answers include:
	Nature of reward:
	• disappointing/minimal
1 mark for nature of reward.	Implied by:
Thereafter, 2 marks may be awarded for reference plus detailed/insightful comment; 1 mark for reference plus more basic comment; 0 marks for reference alone.	• 'just' suggests minimal/a little but no more
	• 'pigeons' suggests users are treated as less than human
Possible answers shown in the 'Additional guidance' column.	• 'a squirt' suggests very small amount of pleasure/ reward
	• 'so-called' suggests questionable whether users do indeed feel good/rewarded

4 Re-read paragraph 6. What was Bogost's attitude to the game he had created, and how does his word choice convey this attitude?   4

Expected response	Additional guidance
Candidates should first state Bogost's attitude to his own game, and go on to analyse how his word choice conveys this.	Attitude:
	• worried/troubled/bothered, etc.
1 mark for attitude	Implied by:
Thereafter, 2 marks may be awarded for reference plus detailed/insightful comment; 1 mark for reference plus more basic comment; 0 marks for reference alone.	• 'concerned' suggests worry
	• 'disturbed' suggests worry
	• 'compulsively (attached)' suggests worry that users have become addicted/unable to quit
Possible answers shown in the 'Additional guidance' column.	

Answers to meaning in context questions on page 72

5 Satire in paragraph 5 and **6** Rapture in paragraph 6.   2

Expected response	Additional guidance
Candidates should show an understanding of the meaning of the term, and be able to demonstrate how this may be derived from the context.	Possible answers include:
	Satire
1 mark for each point from the 'Additional guidance' column: meaning + context.	• meaning: send-up, spoof, mockery
	• context: reference to similarity with Farmville/'you click on a cow and that's it'/obviously banal , trivial or simplistic nature of game
	Rapture
	• meaning: end of the world/mass destruction
	• context: reference to 'eliminated'/'Cowpocalypse'

Answers to understanding questions on page 73

7 Re-read paragraphs 3 and 4. How do the examples given by the writer in paragraph 4 elaborate on the idea of 'variable schedules of reward' as introduced in paragraph 3? **2**

Expected response	Additional guidance
Candidates should provide evidence from the paragraph to show an understanding of the idea of variable reward. 1 mark for each point from the additional guidance column. 0 marks for quotation alone — there should be at least some attempt at gloss.	Possible answers include: • gloss of 'when you click refresh on your email/check your phone/visit Facebook/open Twitter • gloss of 'you might or might not find an update of the sort you'd been hoping for'

8 Re-read paragraph 5. How can the Cow Clicker game be understood to be both 'the funniest' and 'the most horrifying' example of the compulsion to click? **2**

Expected response	Additional guidance
Candidates should provide evidence from the paragraph to show an understanding of both sides of the description. 1 mark for each point from the additional guidance column. 0 marks for quotation alone — there should be at least some attempt at paraphrase but markers should not expect paraphrase of statistical information.	Possible answers include: • funniest: gloss of 'you click on a cow and that's it'/ reference to simplicity/banality of game/reference to silliness of clicking on animated cow to make it moo/reference to only getting response every 6 hours • most horrifying: reference to people being willing to wait 6 hours/people willing to pay (real or virtual) money to play (more often)/more than 50,000 users/people paying $20 (or more)/'pointless improvements'

Answers to tone questions on page 77

1 How does the writer establish a persuasive tone in paragraph 4? **2**

Expected response	Additional guidance
Candidates should analyse how the writer's use of language establishes the persuasive tone. Marks will depend on the quality of comment. 2 marks may be awarded for reference plus detailed/insightful comment; 1 mark for reference plus more basic comment; 0 marks for reference alone. Possible answers shown in the 'Additional guidance' column.	Possible answers include: • reference to and comment on: 'we need to' • reference to and comment on: 'should be' • reference to and comment on: 'could be' • reference to and comment on: 'should be, could be' • reference to and comment on writer's use of 'we/ us' throughout paragraph

2   What is the tone of paragraph 6 and how is this established?   3

Expected response	Additional guidance
Candidates should identify a tone and then analyse how the writer's use of language establishes the persuasive tone. 1 mark for successful identification of tone. Thereafter, arks will depend on the quality of comment. 2 marks may be awarded for reference plus detailed/insightful comment; 1 mark for reference plus more basic comment; 0 marks for reference alone. Possible answers shown in the 'Additional guidance' column.	Possible answers include: Tone: • surprise Established by: • reference to and comment on: 'I'm told that' • reference to and comment on: 'raw wee elegy' • reference to and comment on: 'painful' • reference to and comment on: 'a poem that I might have flinched away from' • reference to and comment on: 'it's not a matter of' • reference to and comment on: '(it's proven to be) quite the reverse'

Answers to word choice questions on page 78

3   How does Lochhead's word choice in paragraph 2 emphasise the challenge of caring for the growing elderly population?   2

Expected response	Additional guidance
Candidates should analyse how the writer's word choice emphasises the challenge. Marks will depend on the quality of comment. 2 marks may be awarded for reference plus detailed/insightful comment; 1 mark for reference plus more basic comment; 0 marks for reference alone. Possible answers shown in the 'Additional guidance' column.	Possible answers include: • 'daunting' suggests care of the elderly is difficult/a lot to face up to/a worry etc. • 'burden' suggests care of the elderly is a heavy responsibility

4   How does the word choice in paragraph 6 convey the experience of loss?   3

Expected response	Additional guidance
Candidates should analyse how the writer's word choice conveys the nature of loss. Marks will depend on the quality of comment. 2 marks may be awarded for reference plus detailed/insightful comment; 1 mark for reference plus more basic comment; 0 marks for reference alone. Possible answers shown in the 'Additional guidance' column.	Possible answers include: • 'universal' suggests we (will) all experience loss (in the end) • 'painful' suggests hurt/grief caused by loss • 'intimate' suggests personal/private/individual experience of loss

Answers to understanding questions on page 78

5 Re-read paragraphs 7 and 8. Identify any four benefits of the poetry sessions with elderly people. 4

Expected response	Additional guidance
Candidates should show an understanding of the two benefits of these sessions. 1 mark for each point from the 'Additional guidance' column. 0 marks for quotation alone — there should be at least some attempt at paraphrase.	Possible answers include: • They take people out of their usual situation; gloss of 'escapism'. • They divert/amuse/pass the time: gloss of 'entertainment'. • They are enjoyable: gloss of 'pleasure'. • They reinvigorate the memory: gloss of 'People who can't remember … learned by heart.' • They bring back other memories as well as the memory of poetry: gloss of 'And then they remember … ' • They improve emotion: gloss of 'shifts of mood' • They help people to become involved: gloss of 'engagement'/reference to man who now joins in.

6 Re-read paragraph 9. Identify two ways in which the writer responds to her own increasing age. You should use your own words as far as possible. 2

Expected response	Additional guidance
Candidates should show an understanding of two different ways in which the writer responds to her own aging. 1 mark for each point from the 'Additional guidance' column. 0 marks for quotation alone — there should be at least some attempt at paraphrase.	Possible answers include: • refusal to accept it is happening: gloss of 'Of course I'm not old'/'denial' or reference to description of (white) hair as 'platinum blonde'. • dressing vibrantly/youthfully: gloss of or reference to description of her 'creepers'. • fear/anxiety/trepidation etc: gloss of or reference to final sentence of passage.

Answers to imagery questions on page 83

1 'a sanctuary' 2
2 'the crest of a wave' 2
3 'a handful of similar projects' 2

Expected response	Additional guidance
Candidates should analyse the writer's use of imagery. Marks will depend on the quality of comment. 2 marks may be awarded for detailed/insightful comment; 1 mark more basic comment Possible answers shown in the 'Additional guidance' column.	Possible answers include: • 'a sanctuary' suggests a place of safety, refuge or calm/an escape from booze culture • 'the crest of a wave': Redemption is first but others are following/suggests momentum or power of dry bar movement • 'a handful' suggests so far very few pubs like Redemption

4   Re-read paragraph 4. How does Catherine Salway's use of imagery convey her feelings about her former career?   2

Expected response	Additional guidance
Candidates should first identify an appropriate image and then analyse the writer's use of imagery. Marks will depend on the quality of comment. 2 marks may be awarded for detailed/insightful comment; 1 mark more basic comment Possible answers shown in the 'Additional guidance' column.	Possible answers include: • 'grinding' suggests dull/relentless/repetitive/unrewarding

5   Re-read paragraph 7. How is imagery used to suggest the importance of alcohol as part of London life?   2

Expected response	Additional guidance
Candidates should first identify an appropriate image and then analyse the writer's use of imagery. Marks will depend on the quality of comment. 2 marks may be awarded for detailed/insightful comment; 1 mark more basic comment Possible answers shown in the 'Additional guidance' column.	Possible answers include: • 'fuelled' suggests seen as necessary to keep London life going/just as a car is kept going by fuel, so London is kept going by alcohol

Answers to meaning in context questions on page 83

6   How does the context help you to understand the meaning of 'omnipresent' as used in paragraph 1?   2

Expected response	Additional guidance
Candidates should show an understanding of the meaning of the term, and be able to demonstrate how this may be derived from the context. 1 mark for each point from the 'Additional guidance' column: meaning + context.	Possible answers include: • meaning: everywhere • context: reference to 'can't even go to the cinema without considering having a glass of wine'

7   How does the context help you to understand the meaning of 'displacement' as used in paragraph 9?   2

Expected response	Additional guidance
Candidates should show an understanding of the meaning of the term, and be able to demonstrate how this may be derived from the context. 1 mark for each point from the 'Additional guidance' column: meaning + context.	Possible answers include: • meaning: substitution/taking the place of/supplanting/ousting • context: reference to 'use of technology'/'kids aren't going out to get drink because they've got so much to stimulate them'

Answers to understanding questions on page 83

8 Re-read paragraphs 8 and 9. **Using your own words as far as possible**, list the evidence that suggests that 'our consumption of booze does seem to be changing.' 4

Expected response	Additional guidance
Candidates should identify and cite evidence that alcohol consumption is changing. 1 mark for each point from the 'Additional guidance' column. 0 marks for quotation alone — there should be at least some attempt at paraphrase, but markers should not be overly punitive if candidates cite statistical information.	Possible answers include: • reported consumption dropping: gloss of 'the share of people who report having a drink in the previous seven days has been falling' • this fall is now well-established: gloss of 'has been falling for at least eight years' • consumption is falling for both genders: gloss of or ref to percentages cited as drinking in last 7 days • volume consumed at any one time also falling: gloss of ' the amount of alcohol consumed by people on their 'heaviest' day had also come down' • younger people reducing their alcohol consumption most of all • younger people replacing drink with other pursuits: gloss of 'displacement (through use of technology)'/'so much to stimulate them'

9 Re-read paragraphs 10 and 11. In what way is the group of customers described both a good and a bad example of the trend towards lower consumption of alcohol as discussed in the article? 2

Expected response	Additional guidance
Candidates should show an understanding both of how the customers embody the supposed trend towards reduced drink, and how they do not. 1 mark for each point from the 'Additional guidance' column. For full marks, candidates must have an answer from both the 'good' and 'bad' sides. 0 marks for quotation alone — there should be at least some attempt at paraphrase.	Possible answers include: Good example: • they are drinking non-alcoholic drinks • one is still sober enough to do her marking • if they were anywhere else they would order a whole bottle, here they drink by the glass • they believe the lack of booze 'makes everything easier' Bad example: • Moule drank with her boyfriend the night before • implication that she drank considerably more than her boyfriend: 'Well, he had a glass, anyway.'

Answers to link questions on page 87

1 How does the sentence, 'It's an opinion shared by British thriller writer Jeremy Duns,' form a link between paragraphs 3 and 4? 2

Expected response	Additional guidance
Candidates should show an understanding both of the link back to previous ideas, and the link forward to introduce new ideas. 1 mark for each point from the 'Additional guidance' column. For full marks, candidates must have an answer from both the 'back' and 'forward' sides of the writer's argument/ideas.	Possible answers include: Link back: • 'It's an opinion' refers back to Edward Champion's beliefs about plagiarism as mentioned in paragraph 3. Link forward: • 'shared by British thriller writer Jeremy Duns' introduces Duns whose experience and opinions come up in paragraph 4

2 How does the sentence, 'The act of uncovering and investigating acts of plagiarism is becoming easier by the day,' form a link between paragraphs 4 and 5? 2

Expected response	Additional guidance
Candidates should show an understanding both of the link back to previous ideas, and the link forward to introduce new ideas. 1 mark for each point from the 'Additional guidance' column. For full marks, candidates must have an answer from both the 'back' and 'forward' sides of the writer's argument/ideas.	Possible answers include: Link back: • 'The act of uncovering and investigating acts of plagiarism' refers back to Jeremy Duns' actions as mentioned in paragraph 4. Link forward: • 'becoming easier by the day' introduces the idea of how this can be done very simply in the digital age, as will be described in paragraph 5.

3 How does the sentence, 'These searches aren't restricted to words' form a link between paragraphs 5 and 6? 2

Expected response	Additional guidance
Candidates should show an understanding both of the link back to previous ideas, and the link forward to introduce new ideas. 1 mark for each point from the 'Additional guidance' column. For full marks, candidates must have an answer from both the 'back' and 'forward' sides of the writer's argument/ideas.	Possible answers include: Link back: • 'These searches' refers back to digital searches to uncover plagiarism as discussed in paragraph 5. Link forward: • 'aren't restricted to words' introduces the idea of plagiarism of images, as discussed in paragraph 6.

Answers to word choice and imagery questions on page 88

4   How does Edward Champion's word choice in the third sentence of paragraph 3 ('When you see … a new form of expression.') convey the strength of his feelings about plagiarism?   2

Expected response	Additional guidance
Candidates should analyse how the speaker's word choice conveys the strength of his feelings. Marks will depend on the quality of comment. 2 marks may be awarded for reference plus detailed/insightful comment; 1 mark for reference plus more basic comment; 0 marks for reference alone. Possible answers shown in the 'Additional guidance' column.	Possible answers include: • 'desecrate' suggests something precious/holy has been defiled • 'wonderful' suggests value/amazing qualities of internet, which therefore should not be plagiarised • 'noble' suggests almost moral/high-minded/personified aspect to internet, which therefore should not be plagiarised

5a How does the imagery of the opening sentence of paragraph 4 ('It's an opinion … a plagiarist's scourge.') emphasise the impact Jeremy Duns has upon the plagiarists he exposes?   2

Expected response	Additional guidance
Candidates should first identify an appropriate image and then analyse the writer's use of imagery. Marks will depend on the quality of comment. 2 marks may be awarded for detailed/insightful comment; 1 mark more basic comment. Possible answers shown in the 'Additional guidance' column.	Possible answers include: • 'scourge' suggests he severely punishes plagiarists/just as a scourge is a whip used to inflict painful punishment, so Jeremy Duns inflicts damage upon the plagiarists he exposes

5b What does the imagery of the final sentence in this paragraph add to the reader's understanding of Jeremy Duns?   2

Expected response	Additional guidance
Candidates should first identify an appropriate image and then analyse the writer's use of imagery. Marks will depend on the quality of comment. 2 marks may be awarded for detailed/insightful comment; 1 mark more basic comment. Possible answers shown in the 'Additional guidance' column.	Possible answers include: • 'like a dog with a bone' suggests determination/tenacity/not giving up/relentlessly seeking out

6 Re-read paragraph 5. What does the word choice of the second sentence ('Search engines … all play their part.') convey about how publicity spreads across the internet? 2

Expected response	Additional guidance
Candidates should analyse how the writer's word choice conveys the nature of loss. Marks will depend on the quality of comment. 2 marks may be awarded for reference plus detailed/insightful comment; 1 mark for reference plus more basic comment; 0 marks for reference alone. Possible answers shown in the 'Additional guidance' column.	Possible answers include: • 'viral' suggests spreads quickly/widely/without anyone trying to make it spread/possible suggestion of harmful

Answers to understanding questions on page 88

7 Re-read paragraph 2. What, according to the writer, are the reasons why plagiarism has now become so common? 4

Expected response	Additional guidance
Candidates should identify reasons for the prevalence of plagiarism. 1 mark for each point from the 'Additional guidance' column. 0 marks for quotation alone — there should be at least some attempt at paraphrase.	Possible answers include: • The internet has made it possible: gloss of 'sheer quantity of online content/new opportunities for digital self-expression'. • Excitement (of having such a large potential audience): gloss of 'With a potential audience of billions), the prospect of contributing can be thrilling'. • Copying has become so easy, we no longer see it as a moral issue: gloss of 'moral responsibility … has been downgraded'. • Technology makes copying easy: gloss of 'technology covertly assists us'. • Candidates may also refer to all of, part of, or items from the list in 'driven by a combination of greed, confusion, ignorance, pressure, laziness and ambition'.

8 Re-read paragraph 5. Why might people be put off discovering and exposing plagiarism? 4

Expected response	Additional guidance
Candidates should identify reasons that might put people off from exposing plagiarism. 1 mark for each point from the 'Additional guidance' column. 0 marks for quotation alone — there should be at least some attempt at paraphrase.	Possible answers include: • gloss of 'laborious' • gloss of 'unpaid' • gloss of 'takes discipline' • gloss of 'sit for hours' • gloss of 'tedious' • gloss of 'exposes you to legal action' • gloss of 'abuse'

Answers to sentence structure questions on page 93

1 How does sentence structure in paragraph 1 engage the reader? 2

Expected response	Additional guidance
Candidates should analyse how the writer's sentence structure engages the reader. Marks will depend on the quality of comment. 2 marks may be awarded for reference plus detailed/insightful comment; 1 mark for reference plus more basic comment; 0 marks for reference alone. Possible answers shown in the 'Additional guidance' column.	Possible answers include: • Use of question, ('Do you fancy …') intrigues reader/makes reader think they would like to earn this much money. • Repeated structure of offers ('one … another …') is engaging/inviting/offers sense of possibility.

2 What is the effect of the author's use of parenthesis in the second sentence of paragraph 3 ('The online education resource … for their children.')? 2

Expected response	Additional guidance
Candidates should analyse the effect of the use of parenthesis. Marks will depend on the quality of comment. 2 marks may be awarded for reference plus detailed/insightful comment; 1 mark for reference plus more basic comment; 0 marks for reference alone. Possible answers shown in the 'Additional guidance' column.	Possible answers include: • allows him to cast doubt on size/value of tuition industry • allows him to cast doubt on reliability of EdPlace as a source/authority

3 How does the sentence structure of paragraph 5 convey the popularity of tutoring as a career? 2

Expected response	Additional guidance
Candidates should analyse how the writer's sentence structure conveys the popularity of this career. Marks will depend on the quality of comment. 2 marks may be awarded for reference plus detailed/insightful comment; 1 mark for reference plus more basic comment; 0 marks for reference alone. Possible answers shown in the 'Additional guidance' column.	Possible answers include: • use of listing/use of two lists — suggests tutoring is popular with a wide variety/large number of people • first list suggests tutoring popular with those who are well-educated • second list suggests tutoring popular with creative people

4 How does the sentence structure of paragraph 6 emphasise the challenges of the graduate job market? 2

Expected response	Additional guidance
Candidates should analyse how the sentence structure emphasises the challenges. Marks will depend on the quality of comment. 2 marks may be awarded for reference plus detailed/ insightful comment; 1 mark for reference plus more basic comment; 0 marks for reference alone. Possible answers shown in the 'Additional guidance' column.	Possible answers include: <ul><li>use of list ('high unemployment, hiring freezes and unpaid internships') emphasises lack of opportunity/lack of reward</li></ul>

Answers to Passage 1 questions on page 101

1 Re-read paragraphs 1 and 2. According to the writer, in what way have Swedish cinemas gone beyond filmgoers usual expectations of movie ratings? You should use your own words as far as possible. 2

Expected response	Additional guidance
Candidates should demonstrate an understanding both of what filmgoers normally expecting from ratings, and how Swedish cinemas have gone further. 1 mark for each point from the 'Additional guidance' column. For full marks, candidates must identify both normal expectations and Sweden's further use of rating. 0 marks for quotation alone — there should be at least some attempt at paraphrase.	Possible answers include: <ul><li>usual expectations: gloss of 'whether a film contains nudity, sex, profanity or violence'</li><li>gone beyond: gloss of 'new rating to highlight gender bias' ('or rather the absence of it)</li></ul>

2 Analyse how the language of paragraph 3 emphasises the gender bias of most films. You should refer in your answer to such features as sentence structure, word choice … 4

Expected response	Additional guidance
Candidates should analyse how the writer's use of language emphasises the gender bias in film. Marks will depend on the quality of comment on appropriate language feature(s). 2 marks may be awarded for reference plus detailed/insightful comment; 1 mark for reference plus more basic comment; 0 marks for reference alone. Possible answers shown in the 'Additional guidance' column.	Possible answers include: Word choice <ul><li>'entire' suggests how totally the Lord of the Rings trilogy is biased</li><li>'all but one' suggests near-total bias of Harry Potter trilogy</li></ul>Sentence structure: <ul><li>listing of names of films/film series shows how very many films are biased</li><li>listing of names of films/film series shows extent to which some of the most famous/successful films are biased</li></ul>

3 By referring to at least two features of language in paragraph 5, analyse how this paragraph conveys the current depiction of women in film. You should refer in your answer to such features as word choice, sentence structure … **4**

Expected response	Additional guidance
Candidates should analyse how the language of the paragraph conveys the current depiction of women in film. Marks will depend on the quality of comment on appropriate language feature(s). 2 marks may be awarded for reference plus detailed/insightful comment; 1 mark for reference plus more basic comment; 0 marks for reference alone. Possible answers shown in the 'Additional guidance' column.	Possible answers include: Word choice • 'rarely' suggests paucity of strong female roles Sentence structure: • listing of possible female role types emphasises how many roles/variety of roles generally unavailable to women • repetition of 'female' reinforces rarity of such roles being played by women Other features: • reduction in status 'superhero … professor … person …' emphasises how poor are the roles offered to women • '(noting that) the rating doesn't say anything about the quality of the film' suggest that even when films do pass the Bechdel test, they may still be of poor quality

4a Re-read paragraphs 9 to 11. Identify two further instances of Sweden's desire to promote gender equality. You should use you own words as far as possible. **2**

Expected response	Additional guidance
Candidates should identify two further instances, beyond the use of the Bechdel test. 1 mark for each point from the 'Additional guidance' column. For full marks, candidates should refer both to the activities of the advertising ombudsman, and also to the Equalisters project. 0 marks for quotation alone.	Possible answers include: • gloss of 'advertising ombudsman watches of for sexism in that industry' • gloss of 'reprimands companies seen as reinforcing gender stereotypes' • reference to/gloss of example of removal of 'skimpily clad women' from adverts • reference to Equalisters project • gloss of 'trying to boost the number of women appearing as expert commentators in Swedish media'

4b How does the sentence, 'For some, though, Sweden's focus on gender equality has gone too far,' at the start of paragraph 10 form a link at this stage in the article? 2

Expected response	Additional guidance
Candidates should show an understanding both of the link back to previous ideas, and the link forward to introduce new ideas. 1 mark for each point from the 'Additional guidance' column. For full marks, candidates must have an answer from both the 'back' and 'forward' sides of the writer's argument/ideas.	Possible answers include: Link back: • 'Sweden's focus on gender equality' refers back to the idea of some Swedish cinemas introducing the Bechdel test/to the actions of the advertising ombudsman/to the Equalisters project. Link forward: • 'for some though/gone to far' introduces the objections raised by Tanja Bergvist in paragraph 10

4c Analyse how the use of language in paragraphs 10 and 11 emphasises the opinions of those opposed to the use of the Bechdel test. You should refer in your answer to such features as sentence structure, word choice, imagery, tone … 4

Expected response	Additional guidance
Candidates should analyse how the language of the paragraphs emphasises opposing opinions. Marks will depend on the quality of comment on appropriate language feature(s). 2 marks may be awarded for reference plus detailed/insightful comment; 1 mark for reference plus more basic comment; 0 marks for reference alone. Possible answers shown in the 'Additional guidance' column.	Possible answers include: Word choice • 'madness' suggests attempts at gender equality have gone too far Sentence structure: • Balanced sentence 'There are far too many films … and lots of films …' used to show issue (of gender in film) is more complex than merely applying the Bechdel test Tone: • 'they should produce' suggests obligation to make better/less biased films rather than criticising/restricting those that already exist Imagery • 'blunt tool' suggests Bechdel test a very imprecise way of examining films' gender • 'point fingers' suggests accusation of others (rather than effecting change oneself)

5 Re-read paragraphs 13 and 14. Identify any four details given in these paragraphs that support the claim in the first sentence of paragraph 13, 'Research in the US … seen as violent.' You should use your own words as far as possible. 4

Expected response	Additional guidance
Candidates should give details that support the claim in the given sentence. 1 mark for each point from the 'Additional guidance' column. 0 marks for quotation alone — there should be at least some attempt at paraphrase, but markers should not be overly punitive of candidate's attempts to deal with statistical information.	Possible answers include: • gloss of 'of the top US films in 2011, women accounted for 33% of characters' • gloss of of the top US films in 2011, women accounted for … only 11% of the protagonits' • gloss of 'ratio of male to female characters in movies has remained at about two to one for at least six decades' • gloss of 'women were twice as likely to be seen in explicit sexual scenes as males' • gloss of ' male characters were more likely to be seen as violent' Candidates might also refer to the fact that two studies are cited as implying that there is a lot of/a variety of evidence to support the claim.

6 Evaluate the final paragraph's effectiveness as a conclusion to the passage as a whole. 3

Expected response	Additional guidance
Candidates should evaluate the final paragraph's effectiveness as a conclusion to the passage as a whole. Marks will depend on the quality of comment. For full marks there must be appropriate attention to the idea of a conclusion. More basic comments may be awarded 1 mark. Possible answers shown in the 'Additional guidance' column.	• The passage concludes with a statement from lead author of a study already mentioned — brings the so-far statistical information cited from the study to life. • Sums up/offers an explanation for the origin of the gender bias dealt with throughout the passage: 'Apparently Hollywood thinks that films with male characters will do better at the box office'/'most of the aspects of movie-making … are dominated by men'. • Concludes by offering reader further/wider/deeper concerns to think about: 'most of the aspects of movie-making … are dominated by men'.

Answers to Passage 2 and comparison question on page 104

7 Both passages consider the application of the Bechdel test to films. Identify the key areas on which they agree, and those on which they disagree. In your answer, you should refer in detail to both passages.

5

Expected response	Additional guidance
Candidates should identify key areas of agreement and of disagreement between the two passages by referring in detail to both passages. For answers earning 3 or more marks, candidates should identify areas of agreement and of disagreement, but the two sides need not be weighed equally — candidates are at liberty to weigh more heavily on one side or the other as long as they do deal at least to some extent with both. Marks will depend on the quality of comment. For full marks there must be appropriate attention to the idea of a conclusion. More basic comments may be awarded 1 mark. Approach to marking shown in the 'Additional guidance' column. Key areas of agreement and disagreement shown below. Other answers are possible.	The mark for this question should reflect the quality of response in two areas: • identification of the key areas of agreement and disagreement • level of detail given in support The following guidelines should be used: • 5 marks — comprehensive identification of three or more key areas of agreement and disagreement with full use of supporting evidence • 4 marks — clear identification of three or more key areas of agreement and disagreement with relevant use of supporting evidence • 3 marks — identification of three or more key areas of agreement and disagreement with relevant supporting evidence • 2 marks — identification of two areas of agreement and/or disagreement with supporting evidence • 1 mark — identification of one area of agreement or disagreement with supporting evidence • 0 marks — failure to identify any key areas of agreement or disagreement and/or total misunderstanding of task

Areas on which the passages agree:

Very few films pass the Bechdel test:

• Passage 1: list in para 3 of films and film series failing the test
• Passage 2: mention in para 2 that when Bechdel test was first proposed, only Ridley Scott's *Alien* (then 6 years old) would have passed

Passing the Bechdel test is not a guarantee of a film's quality:

• Passage 1: para 5 'the rating doesn't say anything about the quality of the film'
• Passage 2: references in para 5 to 'loathsome/whitewash' of *The Iron Lady* and/or to *Savages* being 'not exactly a woman-centric film'

The goal of the current use of the Bechdel test to rate films is to raise awareness among filmgoers:

• both passages use the same quotation from Ellen Tejle about female characters and about 'female stories and perspectives'

Areas on which the passages disagree:

The value of 'Super Sunday'

- Passage 1: mentions Super Sunday in paragraph 6 alongside mention of Swedish Film Institute support, and of how initiative is catching on — overall effect is to imply approval of Super Sunday
- Passage 2: paragraph 5 points out the problematic nature of some of the films to be shown on Super Sunday

Place/level of state involvement

- Passage 1: quotes criticism of Swedish Film Institute for sending out 'signals about what one should or shouldn't include in a movie'
- Passage 2: condemns in paragraph 6 those who complain about the 'nanny state' — dismisses/patronises them as 'guys' and implies they have overreacted — 'knickers in a twist'

Chapter 4

General guidance on answers to Scottish set text questions:

Marking should always be positive. This means that, for each candidate response, marks are accumulated for the demonstration of relevant skills, knowledge and understanding: they are not deducted from a maximum on the basis of errors or omissions.

The wording of questions suggests an approach to answers:

- For questions that ask candidates to '**Identify** …', candidates must present in brief form/name.
- For questions that ask candidates to '**Explain** …' or ask '**in what way** …' candidates must relate cause and effect and/or make relationships between things clear.
- For questions that ask candidates to '**Analyse** …', candidates must identify features of language techniques and discuss their relationship with the ideas of the text as a whole. Features of language might include word choice, imagery, tone, sentences structure, punctuation, sound techniques, versification and so on.
- For questions that ask candidates to '**Evaluate** …', candidates must make a judgement on the effect of the language and/or ideas of the texts(s).

'Waking With Russell' on page 122

1. The poem comes to a turning point after line 6. With reference to at least two techniques, explain how this turning point is made clear to the reader.   4

Expected response	Additional guidance
For full marks, candidates should provide comments on examples showing the 'before and after' of the turning point. This could be done through 2 marks for a detailed/insightful comment on one example OR more basic comments on two different examples.	Possible answers include: Change of address: • lines 1–6 are **about** his son e.g. 'his four-day-old smile'; lines 7 onward are addressed **to** the boy e.g. 'Dear Son' Use of end-stopped line/sentence break: • Lines 1–6 are all one sentence. Line 7 begins a new sentence. Creation of (early) volta: • Poem is divided at an earlier point than conventional sonnets, suggesting that the future (for father and son) is bigger/more powerful/more significant than the past.

2. With reference to lines 7 and 8, explain what the speaker means when he describes himself as 'mezzo del cammin' (line 7).   2

Expected response	Additional guidance
Candidates should explain what Paterson means when he describes himself as 'mezzo del cammin'. 2 marks may be awarded for detailed/insightful comment plus reference; 1 mark for more basic comment plus reference.	Possible answers include: • a translation of the phrase as meaning in the middle of the path • half-way through life • unsure of which way to go (in life) • having a mid-life crisis • going the wrong way/misguided/on the wrong path • about to go the right way/to turn in the right direction etc. • candidates may refer to this being a reference to/allusion to/quotation from Dante — this is not likely to be an explanation of what the poet means unless it is accompanied by some explanation of the idea that he was on the way to Hell until the birth of his son(s) interrupted him in this

3. Evaluate the effectiveness of lines 13 and 14 as a conclusion to the poem. You should deal with ideas and/or language.   2

Expected response	Additional guidance
Candidates should show under-standing of the term 'conclusion' and show how the content or language of the last two lines continue — or contrast with — ideas and/or language from the rest of the poem. A detailed/insightful comment on one example may be awarded 2 marks. A more basic comment would be awarded 1 mark. 0 marks for reference/quotation alone.	Possible answers include: • Use of ! reinforces/emphasises the new excitement about life which poem has shown the speaker now feels • 'I thought' emphasises importance of writer's final idea • 'amongst men' shows poet and son as equals, reinforces the idea of their intimacy/closeness as already established in poem • 'amongst men' looks ahead to son's future as an adult, making conclusion of poem a reference to a life that is not concluded but is still ahead for Russell • 'kissed your mouth' returns to the idea of intimacy as suggested by 'like lovers' • 'pledged' has connotations of solemn/powerful/binding promise — suggests a finality of intent that sits well in a conclusion • 'forever' suggests a finality of intent that sits well in a conclusion

'The Thread' on page 123

1 By referring to one example from lines 1 to 4, analyse how the writer uses a metaphor to clarify one of the main concerns of the poem. **2**

Expected response	Additional guidance
Candidates should analyse how the use of any one metaphor helps to clarify any one of the main concerns of the poem. 2 marks may be awarded for detailed/insightful comment plus reference; 1 mark for more basic comment plus reference. 0 marks for reference/quotation alone.	Possible answers include: Metaphor of ploughing: • conveys the danger to Jamie at the time of his birth as ploughing suggests torn up/damaged • conveys the danger to Jamie at the time of his birth as idea of ploughing suggests Jamie's 'landing' was more of a crash • conveys the danger to Jamie at the time of his birth as suggestion that earth is turned over may allude to a grave being dug Metaphor of thread: • conveys the danger to Jamie at the time of his birth as idea of thread suggests his life was very fragile Metaphor of landing/plane: • conveys the danger to Jamie at the time of his birth as idea of hard landing implies damage/injury

2 By referring closely to at least two examples from lines 3 to 10, show how the language of the poem conveys the idea of uncertainty. **4**

Expected response	Additional guidance
Candidates should analyse how the poet's language helps to clarify the idea of uncertainty. 2 marks may be awarded for detailed/insightful comment plus reference; 1 mark for more basic comment plus reference. 0 marks for reference/quotation alone.	Possible answers include: • 'They don't know' — even doctors/medical staff (who should be experts) are uncertain as to how Jamie survived • 'what higher will' implies that some supernatural/spiritual/omnipotent force was responsible for the boy's recovery but writer is unsure which or how • 'somehow out-revving' — the writer is (still) uncertain how Jamie had become so fit/strong

3 With reference to at least two examples taken from throughout the poem, analyse how the writer conveys the contrast between Jamie now and at the time of his birth. **4**

Expected response	Additional guidance
Candidates should comment on the contrast between earlier (life-threatening) weakness and his current health/strength/vivacity/energy for full marks. Candidates should focus on two examples; 2 marks may be awarded for detailed/insightful comment plus reference; 1 mark for more basic comment plus reference. The contrast should be clear in the commentary. 0 marks for reference/quotation alone.	Possible answers include: • quotation of/reference to, and discussion of contrast between 'his one breath' vs 'lungs somehow out-revving every engine in the universe' • quotation of/reference to, and discussion of contrast between fact that doctors 'don't know how' the thread held at birth vs 'Now the thread is holding all of us' • quotation of/reference to, and discussion of contrast between 'dead' and words suggesting Jamie's current vigour e.g. 'swaying/roaring/out-revving' • quotation of/reference to, and discussion of contrast between idea of crash-landing at birth vs. vigour/energy/movement now

Answers to 'Waking With Russell' comparison question on page 124

Discuss how Paterson uses contrast in 'Waking With Russell' and at least one other poem to highlight the poems' main concerns. 10

Expected response	Additional guidance
Candidates should discuss the use of contrast in this and any other poem(s) by Don Paterson and should refer to appropriate textual evidence to support their discussion. 0 marks for quotation/reference alone. Candidates can answer in bullet points in this final question, or write a number of linked statements.	• Up to 2 marks can be achieved for indentifying elements of commonality as identified in the question, i.e. use of contrast to highlight the main concerns of this and other poems by Paterson. • A further 2 marks can be gained for reference to the poem in question, 'Waking With Russell'. • 6 additional marks can be awarded for discussion of similar references to at least one other poem by the poet. In practice this means: • identification of commonality (2) (e.g. theme, characterisation, use of imagery, setting, or any other key element …) From the extract: • 1 x relevant reference to technique/idea/feature (1) • 1 x appropriate comment (1) (maximum of 2 marks only for discussion of extract) From at least one other text: • as above (x 3) for up to 6 marks *OR* • more detailed comment x 2 for up to 6 marks Thus, the final 6 marks can be gained by a combination of 3, 2 and 1 marks depending on the level of depth/detail/insight. The aim would be to encourage quality of comment, rather than quantity of references. In comments on 'The Thread' the other Paterson poem dealt with in this book, possible references include: • quotation of/reference to, and discussion of contrast between 'his one breath' vs 'lungs somehow out-revving every engine in the universe' to suggest main idea of change in Jamie since birth • quotation of/reference to, and discussion of contrast between fact that doctors 'don't know how' the thread held at birth vs. 'Now the thread is holding all of us' to suggest main idea of change in Jamie since birth/main idea of how Jamie has changed from one needing massive help/support/ intervention to one who can contribute to the family/is vital to the family • quotation of/reference to, and discussion of contrast between 'dead' and words suggesting Jamie's current vigour e.g. 'swaying/roaring/out-revving' to suggest main idea of change in Jamie since birth • quotation of/reference to, and discussion of contrast between idea of crash-landing at birth vs. vigour/energy/movement now to suggest main idea of change in Jamie since birth Other references are possible, especially if candidates have studied further Paterson poems beyond those dealt with in this book. Note however that there is no obligation to discuss more than one other poem: it is possible to gain the full 10 marks, as outlined above, by making a comparison of the poem to just one other Paterson text known by the candidate.

Answers to 'The Thread' comparison question on page 125

Referring closely to 'The Thread' and at least one other poem, discuss how the poet develops the idea of the impact that fatherhood has had upon his life.

10

Expected response	Additional guidance
Candidates should discuss how the idea of the impact of fatherhood upon his life is developed in this and any other poem(s) by Don Paterson and should refer to appropriate textual evidence to support their discussion. 0 marks for quotation/reference alone. Candidates can answer in bullet points in this final question, or write a number of linked statements.	• Up to 2 marks can be achieved for indentifying elements of commonality as identified in the question, i.e. the idea of the impact of fatherhood upon his life in this and other poems by Paterson. • A further 2 marks for reference to the poem in question, 'The Thread'. • 6 additional marks for discussion of similar references to at least one other poem by the poet. In practice this means: • identification of commonality (2) (e.g. theme, characterisation, use of imagery, setting, or any other key element …) From the extract: • 1 x relevant reference to technique/idea/feature (1) • 1 x appropriate comment (1) (maximum of 2 marks only for discussion of extract) From at least one other text: • as above (x 3) for up to 6 marks *OR* • more detailed comment x 2 for up to 6 marks Thus, the final marks can be gained by a combination of 3, 2 and 1 marks depending on the level of depth/detail/insight. The aim is quality of comment not quantity of references. In comments on 'Waking With Russell' the other Paterson poem dealt with in this book, possible references include: • has made a (hard to define) difference: 'Whatever the difference is' • brought him joy: quotation and/or discussion of 'rediscovered' smile/loss of 'old, hard-pressed grin' • brought him an intimate relationship: quotation and/or discussion of 'like lovers'/'kissed your mouth' • has found his way in life: quotation and/or discussion of 'true path was as lost to me as ever' and/or idea of Jamie running ahead to light the path Other references are possible, especially if candidates have studied further Paterson poems beyond those dealt with in this book. Note however that there is no obligation to discuss more than one other poem: it is possible to gain the full 10 marks, as outlined above, by making a comparison of the poem to just one other Paterson text known by the candidate.

Answers to the question analysing the pupil's answer on page 134

The words in the paragraph that show this pupil is trying to stick to the chosen task are: **'One feature of the structure of this poem is its use of contrast.'**

The words in the paragraph that show the pupil is using evidence from the text are: **'the thread of his one breath'** and **'your two-year-old lungs somehow out-revving/every engine in the universe.'** Shorter individual quotations of words and phases from these quotations could also be used.